early gifts

recognizing
and nurturing
children's talents

early gifts

recognizing and nurturing children's talents

edited by

paula olszewski-kubilius
lisa limburg-weber
steven pfeiffer

PRUFROCK PRESS, INC.

Printed in the United States of America.

ISBN 13· 978-1-882664-91-7
ISBN-10: 1-882664-91-4

At the time of this book's publication, all facts and figures cited are the most current available. All telephone numbers, addresses, and Web site URLs are accurate and active. All publications, organizations, Web sites, and other resources exist as described in the book, and all have been verified. The authors and Prufrock Press, Inc., make no warranty or guarantee concerning the information and materials given out by organizations or content found at Web sites, and we are not responsible for any changes that occur after this book's publication. If you find an error, please contact Prufrock Press Inc. We strongly recommend to parents, teachers, and other adults that you monitor children's use of the Internet.

Prufrock Press Inc.
P.O. Box 8813
Waco, Texas 76714-8813
(800) 998-2208
Fax (800) 240-0333
http://www.prufrock.com

table of contents

1

early years, early gifts
how parents and teachers can recognize and develop the young child's talents

by
paula olszewski-kubilius
and
lisa limburg-weber

Most of us believe that a child's experiences within the first few years of life have a great deal of influence on his or her eventual adult development. And much of the research that gets reported in parenting books and magazines supports this notion. Some educational researchers have suggested that children develop 50% or more of their mature intelligence by age 4.[1] On the other hand, other researchers have questioned the belief in the strong influence of the first few years of life by showing that the results of early environmental deprivation can be reversed.[2] These researchers argue that, given the appropriate conditions, intelligence can continue to grow well into adulthood.

While educators and scientists do not have a definitive answer to the questions raised in this debate, most parents simply want to give their children every possible advantage during those early, formative years. How many times have you heard the parents of a young child remark with obvious pride on what they see as their child's special abilities or accomplishments? All parents enjoy observing their child's development and growth, and most parents suspect at one time or another that their child is showing signs of above-average ability in some area.

However, most of these same parents also wonder if their judgment is correct—especially if their child's talent area is one unfamiliar to them. For instance, how does a parent with no special musical gifts or training recognize the early signs of musical interest and talent displayed by a young child? Even parents who have confidently identified special abilities in their children often worry about what to do next. Are private lessons appropriate? Do we need a special teacher? A private school? Exposure to programs in the community? How much should we push our child to develop her area of talent—or should we simply assist her in following the path of her own self-directed interests? And does special ability at a young age mean that our child will excel in this same area when he reaches maturity?

Both parents and teachers can sometimes be overwhelmed by the responsibility of finding answers to questions like these. Giving children the best chance at success in areas of life ranging from physical, to artistic, to cognitive development is a challenge for any adult, but presents a special challenge for adults responsible for a child with high potential. Guiding the obviously gifted young child can be a tremendous joy. But, it can also seem like a tremendous responsibility.

This book is intended to help parents and educators in the task of recognizing and cultivating their children's talents from preschool age through the elementary years. In this introductory chapter, we begin by providing an overview of what researchers know about early talent and its development in various contexts. In subsequent chapters, experts from a variety of fields describe the signs of early talent in young children in the domains of music, language arts, mathematics, the visual arts, science, and athletics; the specific steps families and educators should take to cultivate early talent; and the resources available to help them do so.

What is Talent?

Whether you talk to researchers, parents, or educators of gifted children, one thing is clear: There is no agreed-upon definition of giftedness or talent. Quite to the contrary, in fact, there are many proposed definitions and theories about what these terms mean. As parents investigate various educational programs and options for their gifted children, it is important to understand what definition of talent has influenced the program's design. Parents need to ask program administrators and instructors questions like these:

- How do you define "giftedness" or "talent" in this area?

- How do children qualify for your program, and how were test cut-off scores (if applicable) determined?
- How do the specific aspects of your program (content of the instruction, teaching methods, etc.) relate to the way you select students for the program?

You will probably find that most educators' answers to the question "What is talent?" refer either to IQ scores or to one of the newer theories in gifted education, such as performance-defined giftedness or the concept of domain-specific giftedness, which has grown out of the theory of multiple intelligences.

IQ Scores: Giftedness by the Numbers

In the United States, both researchers and schools have historically identified children as "gifted" or "talented" on the basis of their performance on IQ tests. "IQ" stands for "intelligence quotient," and IQ tests are paper-and-pencil tests that assess aspects of intellectual functioning such as the ability to reason, plan, solve problems, think abstractly, comprehend complex ideas, learn quickly, and learn from experience. According to 52 scientists who study intelligence, IQ is not a narrow academic skill related to learning from books or in school but a "broader and deeper capability for comprehending our surroundings—"catching on," "making sense out of things," or "figuring out" what to do.[3] According to these same experts, IQ tests measure intelligence well and are among the most accurate of psychological assessments.

IQ scores in normal children and adults vary from below 70 to above 150. About 3% of the population has IQ scores above 130, a score which many researchers, schools, and programs use to define where giftedness "begins." Having an IQ in the gifted range certainly does not guarantee success in life. However, it increases the odds considerably. IQ scores have been found to relate most strongly to success in educational contexts such as school, but they are clearly also related to other economic and social ways of measuring success. For instance, adults with higher IQ scores are more likely to perform well in jobs that require them to respond flexibly to complex situations with many changing variables. In our society, these jobs, which include professional and managerial positions, are likely to be higher paid and higher status.[4]

Beyond IQ: Other Ways to Think About Talent

But, there are other ways besides IQ scores to define giftedness and think about talent. Recent thinking on intelligence and giftedness has focused on specific abilities, rather than general intellectual ability, and the role of personality characteristics and motivation in high levels of achievement. For example, Joseph Renzulli,[5] a leading researcher in the field of gifted education, believes that it is more productive to speak of giftedness in terms of behaviors or performances. Rather than talk about a child with a musical "gift," Renzulli would rather say that the child has produced gifted musical performances.

One of the persistent issues within the field of gifted education is whether you can be labeled as gifted if you show high potential (for example, by scoring well on tests such as IQ tests), but do not exhibit high achievement. Renzulli's ideas about giftedness address this issue by recognizing that simply having the intellectual *capacity* to achieve at a high level is not enough to result in exceptional performances. For Renzulli, gifted performances result from three factors: (1) above-average, but not necessarily superior, general ability (IQ-type) or specific ability (such as musical or mathematical); (2) creativity or the ability to come up with unique solutions and different ways of looking at things; and (3) motivation and persistence to achieve at a high level and to produce excellent work.

Another relatively recent theory about intelligence proposes that, rather than one single intelligence, there are multiple intelligences. Howard Gardner,[6] in fact, has proposed that there are at least eight separate intelligences: linguistic, musical, logical-mathematical, spatial, bodily-kinesthetic, interpersonal (knowledge of others), intrapersonal (knowledge of self), and naturalistic (scientific knowledge). Each intelligence enables people to perform well in specific areas. Someone with exceptional linguistic intelligence, for instance, might be recognized by great ability as a poet, while bodily-kinesthetic intelligence is characteristic of a dancer, and spatial intelligence of a chess master. Even though Gardner initially identified only eight distinct intelligences, he has proposed that there may well be others and has suggested criteria that other researchers could use to describe new types of intelligence.

Gardner's theory of multiple intelligences has led to a "domain-specific" approach to thinking about giftedness. That is, rather than viewing giftedness as high general intellectual ability, some researchers prefer to think of it as specific aptitude within a subscribed domain of human activity. After all, when we think of giftedness in adults, we do not usually think of adults with high general intellectual ability or IQ scores. Instead, we think of individuals who are exceptional musicians, artists, or scientists—in other words, individuals who, by virtue of their exceptional achievements, have made a profound contribution to a field or are regarded as working at the top levels of their field. Domain-specific giftedness is a rather new way to view giftedness in children, but it has the value of consistency with the way society typically thinks about adult giftedness.

Another advantage of a domain-specific view of giftedness is that it corresponds to the unevenness we see in most children in terms of their performances in various domains. Ellen Winner, in her book *Gifted Children: Myths and Realities,*[7] argues that the child who is "globally gifted," or equally competent in all or most areas, is one of the great myths of the field. Most children show exceptional ability in one or two areas only. This is a useful point for both educators and parents of young gifted children to keep in mind. Some gifted academic programs assume, for instance, that a child who is reading well above grade level should also be accelerated in the mathematics curriculum. Parents, too, sometimes unrealistically expect a child who is showing extraordinary talent in one area, such as music, to produce similarly extraordinary results in other areas. Gifted children, like all children, respond best to appropriate, realistic expectations of their performance—in both their areas of strength and those areas in which they evidence only average, or occasionally even below-average, ability.

Recognizing and Developing Early Talent

How early does talent emerge? What are the initial signs of talent in young children? How significant are those signs of early talent in terms of later life? There are no across-the-board answers to these questions, since so much depends on the *kind* and the *degree* of exceptional ability we are talking about. A talented young writer may have very little in common with a talented young athlete, just as a child who is a moderately talented musician may look very different from a child with the ability to become a world-class composer. But, some general traits do seem generally applicable to most talented children.

Recognizing Early Talent

One important characteristic is that children who are highly gifted in an area will display what Ellen Winner has called a "rage to master." If allowed to do so, these children will spend the majority of their waking time engaged in the talent area, whether it be music or drawing or reading. Children with a "rage to master" show their intense interest by the hours they spend practicing or playing in the area, their rapid acquisition of knowledge and skills in the area, and their high level of energy and enthusiasm for anything that has to do with the area.

These burning interests of young, highly gifted children very often can help predict their careers and activities in adulthood. For example:

- People who become creative writers as adults often are voracious readers and writers as children. Their childhood writing often displays unusual attention to imagery, an ear for the rhythm and sounds of language, and a playfulness with words.[8]
- Adult musicians tend, as children, to have displayed exceptional sensitivity to the structure of music; strong interest and delight in musical sounds; remarkable musical memory; quick and easy learning of an instrument; and (rarely) early ability to compose, transpose, and improvise.[9]
- Early signs of artistic talent include the ability to draw realistically at an early age and the ability to imitate the style of other artists. More rare among children who will become adult artists is an exceptional sense of composition, form, or color in childhood drawings.[10]

On the other hand, other gifted or exceptional behaviors on the part of children do not point as clearly to a particular path for adulthood. A good example is those children who begin reading at an earlier-than-average age. Surprisingly, early readers do not necessarily have high verbal IQs, nor do they necessarily enter career fields such as writing or publishing as adults.[11] Some children who learn to read at age 3 or 4 seem to be drawing not on high verbal ability, but on an above-average ability to relate sounds and written symbols. These children may later show exceptional talent not in language, but in music. Other early readers are very adept at using visual shapes and cues to learn words; children who use visual-spatial cues to learn to read at an early age may show later talent in mathematics. Precocious reading is an example of an ability that has both diverse roots and diverse outcomes. Parents and teachers who notice above-average interest and ability in their children should remain alert to the possibility that predicting the direction a child's talent will take as he or she matures is a tricky proposition.

What is a Prodigy?

Once in a great while, a child may show extraordinary adult-like abilities in a certain area well before the age when such abilities can normally be expected to develop. We call children like this "child prodigies." Morelock and Feldman defined a child prodigy as "a child who, before the age of 10, performs at the level of an adult professional in some cognitively demanding field."[12] Oftentimes, when people think about giftedness, a child prodigy such as the young Mozart (for music) or Bobby Fischer (for chess) is the image that immediately leaps to mind.

True prodigies are rare, however, for several reasons. One has to do with the nature of different fields of human activity. Child prodigies only are found in fields that, because of how they are structured and developed, are easily comprehensible to a young child. Feldman and Morelock note that the largest numbers of child prodigies have been found in chess and music. Many fewer have been noted in writing, the visual arts, or mathematics. And, in fields such as physics or the natural sciences, prodigies are virtually unheard of.

Another reason that prodigies are so rare is that they emerge only when there is a coming together of a variety of supportive conditions, a process that Feldman has termed "co-incidence." The conditions include not only a young child with high potential working in a domain whose structure makes it available for mastery by a child, but also

- a historical time in which the domain is valued and high-level mastery of it is prized, and
- a family environment that recognizes and supports the ability *and* can obtain resources to ensure its development.

Prodigies provide a fascinating example of the extraordinary range of human ability and developmental timetables, but they are extremely uncommon. It is important to recognize that not all gifted children perform at the same level. A gifted child classified as "above average" might read or reason mathematically several years ahead of most other children his or her age, while a "profoundly gifted" child may display the "rage to master" described above; this child's performances and ability approach expert levels in a specific domain. Prodigies are not the focus of this book. Instead, we will focus on children whose talent, while not at an adult level, is definitely advanced compared to most children their age. These children can be identified by:

- their interest in or curiosity about a topic or domain;
- their ability to focus and concentrate on learning in that area;
- their desire to "play" with the tools of that area; and
- their level of ability, which is advanced compared to that of other children their same age or grade.

While profoundly gifted children and prodigies may be rare and represent the extreme end of a continuum, the same elements necessary for the emergence of a child prodigy—a child with talent, an optimal family environment, and a supportive community—must come together in order to help young gifted children who are developing their talents in a more ordinary time frame.

The Child: Gifted or Talented?

As you read through this book, which brings together experts from a variety of fields, you will note that the terms *talented* and *gifted* are often used interchangeably. Some researchers and practitioners do try to distinguish between the terms. Often, *talented* is used to refer to individuals with abilities in the arts and music, while *gifted* is used to refer to academic types of ability in mathematics or science. One researcher, François Gagné,[13] has proposed a different distinction between the terms. In his writing, *giftedness* refers to exceptional natural abilities observable in young children who have received no special training; *talent*, on the other hand, refers to systematically developed abilities (via schooling or lessons or training) needed for high performance in a certain area.

According to Gagné's theory, one can be gifted and not talented; however, one cannot be talented and not be gifted. A child could be intellectually gifted by virtue of high IQ or test scores, but may not be academically talented if he or she does not display exceptional performance via grades, awards, or other criteria in an academic area. Giftedness is childhood promise, while talent is fulfillment and development of that promise. The process of talent development is then the systematic training and education sought by the gifted individual to develop talent to a high degree. It is that systematic training that is the primary focus of this book.

Developing Early Talent

The Family: Launching Pad for Talent Development

Identifying the presence of natural, raw ability in a child, as exciting as this may be, is only a starting point in helping that child fully develop his or her talents. The myth of the "untaught genius," a child with such strong natural gifts that he or she is able to make significant contributions to a field while bypassing the training and education ordinarily associated with that field, is in almost every case just that: a myth. Even children with prodigious natural ability require much input from their environment in order to develop their talents. Parents, teachers, and coaches all have significant roles to play in the early years of talent development, but the earliest influence comes, of course, from the family.

It is clear from the research on talent development that families play a very important role in whether children's promise and potential are realized.[14] Parents usually introduce the child to the talent area and often serve as the first teacher. At the most obvious level, parents provide the resources to support talent development. These resources include both money (for testing, lessons, instruments, equipment, and outside-of-school educational opportunities) and time spent on arranging instruction, searching out programs, transporting children to events and lessons, and monitoring practices. Some talent areas, particularly those typically not dealt with in schools (such as ice skating or music), require a lot of both time and money, even in the early years of learning and practice.

At a more fundamental level, however, families of talented children are less dependent on these resources than you might assume. Parents who successfully support their talented children usually

- function as a filter through which their young child experiences the world;
- help their child build social relationships that support the development of his or her talent; and
- teach beliefs and values that support, rather than undermine, high achievement.

Parents who are able to do these things, no matter what their economic circumstances, can create a family environment that nurtures their young child's talents and serves as a launching pad for the next level of talent development: that which takes place outside the home.

First, families provide the lens through which young children experience the world. Parents can shield children from stressful events and circumstances, or, if that is impossible, help children understand these things in a constructive and positive way.[15] Difficult circumstances such as poverty, racism, and disability can either limit or energize the development of a talented individual. Did the family's poverty provide motivation for achievement, or did it drown out hope? Creative, productive adults are distinguished not by their families' life circumstances, but by how they as individuals responded to those circumstances.

Have you ever noticed how many eminent public figures can recount stories of difficult childhood years? It is not uncommon to find that highly productive, talented adults have family histories containing circumstances like the loss of a parent, parental dysfunction, neglect, harsh parenting, lack of family stability, rejection by others due to physical handicaps, and poverty. Yet, despite such circumstances—or, perhaps, because of them—these individuals were able to achieve at very high levels as adults. One researcher has pointed out that traumatic childhood events drive some talented adults to choose a field or career and then devote their work in this area to righting a perceived wrong. He called this process of turning stressful circumstances into positive sources of strength "transformational coping."[16] Because of exceptional problem-solving abilities, gifted individuals may be better able to find solutions to problems and obstacles they encounter in life. They may possess unusual resiliency and a broader range of coping strategies.

Does this mean that loving parents who want their children to develop their talents should create opportunities for stress and tragedy? Not according to researchers who have studied the question more carefully. Talented and productive adults tend to come from families where, *despite* difficult circumstances, some supports for talent development were available, such as an orderly home, access to intellectual resources, and supportive adults outside the family.

Another important role for parents is helping their talented child to build supportive social relationships and networks.[17] Social networks consist of the people in our lives with whom we interact, some on a daily basis, some more infrequently. Social networks can be large (like those of working adults) or small (like those of the very elderly or the very young). Social networks can also be identified by the degree to which the members of the network are connected or know one another and the extent to which the members give each other emotional and psychological support. The social world of the child begins with the family; but, over time, as the child matures, it expands to include teachers, coaches, mentors, and a wider scope of peers. Social networks evolve naturally as children move about their world, but parents can help them to build networks that support not only their general social and emotional development, but their talent development, as well.

Finally, families can encourage and cultivate values that are conducive to talent development.[18] These values may include the importance of discovering and developing your abilities, achieving at the highest levels possible, expressing your individuality through independent thinking, and engaging in recreational, cultural, and intellectual activities. In many cases, children learn more from watching their parents live their lives than from listening to their parents talk about their values. For instance, parents demonstrate a love of work and learning by the enthusiasm they show for their own jobs. Parents model independent learning by pursuing activities that take place outside of structured or traditional settings, such as hobbies, community projects, or reading at home. In dealing with the normal events and challenges of life, parents model personality dispositions that are essential to talent development, such as risk taking and coping with challenges, setbacks, and failures. Because children observe their parents closely over a period of many years, parents can demonstrate through their choices, commitments, and attitudes that success requires a great deal of hard work and sustained effort over long stretches of time.

Do Different Families Produce Different Kinds of Talent?

While research generally supports the positive role that families can play in developing talent, some studies have also suggested that different families tend to produce different kinds of talented adults. One key characteristic that influences children's talent development is the degree to which they are free to develop a unique identity within their family—an identity different from their parents—and express their own individual thoughts. Parents who encourage this kind of autonomy are more likely to have children who are creative, independent thinkers who generate unique solutions to problems. As adults, children from these families are more likely to produce new, groundbreaking work in their field (like medical researchers who pioneer new surgical techniques).

In general, parents who produce children who develop independent identities and thought are those who create more emotional freedom between themselves and their child, monitor their children less closely, and practice less-conventional childrearing. This type of family environment can result from negative circumstances, such as parental alcoholism or mental illness, but it can also result from other factors, such as parents who are involved with their own interests or careers[19] or those who simply offer their children more emotional latitude and leeway.

Independent and autonomous children often are more willing to spend time alone. Being able to tolerate solitude is an important component of the talent-development process. The voracious reading or practicing required to reach high levels of mastery in a field necessitates time alone. The inability to be alone for long periods of time can thwart the creative process, which involves incubation periods for ideas. Oftentimes, gifted and creative individuals develop a "taste" for solitude and use internal fantasy, daydreaming, and mental problem solving as coping strategies to deal with it.[20]

This research does not mean that parents should work at achieving emotional distance between themselves and their talented children! Some researchers have suggested that high levels of talent development depend on a *balance* of support and tension within the family. Families that provide this balance can be described as both "integrated" (family members are emotionally connected to and supportive of one another) and also "differentiated" (individual thought, expression, and development of talents are encouraged).[21] Parents who overemphasize differentiation can produce children who accomplish great things as adults, but are not well adjusted. An overemphasis on integration, on the other hand, can lead to adults who are very well adjusted, but not necessarily talented or creative. Families who effectively balance these areas are more likely to produce children who are self-motivated and self-directed to achieve in their talent areas.*

---

* More research still remains to be done in this area. One researcher has found, for instance, that creativity can develop both in talented individuals who experience great misfortunes and those who do not. However, those talented, creative adults who were "challenged" (by having to deal with misfortunes, although they received some kinds of family support) may be "more overtly driven to prove themselves and to receive recognition".[22] In addition, family environment factors interact with others, such as a person's basic constitution, which may make one more or less vulnerable to stress.[23]

How Can Parents Put This Research to Work?

Parents of gifted children need to establish and maintain bonds with their children, but also allow them autonomy, independence, and psychological and emotional space. To increase the chances of your gifted child's becoming a healthy, productive gifted adult, the research suggests that you should

- help your child to find his or her own identity;
- allow for open expression of ideas and independent thought;
- provide support in the presence of stressful events; and
- remain involved in supporting your child's achievement, but avoid emotional overinvestment in his or her accomplishments.

Parents also help children to succeed by allowing them to experience and cope with challenges and difficulties in their lives. Parents should not shield or try to protect children from all risks or hard work. Parents also need to allow children to experience the tensions that arise from challenging ideas and high expectations. They can support the development of coping strategies for stress, which include a rich internal fantasy life, use of time alone to decompress and rejuvenate, expression of emotions through creative work, and active use of leisure time.

Finally, parents can also be assured that it is not all up to them! "It takes a village to raise a child" is a saying that has been overused to the point of triteness in the popular culture of our connection-starved American lifestyles. The wisdom behind the proverb, however, holds especially true for the talented child. No matter what the child's natural gifts and no matter how optimally the family environment supports the development of these gifts, the gifted child needs input and involvement from a larger community if he or she is to develop into an adult who is fully engaged and productive in his or her talent domain.

The Community

In our discussion, the word *community* refers to the collection of people, institutions, and organizations that surround and affect a growing child. We can easily think of a number of small communities that directly influence our children: neighborhood, classroom, school, Scouts, sports team, church or religious organization, and town or city. Children also participate in larger, less easily visualized communities. For instance, they are residents of a geographical region, members of a gender group, citizens of our country, and inhabitants of the western world. The gifted child's community, unique to each child, is the complex configuration of nonfamily influences on his or her life, work, and play.

How do communities help the young gifted child develop his or her talent? Minimally, the child's community must recognize and permit the development of the talent area in general. We have talked about the fact that a child prodigy will emerge only at moments in space and history when the community is prepared to value the talent domain. The same holds true for children with other levels of potential in a domain. The child gifted in movement, rhythm, and bodily awareness will not become a talented dancer in a religious community that does not value or practice the art of dance, just as an Einstein born into a preindustrialized society could not have developed into the mathematical theoretician he became.

Beyond this minimal requirement of a community that recognizes and values the talent area, however, the young gifted child also needs access to specifically talent-related relationships and opportunities outside the family. Most gifted children further their talent development by participating in both school-based and other, nonschool-based activities.

Talent Development in School

As children grow older, much of their waking hours are taken up by a cultural institution charged with preparing children for productive adult labor—the school. A clear division of educational labor has for years existed in our country: Parents supervise their children's after-school learning, such as music and sports, while trusting that the local public school will wisely and efficiently meet their academic needs. Except, perhaps, for those who chose parochial or expensive private schools for their children, many parents of previous generations never gave a second thought to evaluating whether their children's school provided a "good match" or the "right fit" for their individual child's needs. Children were expected to conform to what the school had to offer, not the other way around. In 21st-century U.S. society, however, with many public school systems in crisis and school choice a political hot potato, many parents have been sensitized to the possibility that the age-appropriate class in the neighborhood school might not, in fact, be the right place for their child to learn and develop. Parents of gifted children may feel particular pressure to discern whether, and how, their children's school can truly meet their special learning needs.

The first thing that families must realize is that, while schools are responsible for developing expertise in content areas and educational techniques, parents also need to develop expertise in a particular area: their son or daughter. Research has shown that parents who understand their child's needs and who advocate for those needs to be met can help ensure that the school works effectively with their gifted child.

Schools that are sensitive to students' varying abilities can be an invaluable resource for young children's talent development. Often, children's talents are first identified by teachers at their schools. Other times, schools provide parents with a way to notice the extent to which their children are accelerated in a certain area, as they compare their child's achievement with that of peers. Schools can also be excellent sources of information about talent development opportunities and can provide networking opportunities with other children (and their parents) who share similar interests and have similar abilities. And, of course, the school plays a large role in instruction for talent development, particularly in fields such as mathematics and science, where most instruction tends to take place in the classroom. Schools that provide an appropriate instructional "match" for gifted children's abilities—in which children are being appropriately challenged—can help them excel.

However, while finding a school that accommodates the gifted child's exceptional abilities is important, parents cannot rely only on schools for their children's talent development. Some schools simply fail to identify the gifted student's abilities, either because the school doesn't provide appropriate testing or because the child's ability is masked by behavior or learning problems and is therefore difficult to detect. Other schools are reluctant to allow the gifted child to progress at his or her own accelerated learning rate, while still others would be willing to accelerate the gifted child, but do not have the resources needed to provide differentiated instruction (appropriate for the gifted child's learning level and rate) in the appropriate area. At some schools, particularly small ones or those that do not group by ability, gifted children have trouble finding other gifted children with whom they can have truly peer relationships. And, finally, some children whose talent area requires long hours spent in out-of-school practice (e.g., music) experience difficulties because long school days make finding practice time difficult. Parents whose gifted children experience a good fit in their schooling and receive needed school services tend to be those who have worked to know their children and learned to advocate for their needs.

Talent Development Outside of School

Schools are certainly not the only place to which parents can turn to help their children develop supportive social networks in their talent areas. If we examined talented children's social networks further, we might find that they ideally include not only teachers or coaches, but also

- peers at a similar level of talent development;
- practitioners at different ages and levels of talent development, including both older children and teens who can help give the young child a realistic idea of how talent develops over time through practice and adults who are actively engaged as professionals or talented amateurs in the talent domain; and
- other families of talented young children (on whom parents can draw for carpooling, resource sharing, and advocacy).

Meeting and maintaining contact with people in this talent development network can take place through a variety of contexts and institutions, including

- school services, both classroom-based and pull-out programs;
- contests and competitions at various levels (neighborhood, city, regional, state, national) that are sponsored by schools or other organizations;
- summer/weekend/after-school group-based programs sponsored by schools, cultural institutions, or universities;
- private lessons given by individuals or available through cultural institutions;
- the Internet, where children, supervised by their parents, can access (through posting questions on listservs or participating in chat rooms and other electronically facilitated communities) both peers and experts in the field; and
- less-formal, privately arranged contexts, usually facilitated by parents, such as play dates with talented peers, arranging for a young child to visit the place of employment of an adult practitioner, and family visits to events such as concerts, art shows, and athletic events.

Children who participate in special activities such as these can develop relationships with peers that provide specific emotional support for achievement in the talent domain. Friends and companions who are also involved in the talent field can be essential to sustaining the child's commitment to the domain during critical times, such as when practicing seems boring, or the child experiences failure, or peers devalue the talent or ability.[24]

Motivation, skill development, and performance opportunities can all stem from contacts made in a variety of school and community settings. No gifted child needs *all* of these opportunities for talent development, but every gifted child needs *some* form of community involvement beyond the support of his or her immediate family. In most cases, the number and intensity of these relationships and opportunities should increase as the child grows older and approaches adolescence. In most cases, too, the talented child will gradually take over responsibility for seeking out and maintaining such opportunities as he or she matures both socially and in the talent area.

Each of the following chapters will explore, in the context of a specific talent domain, the general concepts reviewed in this chapter. For the child gifted as an athlete, or a musician, or a dancer, our chapter authors address the following questions:

- How do experts in this area test for and define giftedness and talent?
- How are young gifted children in this area first recognized?
- What specific family and community resources help the young gifted child develop his or her talents in this area?
- What stages of development does talent in each domain traverse through and what are the significant influences that promote progression through these stages?

We want to caution you that the information contained in these chapters should be seen as introductory in nature. Parents with a child who continues to be interested and engaged in a talent area will want to seek out additional sources of information—including full-length books, the Internet, their children's teachers or coaches, other parents, and adults talented and practicing in the area—to help them learn more about what their young children need to develop their talent. Our hope as authors of this book, however, is that this introduction to the topic of developing your young child's talent will inspire you, reassure you, and motivate you to continue to meet your unique, and uniquely gifted, child's needs in the very best way you can. Good luck!

nurturing talent development in science

by

cheryll m. adams

Young children are naturally curious about the world around them. Add to this natural curiosity some of the traits associated with gifted children—persistence, intense interest in a topic or area of study, ability to see connections others might miss, high cognitive ability—and you have the makings of a young scientist. This chapter will give you an idea about some of the characteristics of young scientists, the role of creativity in science, important science processes, the special case of gifted girls in science, and ways that you, as parents, can support, assist, and nurture your young scientist.

Unfortunately, the nurturing of the young scientist falls mainly on the parents and others outside the school, or at least outside of the school day. To understand why this is the case, let us look at the current state of science in the schools.

Science in the Schools

In the late 1980s, efforts to make schools accountable for the academic success of their students resulted in a wave of school reform. These reform efforts insisted that public schools address specific academic standards for each content area. This movement toward high academic standards spurred the development of "benchmarks," the minimum level of competence students should attain for nearly every content area. In science, two very similar works are excellent guides for what students should know in science. Both Project 2061's *Benchmarks for Science Literacy* and the *National Science Education Standards* form the basis for many of the state and district standards developed for school systems across the country.[1] If we have standards that identify what our children need to know and be able to do in science at each grade level, why should we be concerned that our children with a bent toward science will not have their interest nurtured in the school setting?

The Syndrome of 10

In his monograph on science talent for the National Research Center on the Gifted and Talented, Paul Brandwein, noted biologist, teacher, and researcher, recently reviewed the state of science education and surmised it to be nearly the same as in 1983.[2] In that year, the National Science Teachers Association identified 10 recurring problems in science education. Among this "Syndrome of 10" were indications that the science curriculum in most schools consisted of the textbook; lecture was the main form of instruction; science was removed from the world outside the classroom; supplies, equipment, and resources were severely limited in most classrooms; and science content was nearly nonexistent in the elementary school.

Standardized Testing

Currently, *accountability* is a constant buzzword in education. Administrators are pressured to use test scores obtained from annual student testing as "proof" that students, teachers, and schools are or are not meeting the state's academic standards. Today's legislative and administrative emphasis on decision making based on scores obtained through statewide standardized tests of achievement has contributed to the lack of progress in overcoming the "Syndrome of 10" nearly 20 years later. In most states, reading, language, and mathematics are stressed on these statewide tests of achievement. Unfortunately, many schools operate under the belief that "We treasure what we measure." Simply put, if a subject is not "tested," it receives little attention at the classroom level, since teachers must spend much of their time covering the information to be tested. Generally, science is not currently a tested subject on statewide standardized tests.

Furthermore, the results of the last National Assessment of Educational Progress released in November, 2001, indicates that the performance of our 12th graders on the science portion was slightly worse than 4 years ago.[3]

Seventy-one percent of fourth graders and 68% of eighth graders scored below the proficient level, indicating that they lack the knowledge necessary to apply scientific concepts and principles.

Teaching Science

In many elementary schools, as little as 20 minutes a week is allotted to teaching science. At the elementary level, it is not uncommon for teachers to relegate science to the back burner because they do not feel comfortable teaching the subject, having had little experience with the subject outside of the one or two basic science classes they were required to take at the college level, lack interest in the subject, or both. Never would the teaching of reading or mathematics be given such treatment!

Generally, science doesn't become a legitimate subject until middle school. High schools traditionally offer biology, chemistry, and physical science, adding more courses when interest warrants it and funding supports it. At the sixth-grade level and beyond, however, a shortage of science teachers has often led to the employment of underqualified teachers and, in many cases, unqualified teachers to teach science classes.

Science is best taught when students are solving real problems and working as a scientist would. For example, the teacher can pose the following problem: "Here are six different kinds of batteries and a variety of items that use batteries. What might we want to find out?" Students may respond with answers such as, "Which battery really runs the longest?," "Is one kind of battery better for electronic items and another battery better for flashlights?," or "Is there really a difference among alkaline, lithium, and super batteries?" Students might then design experiments to test each hypothesis. While there are excellent programs and materials that support this style of teaching and learning, many teachers still use the lecture method followed by a lab to verify the material presented through the lecture. The lab often lacks any aspect of open-endedness, and the result is as predictable as having a tasty apple pie after carefully following Grandma's recipe for apple pie.

Most states adopt one or more textbook series, and schools must use a series from the official adoption list. While many of the newest science texts have colorful illustrations, graphics, hands-on activities, and other support materials, some school systems purchase the texts only. Funding is not available for the "extras," such as materials for activities. Furthermore, a participant in a recent study of science texts indicated that the millions of dollars to produce them must have gone for the graphics, pictures, and colorful layout, not for accurate science. Many texts have glaring errors, such as the equator running through the southern United States![4] While I can't recommend a particular textbook series as exemplary, there are some materials that can be used to craft an inquiry-based science program. One excellent set of materials comes from Joyce VanTassel-Baska and her colleagues at The College of William and Mary. This problem-based learning series was developed specifically for gifted children. A list of these and other materials is included in the Appendix at the end of the chapter.

In summary, particularly at the elementary level, there are far too many instances where unqualified, uninterested teachers are leaving the study of science to Friday afternoons, 30 minutes before school is out, rather than doing an exemplary job of preparing future scientists and scientifically literate citizens, exposing students to a variety of real-world issues and problems to solve, and providing opportunities for using critical and creative thinking skills.

Finding Gifts and Talents in Science

Factors

Three factors for predicting high ability in science are genetic, predisposing, and activating.[5] The genetic component includes high verbal ability, high mathematical ability, and good neuromuscular abilities. These neuromuscular abilities are what allow us to handle delicate scientific equipment without dropping it, calibrate instruments with precision, and, in general, keep us from being klutzes! While genetics plays an important role in these factors, early exposure to a variety of rich and engaging materials can stimulate the development of these abilities.

The predisposing factor includes two personality-based attitudes: questing and persisting. Questing may be best personified by the child who "needs to know." This child pursues answers with a vengeance and is not satisfied by pat answers to sophisticated questions. In addition, the child will evaluate answers, rather than taking them "on authority." Persisting includes the willingness to continue working on a project despite setbacks, to experience failure, and to become absorbed in a project. Children exhibiting high persistence may even have to be reminded when it is mealtime and bedtime.

Parents can influence the last factor perhaps more than the others. The activating factor is simply the opportunity for children to use their talent.

Putting your child in touch with a mentor is a good plan, or perhaps your child has a teacher who shares his or her interest in a particular area of science and encourages him or her to delve deeper. Scientists can nearly always name one or two teachers who encouraged them to persist and supported their curiosity. Providing materials for investigations; books on science topics; computer software and other media; and trips to museums, science centers, laboratories, environmental stations or any other place that might spark or sustain a science appetite are ways parents can assist in the development of science talent. At the end of this chapter is a list of books that might be helpful to you as you encourage your young scientist.

How Can I Tell if My Child is Gifted in Science?

First of all, there is no test for "scientific giftedness." There are, however, some standardized instruments that we might use to help us get a good idea of science talent. Most standardized achievement tests given by a school district will have a science component. Unless science is a "tested" subject in your district, the science portion may not be given to the students. If your child has performed at the 95th percentile or above, there is a chance that he or she has talent in science. A better indication would be to have the child take an out-of-level test (a first-grade student takes the second-grade test) and look at the percentile. There is no set number that means "gifted," but I generally use the 80–85th percentile on an out-of-level test. That is, if the first grader scores better than 80% of the second graders, he or she has achieved at a level much higher than we would expect for a first grader.

One test that shows promise is the Screening Assessment for Gifted Elementary Students– 2.[6] The beauty of this instrument is two-fold. First, we can see how the child stands when compared to other children in the typical classroom and also how he or she compares with the gifted population. Secondly, the test is not timed and is easy to administer. The drawback is that one test is used for both mathematics and science achievement, so one cannot isolate the science portion. Having said that, science and mathematics go hand-in-hand and it is very difficult to do science without a solid knowledge of mathematics.

The Group Embedded Figures Test (GEFT) measures field-dependence/independence, and the literature supports its linkage to a student's ability to design a controlled experiment.[7] The Diet Cola Test can be used as an evaluation instrument to determine the effectiveness of direct instruction in basic and integrated process skills.[8]

If you are interested in having your child's science achievement and ability assessed, check first with his or her school to see what is available. If outside testing is needed, contact the educational psychology, clinical psychology, or assessment department of a nearby college or university. You may be fortunate enough to have a university with a department of gifted education and an affiliated testing center. Many offer free or inexpensive testing services as part of the training given to their graduate students.

Creativity's Place in Science

Creativity and Science Process

We usually think of science as an exacting, analytical field. If this is indeed the case, does creativity have a place in science? Often, there is a mismatch between how scientists actually do science and how we describe the process of science in our classrooms. We are spending too much time learning about the products of science (e.g. nuclear reactors, quantum theory, cell theory, machines, light) and too little time on the processes that allowed the products to happen.[9] According to R. Pollack, "the statement of science is the testable prediction. The creative event of science is the demonstration that the prediction was correct."[10] So, creativity in science plays out in the process of actually doing science and thinking about solving problems, not simply reading about science. Creative thinking, then, is similar to the processes scientists work through as they solve problems.

I'm not advocating telling your child's teacher to throw away the texts and ignore content in favor of process. We can't have one without the other. However, in many science classrooms, we are spending too much time on content to the near exclusion of process. "But, I thought the 'scientific method' that we all learned in our science classes *was* process. If teachers teach that, haven't they covered process?" Yes, the "scientific method" is in nearly every science text, and often teachers require our children to memorize the steps. But, there are two flaws in this approach. First, there is no one process which could be called *the* scientific method, but many methods that scientists use to solve problems. Second, we usually teach the method in our texts as a set of steps—a linear process. In fact, the process of doing science is cyclical. The various stages feed back into each other many times before the problem is solved.

Paul Brandwein has suggested that creativity and process play major roles in identifying and nurturing those students who are gifted and talented in science. He advised that paper-and-pencil creativity tests and IQ tests will not necessarily help us find these students. Other factors such as personality traits (the persisting, questing, and activating factors), competency in science, and previous opportunities to practice the skills of a scientist are not reflected in the scores on these tests. Actually working through the process of science as a scientist does and completing an experimental design is a sign of talent in science.[11]

The Creative Process in Science

In the classroom, we cannot separate process from content, product, and environment. The same holds true in a discussion of creativity. We look at the creative process within a context of personality, product, and environment. Before we can talk about the creative process in science, we need to mention the personality traits of creative scientists. Below is a list of personality traits of creative scientists gleaned from several works.[12] Which of the personality traits of creative scientists do you see and can you foster in your child?

- risk taker
- autonomous
- unconventional
- original
- persistent
- looks at unusual details
- independent
- playful
- rational
- dislikes ambiguity
- interest in art/humanities
- energetic
- broad aptitude
- curious
- intellectual courage
- daring

An example will show more closely what is meant by looking at personality, process, product, and environment: The famous chemist, Kekule, solved his dilemma of determining the shape of benzene molecules while daydreaming before a fireplace. He "saw" a snake swallow its tail and, from that, made the connection that the shape of benzene was not a chain of carbon molecules, but a ring instead.[13]

Alexander Fleming told another biographer that "I was just playing" when he discovered penicillin. And, in 1945, shortly after receiving his Nobel Prize, Fleming said again, "I play with microbes. There are, of course, many rules to this play . . . but, when you have acquired knowledge and experience, it is very pleasant to break the rules and to be able to find something nobody had thought of," just as he often did in his games.[14]

There are many who have proposed theories to explain the creative process—Abraham Maslow, Carl Rogers, Lawrence Kubie, and Sarnoff A. Mednick, to name a few. In most cases, personal descriptions and accounts of scientists' own thinking must suffice. Providing children with biographies and autobiographies of scientists will help them get a sense of these thinking processes. Some suggestions are provided in the Appendix at the end of this chapter.

As we have already discussed, there is no single "scientific method" or process of doing science, so next we will take an in-depth look at one model of the creative process in science.

A Model for Creative Process in Science

I chose Mansfield's model of the creative process in science for two reasons.[15] First, the terminology is different than the model usually presented in science texts. Hopefully, this will help us stop buying into the notion that there is *one* scientific method that exists as a set of linear steps. Second, the model is relatively simple and easy to follow, and you should be easily able to use it with your young scientist.

There are five processes in creative sciencing:

1. selection of the problem;
2. extended effort to solve the problem;
3. setting constraints;
4. changing constraints; and
5. verification and elaboration.

We'll look at each one individually, remembering that we can cycle through the process or individual steps many times before the problem is solved. Even upon reaching the verification and elaboration phase, the scientist may simply have found a new problem in solving the old one, and the cycle continues.

Selection of the Problem. First, the problem that is selected should be ready to be solved, or its solution should be remotely possible given our present state of technological knowledge and instrumentation. Scientists find problems by noticing gaps and places where new observations are incompatible with known phenomena. Students who have studied a particular topic in-depth will have a better chance of finding a real problem. Helping your child identify real-world problems, rather than contrived exercises, will help ensure that he or she is working as an actual scientist would. Take some time and observe the world around you. For example, most children have some kind of battery-operated toy. Let's take a second look at the battery problem mentioned earlier. Suppose the child must spend her allowance to replenish the batteries after the original set wears out. It would be beneficial, then, to figure out which batteries were the best buy based on cost and longevity, thus making this a personally relevant problem for the child to solve.

Extended Effort to Solve the Problem. One characteristic of creative scientists mentioned previously was "commitment to work" or persistence. The extended effort needed to solve a problem is so great that usually only the highly motivated can persevere. This extended effort may also allow chance time to operate, as noted in Louis Pasteur's famous quote, "Chance favors only the prepared mind." This effort over a period of time helps the scientist see clues to the answer that don't seem to be directly related to the problem. In our battery problem, time and effort, trips to the store, cost comparison, and an analysis of the various brands and kinds of batteries must all be completed before the actual investigation can begin. Working around extracurricular activities, finding an adult with time to spare and the availability of a car must all be planned well ahead of time. Coordinating these arrangements will test your child's persistence, creativity, and patience.

Many famous discoveries might not have been made if the scientists had not worked on the problem for an extended period of time. Particular examples of this that come to mind are Louis Pasteur, Alexander Fleming, Marie and Pierre Curie, Albert Einstein, Thomas Edison, and Barbara McClintock. For example, Barbara McClintock spent 3 years studying just one chromosome on a corn kernel! Translated into use, this means that investigations will rarely be finished within the timeframe of a Saturday afternoon. Instead, it will be necessary to arrange times for your young scientists to continue their work for extended periods of time.

Setting Constraints. A constraint is anything that restricts or limits our ability to solve the problem. These constraints may be present at the beginning of the investigation or appear as new information is gathered. Constraints occur when scientists find that their observations of a phenomenon differ markedly from what is expected. Scientists may place constraints on themselves when they choose to work within a particular theory or model. A working hypothesis is an example of this. Sometimes, scientists have to change the hypothesis and must be flexible enough to do so. Scientists have to work within the constraints of the technology, too. They may have to modify their choice for data collection if the required instrumentation or technique is not yet available, or they may choose to create the proper tools themselves. In our battery problem, contrary to television advertisements, a particular battery may not be the one that keeps going, and going, and going in your child's investigation. Now the child must figure out what to do. Do I go with this result, repeat it, leave this battery out of the investigation, or what?

For most of their school career, students have been taught that there is one right answer to a problem. It will probably take quite a bit of support from you or a mentor before your child will stop buying into that notion. There may be many right answers and many ways to approach a problem. Children need to think through other constraints that may be placed on the problem, such as time, equipment and, cost. This may result in negotiations for an extended bedtime or an advance in their allowance.

Changing Constraints. The ability to move from one idea to another when trying to solve a problem, rather than getting bogged down in a rut, is called "flexibility of thought." The personality characteristics of openness and flexibility of thought help one break a particular mindset and try a different spin on the problem. Robert Root-Bernstein has pointed out that scientists who engage regularly in highly personalized, nonscientific activities do a great job of leaving the problem for a time and going on to other things. Later on, the solution hits—the "A-ha!" or "Eureka!" Dreaming, unconscious thought, imagery, and transformational thinking all place no constraints on the solution. He listed over 300 scientists of the 19th and 20th centuries who were also accomplished artists, writers, or musicians.[16]

Even though an experiment is in progress, nothing is written in stone. Changes occur and modifications must be made, reflecting the cyclical nature of the process. This may be difficult for the child who has been taught using a linear model. Allowing your child to take time to "incubate" his or her thoughts may help in changing constraints. Activities involving metaphorical thinking and analogies may facilitate the ability to break set. Brain teasers, board games, or reading a book are other suggestions. Even going outside to take a walk in the woods or play a game of soccer may be just the prescription needed to help your child change constraints.

Verification and Elaboration. This phase may be long or short. Weeks, months, or years of frustration over a solution to a problem has finally ended. The scientist must verify the solution and communicate the discovery. Quite often, the solution leads to another problem, so the creative processes continue to recycle.

Not only do children need to verify their results, but they need to communicate them. For example, a child working on enzymes and pH may present his or her paper to a group of biochemists. A child whose research involved cross-pollination and propagation of a new plant species may choose to bring the results to the attention of the botanical society. The results of the battery investigation might be shared in a letter to the various battery companies, along with data tables and suggestions. Your child's school may also participate in science fairs, Science Olympiad, Future Problem Solving, or other scientific or creative competitions.

Implications for Home and School

At School

A recent study of science textbooks and curricular materials found that there is no basal science program that is appropriate for gifted students at the elementary or junior high level.[17] The results of this study, the issues presented earlier dealing with time and attention paid to science in the classroom, and the lack of materials for activities in many schools are real issues. Taken together, these school-related factors do not favor nurturing children who are talented in science. How can you tell if your child's program is adequate to nurture science talent? The following nonnegotiables will give you a place to start:

1. Children are exposed to science in some way everyday.
2. The classroom contains a rich collection of books, manipulatives, and other materials, both natural and human-made.

3. Children have time each day to pursue their interest in science by reading books with a science focus, investigating their own self-selected projects, or spending time with science-related materials.
4. Science investigations are inquiry-based, student-centered, and open-ended.
5. A broad range of ability and reading levels are addressed by the materials used in the science classroom.
6. The teacher has advanced knowledge of the science topics taught at the particular grade level.
7. There are provisions for enrichment and acceleration in each topic studied.
8. The science content is taught using concepts, principles, issues, and themes.
9. There are opportunities to work in homogenous groups.
10. Assessment includes both traditional paper-and-pencil tests and alternative assessment options (e.g., performance assessments, portfolios, student-selected projects).

At Home

If you child's school science program does not adequately meet his or her needs, you may have to attend to your child's talent development at home. Here are some ideas you might incorporate: First, consider science as action. We learn science by doing science using real-world problems and working like a scientist does. That's the real key to the issue. The content, process, product, and environment must all interact. One of those elements can't be missing or taught in isolation. Children can't learn to look for solutions and discover without opportunities to explore, question, investigate, examine, and probe. Hence, you will need to search for materials that are open-ended, not the type of materials that usually come with most textbook series adopted by schools. Avoid "follow the directions" labs or "cookbook" labs. They usually have step-by-step instructions, complete with pictures that show typical results, leaving little for the student to do other than manipulate the equipment.

Have your children read essays by, and biographies and autobiographies about, scientists, paying close attention to the process by which they sought solutions, not just who they were and what they discovered. Take your children to the science museum on special "talk to the scientists" days. Allow them opportunities to interact with practicing scientists in the family or your circle of friends. Help your children with high ability and interest in science to find mentors in their area of interest. Allow your children the freedom to self-select a research problem and carry it through. Have them record and observe everything. Don't praise them purely on the "correct" answer. Check out your children's thinking by asking them to explain to you how they arrived at the answer. Ask "why" and "how." Have them defend their reasoning. Encourage flexible thinking and interpretation. Permit them to study a field of interest in depth. Foster the characteristics of creative scientists.

The next section will give you an in-depth look at the processes of science. This may serve as a primer for you as you develop or seek activities to nurture you child's science talent at home.

The Processes of Science

The methodology of science consists of a number of basic and integrated science processes or thinking skills. We sometimes ignore content in favor of process and vice versa. Ideally, we want a nice marriage of content with process. Rather than just working on a particular process with your child in isolation, do it within content instead. This is a good rule of thumb to remember throughout our discussion of science processes.

I will explain each skill and give some examples to assist you in developing your own activities to use with your child. The examples presented are just guidelines. You should modify each to meet the needs of your own child's developmental level. A gifted child's cognitive, social, emotional, and motor ability are most likely at various "ages" at any given time. Perhaps your child's mental age is 12, but chronological age and motor skill development is about age 5. Due to this asynchronous development of gifted children, you may need to go with the child's cognitive ability and modify the activity until the motor ability catches up.

Basic Scientific Thinking Skills

First, let's look at the basic scientific thinking skills: observing, communicating, classifying, using numbers, measuring, inferring, and predicting.

Observing. This is a good first process with which to engage your child. Observing allows the child to use all his or her senses. Start with something familiar, such as a favorite toy. Ask, "What can you tell me about Mr. Bear?" "What color is he?" "Tell me about his covering." Depending on the sophistication of the child, you may be able to enter into a discussion of quantitative (those attributes that can be counted, measured, timed, etc.) versus qualitative (those things that are described) observations.

Communicating. Communication may be oral, pictorial (drawing pictures), graphic (making graphs, charts, diagrams), or written. Your child's cognitive and motor development will help you determine which form you might want to introduce. Simple descriptions, drawings of objects found on a walk through the park, or a graph depicting the favorite ice cream flavors of friends and family members are good first choices.

Classifying. Classifying objects is the basis for a number of commercial games. Children enjoy placing items in piles according to their attributes. An assortment of buttons, cereal prizes, or natural objects accumulated from a nature walk are great collections for classifying into groups. If your child's ability to classify objects is more sophisticated, you may want to find some classification keys (sometimes called dichotomous keys) to natural objects such as trees, flowers, insects, or seashells. These will generally provide a challenge to an elementary-level child.

Using Numbers. The importance of mathematics to science is easily demonstrated here. We need numbers to quantify our data. All basic math skills, such as counting, adding, subtracting, and finding averages, must be sharpened. Some children may move rapidly through these basic skills and show interest in learning about powers of 10, decimals, and other number bases well before these topics are introduced in school.

Measuring. Very simple measurement activities might include ordering a set of pencils from longest to shortest, measuring items with nonstandard measurements (how long is the kitchen if we measure it by your feet?), and measuring water (over the sink!) with 1-, ½-, and ¼-cup measures. More sophisticated forms of measurement are mass, area, volume, and temperature, and your child's developmental level will guide you in introducing these ideas.

Inferring. Inferences are basically explanations of observations. This process entails being able to draw upon relationships among what is being observed and then generalize. Inferences must be logical, and we need to remember that they are also not final. Often, more observations lead to a new inference. For example, the sky darkens at noon. This is an observation that you and your child might make. See if your child can draw an inference based on this observation. What inferences might be made upon walking out of the mall and seeing the sidewalk pavement is wet?

Predicting. We make predictions based on what we have observed in the past or the data we currently have available. We can make some accurate predictions, such as the sunrise, while other predictions, such as what the weather will be tomorrow, cannot be made with such precision. Giving your child experiences with both kinds of predictions will increase his or her scientific thinking. For example, children may have noticed that potato chips leave a greasy spot on their brown lunch sacks. Perhaps they can select several different types of material, such as copier paper, newsprint, waxed paper, and plastic wrap, and predict which ones will allow the oil in the potato chips to pass through. Then, have them test their predictions.

Integrated Scientific Thinking Skills

The integrated skills are more complex and involve higher levels of thinking. These skills include controlling variables, defining operationally, interpreting data, and experimenting.

Controlling Variables. When you and your child conduct an investigation, you need to be able to figure out what affected the outcome. For this reason, we need to control the variables, those things we manipulate or hold constant during the investigation. In our investigations, we want to hold all but one of the variables constant each time we perform the experiment. To determine what plants need to live, we might set up an investigation in this manner: Plant A gets good soil, water, air, and sunlight. Plant B gets everything except water. Plant C gets everything but air, and so on. By recording the data from our observations of each plant, we can compare our results and begin to get an idea about the needs of plants. Of course, we would want to repeat the experiment several times to be sure. Note, however, that this is a very brief condensation of a quite elaborate investigation. We would want all plants to be of the same variety, have a standard for the amount of water given, amount of sunlight . . . you get the picture.

Defining Operationally. Children with science talent will spend much of their time investigating anything and everything. However, they need to be precise when communicating their problem, procedure, results, conclusions, and so forth. One way to be precise is to define operationally the terms used in the experiment. For example, if we are investigating the question, "Do earthworms like light?," we need to define what we mean by "earthworm," "likes," and "light." Does "like" mean they turn toward it, move 2 inches toward it, or move 2 inches toward the light within 5 minutes of turning on the light?

Interpreting Data. This skill is the sense-making part of thinking scientifically. Once all the data have been gathered and organized, interpreting them means figuring out what the data all means. If we want our young scientists to make valid conclusions, then we must help with data interpretation. Suppose you kept a count of the birds visiting the bird feeder at the same time each day. How could this data be displayed to ensure accurate interpretation? What conclusions might be drawn once the data were interpreted?

Experimenting. In its simplest form, experimenting is just messing around with materials. What happens if I manipulate this? What might happen if . . . ? How can I . . . ? What if I put these together? Take them apart? Giving children a variety of safe materials with which to experiment allows them to develop their own questions and figure out ways to find answers. Experimenting involves trial and error, and young children with science talent need a safe place to work through these processes.

Affective Skills

Affective skills are those that deal with valuing, appreciating, feeling, and interest—the heart, rather than the head. Although the scope of this chapter does not allow a complete discussion of these skills, I think it is important for parents to know that there are skills beyond the cognitive ones that must be fostered in their child talented in science. These affective skills include curiosity, a desire for knowledge, patience, self-discipline, craftsmanship, having confidence in and relying on data, comfort with ambiguity, willingness to modify explanations, cooperation, respect for and trust in the thinking process, and honesty.[18]

Thinking Conceptually

Question: If the science curriculum in any one of the nation's 107,000 schools were a body of water, which one would it be? Answer: Utah's Great Salt Lake, 83 miles long, 51 miles wide, but only 13 feet deep on average.[19]

While this question wasn't really found on a test, it serves to illustrate what has become of science curricula. In classrooms where science is taught, quite often a variety of topics are covered superficially, rather than a few in depth. At the national level, the movement is toward teaching using concepts. Concepts are the "Big Ideas," the framework upon which we can hang the generalizations, principles, skills, and facts in a course of study. Concepts should come from all areas of science—life, earth, physical, and technological science. Many concepts cut across areas and even disciplines. Consider engaging your child's interest in science through the use of concepts, rather than only learning a large body of factual knowledge. Here are some examples of concepts: Change, Cause and Effect, Systems, Scale, and Patterns.

A Final Note: The Special Case of Gifted Girls and Science

Girls do not take as many advanced science classes as boys, and they are less likely to choose careers with a science focus. As parents, it is important that we encourage our daughters in the areas of math and science. We need to help them understand that they can enjoy and be successful at math and science. Because the paucity of women in science fields continues to be an issue, parents need to be aware of some of the causes so that interventions with their own girls can begin in time for changes to be made.[20]

The Leaking Pipeline

The science pipeline is leaking women. This phenomenon, in which gifted girls lose interest in science, starts slowly during the elementary school years, where it is barely perceptible. By middle school, the leak becomes evident, and, by high school, there is a steady drip that can no longer be ignored. By middle school, girls show a marked decline in interest in science, and that interest continues to wane throughout high school. Young women, more often than young men, choose not to continue advanced coursework in math and science beyond what is required for high school graduation. Math is the critical filter: If a student does not take 4 years of mathematics, including calculus, there is little chance of being able to declare a major in science or a science-related field in college. It is crucial that you encourage your daughters to take 4 years of math in high school. Otherwise, they will not have the foundation for advanced science classes.

Personality Factors

Girls who conform to the stereotypical ideal of the well-behaved, quiet young lady are often rewarded by parents and teachers. Boys are often reinforced for being assertive, curious, questioning, and active. These characteristics map onto some of the attributes of successful scientists. Unfortunately, girls exhibiting these same characteristics are often labeled as "obnoxious" or "bossy," and these behaviors are subsequently discouraged. In addition, there is evidence that teachers give low ratings on academic evaluations to high-achieving girls who are analytical and prefer original, rather than traditional, approaches to their studies, which are the characteristics that support success in quantitative fields.

Attitudes Toward Science

Girls' attitudes toward science decline steadily from upper elementary grades through high school. Girls start school with a positive attitude toward science and something causes this attitude to drop. The resulting negative attitudes can discourage girls from electing to continue advanced coursework in math and science. This, in turn, reduces their chance of pursuing a career in science.

What Parents Can Do

In concert with your daughter's guidance counselor, insist that she take 4 years of advanced math, including calculus, and 4 years of science, including physics. Help your daughter be proud of her gifts and talents, especially in math and science. Help her connect with strong female role-models in science careers, such as an industrial chemist, physician, or biomechanical engineer. Empower your daughter to take risks, experience failure, and problem solve in a safe, supportive environment. Celebrate and encourage her assertiveness; this is a quality of a good leader, not bossiness. Foster positive attitudes toward science by providing hands-on, minds-on activities that demystify science at an early age.[21]

Suggested Materials for Nurturing Science Talent

Berger, Melvin and Gilda Melvin, *Do Whales Have Belly Buttons? Questions and Answers About Whales and Dolphins.* New York: Scholastic, 1999.

Cash, Terry, Steve Parker, and Barbara Taylor, *175 More Science Experiments.* New York: Random House, 1989.

Center for Gifted Education, *Dust Bowl.* Dubuque, Iowa: Kendall/Hunt, 1989.

Center for Gifted Education, *The Chesapeake Bay.* Dubuque, Iowa: Kendall/Hunt, 1997.

Center for Gifted Education, *Hot Rods.* Dubuque, Iowa: Kendall/Hunt, 1997.

Center for Gifted Education, *Acid, Acid Everywhere.* Dubuque, Iowa: Kendall/Hunt, 1997.

Center for Gifted Education, *What a Find.* Dubuque, Iowa: Kendall/Hunt, 1997.

Challoner, Jack, *My First Batteries and Magnet Book.* New York: DK Publishing, 1992.

Claiborne, Michele, *Mindbenders: Optical Wizardry.* New York: DK Publishing, 1997.

Cooney, Barbara, *Miss Rumphius.* New York: Puffin, 1982.

Demi, *The Empty Pot.* New York: Henry Holt, 1990.

Earle, Silvia A., *Dive! My Adventures in the Deep Frontier.* New York: Scholastic, 1999.

Kneidel, Sally, *Creepy Crawlies and the Scientific Method.* Golden, Colo.: Fulcrum, 1993.

Macaulay, David, *The New Way Things Work.* New York: Houghton Mifflin, 1998.

McDonald, Megan, *Insects Are My Life.* New York: Scholastic, 1995.

Merriam, Eve, *The Wise Woman and Her Secret.* New York: Simon & Schuster, 1991.

Ruef, Kerry, *The Private Eye.* New York: Atlantic Monthly Press, 1998.

Schwartz, David M., *Q is for Quark.* Berkeley, Calif.: Tricycle Press, 2001.

Showell, Ellen and Fred Amram, *From Indian Corn to Outer Space.* Peterborough, N.H.: Cobblestone Publishing, 1995.

Smith, Alastair, *The Usborne Big Book of Experiments.* New York: Scholastic, 1996.

Steptoe, John, *The Story of Jumping Mouse.* New York: Mulberry Books, 1972.

Walker, Sally M., *Mary Anning Fossil Hunter.* New York: Scholastic, 2001.
Watson, Philip, *Light Fantastic.* New York: Walker Books, 1982.
Wells, Robert E., *What's Smaller Than a Pygmy Shrew?*, Morton Grove, Ill.: Albert Whitman, 1995.

3

developing talent in language arts during the elementary years

by
michael clay thompson

The general objects—are to provide an education adapted to the years,
the capacity, and the condition of everyone, and directed to their freedom
and happiness—we hope to avail the state of those talents which nature
has sown as liberally among the poor as the rich, but which perish
without use, if not sought for and cultivated.
—Thomas Jefferson, *Notes on Virginia*[1]

What is language? Language is the commu-
nication that we create with words, whether spoken, written, or thought. We
think with words, and we make our thoughts known to others through
words, both in casual and formal situations, including in school and in our
professional lives. To be good at language is to be stronger in almost everything we do.

Not only are the language arts important as knowledge in themselves,
but they are the path to advancement in other disciplines. If a child is strong
in the language arts, he or she has a beginning for progress in history, foreign
language, science, the arts, and even mathematics.

Strength in language arts requires a long-term, challenging program that
exposes students to things they think are difficult—so difficult that they are
unable to do them without learning and growing. It is in the nature of *challenge* to accomplish what you were not able to do at first, but what you equip
yourself through strenuous effort to do only after you encounter the challenge.

Unfortunately, in many programs, the level of challenge in language arts is low. This is particularly so in those language arts that are the basis of professional success and serious scholarship. The quality and quantity of rigorous reading, sound instruction in grammar, development of advanced vocabulary, and training in formal writing are sometimes sacrificed to popular educational philosophies that emphasize building self-esteem through avoiding challenge. These easier programs feature unevaluated activities such as informal journals that anyone can do without learning or correction, a disdain for instruction in vocabulary and grammar, and a sustained avoidance of real reading. The reading that is assigned is often characterized by the reliance on dumbed-down anthologies, the low number of novels assigned, and the focus on popular, but vocabulary-deficient books and stories. Parents of gifted children must regard such programs as unsatisfactory. Gifted children need sharp challenge, with the constant experiences of more and stronger reading, formal writing, demanding standards in the correct use of grammar, and a continual extension of their vocabulary base.

The good news is that, whether there are strong programs available to the child or not, it is possible for parents to guide their children in ways that develop language talent. In this quest, the central goal involves reading.[2] Even in this age of multimedia and computers, reading books is the basis of intellectual growth. In fact, the attraction of electronic alternatives—not to mention the cap on learning placed by many school systems—has created a situation in which *reading books is more important than ever.*

Books, unlike textbooks, are not controlled. Books are not confined to grade level. From real books, children encounter a diversity of ideas and experiences. In real books, children grapple with tragedies and ethical choices; they hear correct grammar; they receive wonderful ways to spend personal time. They learn a vocabulary beyond anything heard in the school or home; they make fictional friends similar to themselves who befriend them all their lives; they absorb how writing should sound; they gain the basis for strength in all of their school subjects. For these and other reasons, creating an enduring love of books is the key, and parents of gifted children have every opportunity to do this for their children.

Content of a Language Arts Curriculum

High scholarship is not necessarily popular. Many have commented on the anti-intellectual tone of U.S. culture, which extends, ironically, even to the school environment. In a culture that emphasizes easy reading and high-interest stories, it is important for the gifted child to move against the current. Gifted children must seek out the strenuous content from which mediocre programs gravitate away. Gifted children need serious knowledge, including a direct acquaintance with the giants of literature, a mature competence in the revelations and applications of grammar, and a vocabulary that simply does not exist in soft stories and dumbed-down textbooks. Parents should actively seek out challenge programs, honors programs, and other special programs that feature exceptionally strong language arts curricula. Key elements include classics, grammar, vocabulary, writing, biography, and foreign language.

Classics

Joyce VanTassel-Baska has said that "The gifted child's major contact with the world of ideas is through literature."[3] Therefore, it matters what literature students read, and heavily included in what they read should be the classics, meaning not just the ancient classics like *The Iliad*, but modern and young children's classics, such as *The Wind in the Willows* and *Peter Pan*. Typically, classics are read by children all over the world, in dozens or even hundreds of languages. Classics are part of the global experience that bright children everywhere share. Every major publisher has a classics division, and parents should familiarize themselves with the children's classics section of their favorite bookstore. From children's earliest years, parents should begin to read children's classics, such as the Mother Goose stories and the great fairy tales, to their children. Precocious young readers will soon begin reading them on their own. Through the classics, students become directly acquainted with the world's beloved writers, with the themes and questions that have concerned humankind for centuries, and with characters known all over the world. Academic life is filled with references to the classics that only students who have read these books will understand. Classics also fill students with thousands of well-made sentences that become templates for their future writing. Classics also use good words, above the artificial limitations of age-graded vocabulary. In James M. Barrie's *Peter Pan*, for example, we find these words: *diffidence, placid, adhere, quietus, miscreant, quixotic, reproof, condescend, somber, enigma, phlegmatic, undulate, sublime, resolute, strident, din, amicable, amorous, raconteur, profound, dejection, placid, amiably, tedious, mea culpa, perplex, impede, interpose, incisive, impassive, admonish, aperture, avidly, perfidious, miasma, abject, portal, fain, sanguinary, retort, imperiously, hauteur, patronize, aloof, blithe, boon, cypher, wince, defray, genial, cadaverous, remonstrate, nether, upbraid, solicitous, conveyance, mauve, hitherto, succulent, artifice, proffer, ardent, tremulous, recriminate, assail, virulent,* and *insinuate.*[4]

Some of the strong-vocabulary titles that older elementary gifted children might read include Mark Twain's *The Prince and the Pauper* and *Tom Sawyer,* Jack London's *White Fang* and *The Call of the Wild,* Robert Louis Stevenson's *Treasure Island* and *Kidnapped,* H. G. Wells's *The War of the Worlds,* James M. Barrie's *Peter Pan,* Arthur Conan Doyle's *The Hound of the Baskervilles,* Sir Walter Scott's *Ivanhoe,* Kenneth Grahame's *The Wind in the Willows,* Kate Wiggin's *Rebecca of Sunnybrook Farm,* and L. M. Montgomery's *Anne of Green Gables.*

Other titles, especially for the very youngest readers, might include the Mother Goose stories, the great fairy tales; books by Beverly Cleary, Shel Silverstein, Eric Carle, or Roald Dahl; Enid Blyton's *Famous Five* series; the Dr. Seuss books; *Pippi Longstocking, Mr. Popper's Penguins;* and *Little House on the Prairie.* Parents can also consult *Some of My Best Friends Are Books: Guiding Gifted Readers From Preschool to High School,* by Judith Wyn Halsted or *Books for the Gifted Child,* Volumes 1 and 2, by B. H. Baskin and K. H. Harris for additional suggestions (see the resource section at the end of this chapter).

Parents who wish to accelerate their child's literary vocabulary can begin with this list of 50 words, which are prominent in the classics of American and British literature; these words do not look like children's words, but they are found even in children's literature: *countenance, profound, manifest, languor, serene, prodigious, acute, exquisite, melancholy, perplex, amiable, grotesque, clamor, condescend, singular, placid, sublime, allude, abate, incredulous, tremulous, vex, odious, venerate, vulgar, apprehension, vivid, wistful, subtle, pallor, visage, repose, tedious, traverse, remonstrate, retort, undulate, martyr, articulate, rebuke, prostrate, tangible, placate, pervade, superfluous, abyss, genial, sagacity, derision, somber.*[5]

Grammar

In *Teaching the Gifted Child,* James Gallagher urged language arts teachers to "go beyond the rather sterile presentation of grammar and syntax."[6] This should not be construed as deleting grammar and syntax from the curriculum, but as encouragement to explore grammar in exciting and creative ways, realizing that grammar gives gifted students a way to think about language.[7] Gifted students must know that their futures depend on their ability to use pronouns correctly, to match their subjects to their verbs, to avoid misplacing modifiers, to keep their tenses parallel, and to write sentences, rather than sentence fragments. These standards of correct English must be understood and applied. They are a requirement of professional language. Good writing, punctuation, and speaking all depend in part on a solid competence in all four levels of traditional grammar:

- parts of speech;
- parts of sentence;
- phrases; and
- clauses.

Parents should seek out teachers and programs that emphasize classical grammar, beginning in early elementary school. It is advisable to inquire in detail, since some programs only include the parts of speech in their grammar curriculum, even though the parts of speech alone are insufficient for children to make most of the important grammar decisions. Gifted children from at least third grade on are capable of mastering the fundamentals of the four levels of traditional grammar.

Vocabulary

For decades, educational philosophy has been in the grip of Horace Mann's age-graded concept that gives all children of the same age the same curriculum. Gifted children are ignored by this approach, and, in the area of vocabulary, the effect has been a national intellectual catastrophe. When we examine the vocabulary of children's classics written a generation ago, such as *Peter Pan*, *The Wind in the Willows*, *Alice in Wonderland*, and *Tom Sawyer*, we see strong vocabularies that are needlessly excluded from elementary curricula today. The truth is that every third grader in the land can pronounce and define *Tyrannosaurus Rex*, and all of those children are surely capable of learning words such as *serene*. In obedience to the age-grade dogma, however, we have reduced the vocabulary of all elementary texts to the simplest, least-educated words, and then we despair over low test scores! As a nation, we have forgotten that children won't learn what they haven't encountered. For gifted children, the age-graded vocabulary limits are grossly unrealistic. Parents should expose their children to a strong vocabulary from the beginning, both in conversation and in what they read to them, and they should seek programs that will extend this effort.

Additionally, some educational philosophies—one thinks of the whole language movement—ban direct instruction in vocabulary in favor of discovering words in literary context, so that the word is encountered in a living story where it will have authentic meaning for the child. While discovering words in context is good, banning direct vocabulary study is a mistake. Gifted students need a strong foundation in the Latin and Greek basis of English diction,[7] and they should also learn the advanced English vocabulary of the classics of American and British literature, including such words as *countenance, serene, manifest, sublime, odious,* and *grotesque.*[8]

Writing

Although writing is sometimes approached as a separate skill, the truth is that reading is the beginning of writing. Young children whose parents have read children's classics to them from their preschool years will have developed not only their own reading abilities, but a right sense of how sentences should sound and a classical level of exposure to vocabulary. As children learn to write, parents should encourage them to write in many ways and for many reasons. Parents should write notes to their children and encourage them to write down their feelings about things they learn. Children can keep diaries and write their own stories. There is no reason to avoid helping them write correctly, so long as it is done in a supportive manner. Children can also begin using computer word processors at very early ages and can enjoy the ease and fluency that this technology brings to the editing and revising process.

Biography

Many researchers have noticed the benefits of biographies for gifted children. James Gallagher wrote that "In particular, the study of biographies is a strongly suggested program for the gifted, on the very sound grounds that some degree of identification and career interest may be stimulated when a particular biography hits a particular youngster just right."[9] This is worth emphasis in an educational culture that ignores biography; few classes in any subject, including history, assign biographies; yet, for gifted children, biography meets their need for depth and their intense identification with humanity.

Foreign Language

It is difficult to exaggerate the increasing importance of foreign language for gifted children. Spanish, in particular, has a social and intellectual imperative unprecedented in U.S. education. From foreign language, children receive numerous benefits, including grammar, vocabulary building through cognates (words related to words in the other language; *biography* in English is a cognate of *biografía* in Spanish), direct encounters with poetry and literature in the second language, multicultural education, and an inherently interdisciplinary curriculum.[10] One of the special characteristics of Spanish is that hundreds of ordinary words in Spanish have English cognates that are advanced, making Spanish a secret strategy for vocabulary building in English.

The tradition in U.S. schools has been to de-emphasize foreign language by treating it primarily as a college admissions element, deferring the introduction of foreign language until the high school years. Today, many school systems begin foreign language in the middle school grades, but this is too little, too late. School should emphasize foreign language beginning at elementary grade levels. Then, actual fluency should be the goal because today's students are not studying foreign language just for college admissions, but to be functional in a multicultural and bilingual society.

Behavioral Indicators of Language Talent and Stages of Development

The behavioral indicators of talent in language, not surprisingly, are revealed through language. This precocity in language is evident from the earliest years. According to Barbara Clark,

> Gifted ability in language arts is one of the easiest areas of ability to discover. Children with high ability in this area often use complex sentence structures before two years of age. Their conceptual development is reflected in the questions and observations they make and the vocabulary they use at this age. Their memory for events seems unusual, and they have a growing body of information they enjoy sharing even before the age of three.[11]

As children approach school age, parents will observe numerous behavioral indications of potential talent in language arts:

> Early word recognition and reading, rapid and easy learning, large vocabulary, ability to deal with complex and abstract concepts, ver-

bal expressiveness, voracious reading, and precocious reading comprehension frequently are listed as characteristics of gifted children.[12]

One of the most striking examples of early potential comes from
Barbara Clark, who reported the following conversation between a grand-
mother and granddaughter:

"I'm playing with my chalkboard."
"You are?"
"Yes. I played with it yesterday, too."
"Really?"
"Don't you remember? You gave it to me for my happy birthday last
Wednesday."[13]

The little girl is only *22 months old,* and she illustrates many of the characteristics that indicate giftedness in language arts. In addition to precocity
in vocabulary, early use of complicated word order, and intense involvement
with literature, books, and libraries, gifted children may express their need
for depth through obsession with reading numerous books on a single topic.
Gifted children are known for "going off the deep end" on subjects that fascinate them. This makes sense: While others struggle at the edge of new
knowledge, trying to understand, gifted children understand immediately
and want to know much more, often immediately. Their initial comprehension suggests meanings to them, implies applications, and ignites curiosity,
spurring them to learn more, which ignites greater curiosity, which becomes
a self-propelling hunger to learn more. By the time some students would
have turned back, confused, from the initial encounter with the knowledge,
gifted children might be many levels deeper and enthralled. They may have
read every book in the school or public library on the subject!

Gifted children often read before they reach first grade or even before
they reach kindergarten. Inflexible programs that insist on "teaching" such
students to read can create damaging misalignments between the child's
needs and the mandatory reading program. Even moving the student to
the so-called high group may not be the answer; the class's advanced reading group—designed for the best regular readers—may be woefully below
the reading needs of a gifted child. They are not regular readers. Clark
wrote that:

Often gifted children will come to school reading significantly beyond their age peers. Care must be taken, however, that the scope of material presented is difficult enough to tap the extent of this growth. "Top" reading groups may still be far below the gifted reader's capability.[14]

The gap between the gifted child and the rest of the students is not infrequently far greater than what may be popularly assumed. One mother reported: "My son has been studying acting (mostly Shakespeare) since he was 4 years old. Once when he was 5 or 6, he memorized an entire script (90 pages)—everyone's parts—by the second time he heard it."[15]

Stages of Development From Novice to Expert

Intelligence and language are merged so intimately that high intelligence produces an exceptional, noticeable, and rapid acquisition of language. Gifted children frequently exhibit language maturity that appears early, distinguishes them from other children their own age, and continues to develop with a self-propelled energy, placing greater distance each year between the child's educational needs and the school curriculum. Gifted children who do not receive challenging books or elaborate writing assignments at school may respond by developing extraordinary private reading and writing habits or hobbies. They may amass large personal libraries and write their own plays, poems, and novels.

There are some characteristics that, while not applying to every gifted child, do pertain to most, and that constitute stages in a gifted child's language development:

1. *Early language fluency.* Gifted children often display language ability as infants, cooing responsively, learning first words rapidly, using grown-up-sounding sentences early, and speaking to adults with striking presence and equality, before they have learned to read. They may exhibit strikingly advanced vocabulary and a full recall of stories read to them. They may express shockingly mature ideas at very early ages. At the age of 2½, one young girl commented, as the family was driving over a railroad overpass, "I'm on a bridge and there's no water beneath me."[16]

2. *Reading prior to school.* If their parents read to them frequently, gifted children may learn to read through osmosis, moving quickly from fin-

ishing their parents' sentences to reading their own books independently. In a positive, book-filled environment, this effect snowballs, and gifted children can become accomplished readers well before they reach school. Ken W. McCluskey described a visit to his office by a 4-year-old boy who, upon walking into the room, looked at a piece of equipment and asked, "Impedance audiometer. What's that?"[17]

3. *Need for language, and preference for above-grade-level literature.* From the first school years, gifted children may exhibit a marked preference for above-grade-level literature. The quality, maturity, and quantity of standard reading programs will be inadequate—usually grossly inadequate—for them. Ordinary school texts and literature books will be too easy. Gifted children may act out their boredom and be misidentified as discipline problems, rather than as children with accelerated learning needs. If they can find a program that will challenge them, they can become highly experienced readers by the middle school years. Gifted middle schoolers not uncommonly read beyond what is typical of some college students. This above-grade-level preference may also be visible as an above-grade-level preference in language generally; gifted children may prefer to converse with adults, rather than with children their own age, whose conversation and interests may seem boring. They may love listening to adult conversations that other children their own age would not comprehend. They may find talk programs on public radio stations attractive. Some gifted children may prefer staying in church and hearing a sermon over going to Sunday school. Parents should note these indications of need for language.

4. *Unusual concern over issues of justice and morality in literature.* Gifted children often have a rapid moral development that affects their relationship to literature. Even in the elementary years, they exhibit a mature sense of fairness and justice not characteristic of other students their age. This can isolate them from their perplexed friends, who do not understand what they are upset or excited about and who may ridicule them. In language arts, their moral maturity can cause them to be deeply involved in certain literature (or current events) that other students their age find boring. Parents and teachers must be vigilant to respect and respond and to protect gifted children from any potential negative reactions to this impressive and valuable characteristic.

5. *Intense desire to read deeply in one subject.* As noted above, gifted children frequently develop overwhelming fascinations with things that interest them, fascinations that obsess them for extended periods of time. They sus-

tain longer than other children. They persist in studying their topic with great self-discipline to the dismay of others who do not understand their enthusiasm. A program that understands the intense enthusiasm of gifted children will find ways to honor this need for depth, and parents have an opportunity to respect it at home by helping their children acquire books and other material.

6. *Advanced studies in high school.* Joyce VanTassel-Baska has observed that "Because gifted learners have mastered certain basic content skills so well that they can do them automatically and earlier than other learners, they have the learning time to invest in more advanced and complex concepts and skills."[18] The benefit of this learning time becomes especially important in the high school years, when acceleration during the elementary and middle school years gives these students a chance to qualify for more advanced high school classes, such as Advanced Placement classes, more years of foreign language, and higher mathematics and science classes. Many middle school and high school gifted students also dual enroll by taking college classes either through local universities or through distance learning, including over the Internet.

7. *Fully developed talent.* Their combination of accelerated pace, extraordinary quality and quantity of reading, and propensity for exceptional depth, as well as their ability to retain most everything they read, frequently leads gifted children into accomplished lives as adults. Tellingly, Harry Passow defined the gifted person as "an individual with potential for outstanding achievement in a socially valuable area,"[19] emphasizing the benefit to humanity that can result when a gifted child's talent is fully developed. Since language fills so many areas that are essential to human happiness and progress, full development of language talent would seem to be an especially important goal for parents of gifted children.

Beginning the Enrichment Experiences Early

Parents of gifted children should actively enrich the language experiences of their children from the earliest days of their life. Enrichment begins in the home by avoiding talking down to children, employing a mature vocabulary in conversation, providing a literary environment, encouraging writing and appropriate computer use, and coaching children in an educational use of television. Children today have entertainment opportunities unknown a generation ago, with high-energy television programs, movies, and video games. If books are going to be a powerful factor in children's lives, it will have to come from an early habit of parents reading books to children.

In school, the question of enrichment is complicated. Some school systems understand the importance of gifted education and commit resources to teacher training that results in challenging, differentiated learning experiences. Other programs do not understand the real nature of differentiation for gifted children. An overemphasis on concept-poor, time-consuming projects is not beneficial to gifted children, and enrichment activities that do not feature complexity, concepts, and rapid learning are not appropriate. VanTassel-Baska has noted that

> programs, especially pullout-resource-room-type programs, stress enrichment projects and activities that are often not presented at a high or fast-paced level. The term *enrichment* often is used to characterize programs in which there may even be a purposeful avoidance of higher level content because of complaints from teachers at higher grade levels that they will have nothing left to teach if advanced content and skills are introduced earlier.[20]

The Role of Practice or Study

Studies of advanced development have found that verbal or linguistic giftedness develops where it is systematically encouraged and nurtured. Where language use is valued in the home and community and where academic experiences are provided with adequate time and attention to progress, linguistic competence may be viewed as predictable.[21]

Practice and Study

If a child played tennis for three weeks a year, scattered out over the calendar, no one would expect him or her to improve in tennis, yet that is what many programs do with books. They teach several books—three or four—during the year. Often, even those titles are weak, with mediocre challenges of interpretation and low vocabularies. These programs are then shocked to learn that their students have low vocabularies and that test scores are down! They devote months of class time to teaching students the "skills" needed to get higher scores on achievement tests.

First, programs that assign challenging books at every grade level do not need to remediate their curricula; and second, all students, including gifted students, need practice. Experience limits accomplishment, and students who have experienced few books will accomplish little. Gifted children cannot grow in a regular program that offers only a handful of grade-level titles; they need a gifted-level literature program that features quality and quantity. At a minimum, gifted children should be reading several strong titles of fiction and non-fiction every month in order to acquire the level of reading experience necessary. Typically, this involves a strong in-class literature program accompanied by an outside reading program that lets students select some of their own titles.

Choice

This element, letting students choose some of their titles, is important. Choice is for gifted children what oxygen is for lungs. Filled with raging curiosities and preferences fired by their intense minds, gifted children need freedom to chase their interests—to a degree that would seem nonsensical in ordinary life. This positive characteristic can be frustrated in programs where a controlling teacher selects and assigns all reading titles. A better approach is for the teacher to select some and to let students select others (perhaps for outside reading) within guidelines.

Practice and study are particularly important for the mastery of grammar. The four levels of traditional grammar, including the parts of speech, parts of sentence, phrases, and clauses, are easily learnable if students work with them regularly. In contradiction to the stereotype of grammar as a tedious, endless subject, it is actually quite small in its essentials; students need to learn about 60 terms to learn the fundamentals of grammar. This does require disciplined study of all four levels of grammar. The basic terms that organize the four levels of traditional grammar, organized by the four levels, are:

- parts of speech: noun, pronoun, adjective, verb, adverb, conjunction, preposition, interjection;
- parts of sentence (subject, predicate, direct object, indirect object, subject complement);
- phrases (prepositional, appositive, verbal); and
- clauses (independent, dependent).

Each of these terms is accompanied by other terms that elaborate its qualities. Nouns, for example, can be proper or common, singular or plural.

Even so, grammar is a short and easily learned subject. With practice and study, even young gifted students can master it quickly and permanently to their great advantage.

Parents should seek out programs that emphasize grammar and apply it to various language arts experiences, rather than just teaching it as a unit and ignoring it at other times. It will be important to find or advocate for programs that adopt an accelerated approach to grammar content compared to the typical age-graded topics. Gifted first graders can be introduced to the parts of speech, the eight kinds of words. Second graders should also study the basics of the sentence and learn that it has two sides, a predicate about a subject. By the third grade, students can learn about direct objects and subject complements, as well as about prepositional phrases, and they should learn that a sentence can have more than one clause (a subject with its verb), making a compound sentence. From fourth grade on, students should also know about indirect objects, appositive and verbal phrases, and both independent and dependent clauses, which will let them learn not only compound sentences, but complex sentences, as well. With this foundation, students will be able to make competent grammar decisions from their mid-elementary years on, and they can practice and study grammar by applying it to the rest of their language arts tasks.

Study is also essential in learning the etymological (word origins) foundation of the English language. Students must memorize the definitions of most Latin and Greek stems that are found in English because knowing the stems will not only help them define words, but also spell them and appreciate them. Asking gifted children to memorize may sound like heresy in the face of decades of theory that gifted children should concentrate on higher order thinking, but that is a misunderstanding. There is nothing low about learning, and the alternative to remembering is forgetting. We want gifted children from the mid-elementary grades on to know the meanings of the most important Latin and Greek stems, and we must not be impeded from this or other critical high knowledge by superficial prohibitions.

Overall, practice and study are more congenial to gifted children than to most children, particularly when choice has been involved or when the child sees why the subject is important or meaningful. Self-motivated study is one of the typical characteristics of gifted children, who study their own hobbies and obsession-topics with determined persistence. This can provide the basis for general study habits.

How to Choose or Evaluate a Program or Teacher

Gifted youth find instruction that covers material they already know or that is adjusted to the pace of the slowest student in the class particularly onerous.[22]

As a rule of thumb, parents should look for programs that are *intended* for gifted children and that are developed and implemented by trained professionals. Parents should look for sincere flexibility and modification of regular programs to accommodate the exceptional needs of gifted children, or even for an entire program or school developed for gifted children. Simple acceleration may not be the answer. Young gifted children may be advanced in their cognitive development, but still not prepared to participate in a class of students several years older than they are. Gifted elementary students may be able to understand an advanced lecture or read high school texts, but may be unable to write at the higher grade level. One good source of programs comes from the National Association for Gifted Children. On its Web site (http://www.nagc.org), NAGC maintains an annual list of summer and enrichment programs that parents can consider, listed by geographic region.

Whatever program parents consider, it will be important to study its philosophy. Some programs claim to accommodate the needs of gifted children, when in truth their teachers are untrained and the modifications are minimal or misguided. One indication of quality is language in the program's philosophy that addresses giftedness or the extreme range of learning needs. Van Tassel-Baska has noted that

> There are a few core questions they [parents] should ask. One would be what is the philosophy of the school in terms of teaching and learning and how does the school see gifted education fitting into that philosophy? I think that is very important. Secondly, what is their policy on acceleration of students? By that I mean acceleration broadly defined, like how do they handle kids at different levels within a curriculum? Thirdly, how they select teachers in that school? What are the criteria they use to select them?[23]

Grouping

Typical practice in gifted education varies with vogue. Even though research supports ability grouping for gifted children,[24] there are periods when programs disregard these findings and eliminate ability grouping.

Parents should seek out programs that group gifted students together with their gifted peers, where their similar abilities let them talk, read, and write with a natural freedom. They need time to be with other kids who read the kinds of books they read. Like all children, gifted children need a chance to be themselves.

> Gifted youngsters enjoy more than almost anything else the opportunity to exchange ideas among themselves without fear of being laughed at or scorned. Some programs group youngsters only periodically or for a certain time each day. However, extensive grouping by interest and ability is needed for gifted students to fully develop their potential.[25]

Parental Involvement: When, Where, How Much?

Parents of gifted children should plan to be involved in their child's education, from the beginning, both at home and at school. Society at large—and this includes many school systems—is not informed about, or supportive of, gifted education, and the parent will need to function as advocate, watchdog, friend, and mentor to the child.

It is crucial that parents intentionally develop a strong language environment in the home, one that envelops children in good books, grown-up words, and elaborate sentences. A baby-talk tradition should be avoided. Parents should read to their young children. This should be a daily event and should begin early. Jeanette Plauché Parker has stated that "Regardless of the age of the students, read aloud to them often, using the best available examples of the type of literature you are introducing."[26] The selection of books should include the child's choices, but should also employ guidance from the parent. The parent of a young gifted child should include outstanding works of children's literature, including famous fairy tales and children's classics. In the process, the parent should model reading and the love of reading and should serve as a positive role model for literary taste. There should generally be an emphasis on books in the home; there should be a home library, and the parent should also help the child to build up his or her own library. Parents should give books as gifts on birthdays and holidays. Trips to the bookstore should be special rewards. Stories should be talked about, recalled, and used as ways of explaining things. Both fiction and nonfiction books should be a part of children's lives. Once children develop the ability to read, parents should write to their children and develop a family habit of notes and letters. Gifted children should see their parents reading and writing frequently.

In addition to reading, there are exceptional media opportunities for language development that promote strong syntax and educated vocabulary, such as filmed versions of the classics of literature, including Franco Zeffirelli's film of *Hamlet* (1990) starring Mel Gibson (a ghost story!), *To Kill a Mockingbird* (1962), and the animated and live-action versions of *Animal Farm* (1954 and 1999, respectively). With each passing year, more outstanding examples of these great works become available on video or DVD, and a judicious use of these films will expose children to a stratum of the English language they are unlikely to hear in their ordinary lives. DVD technology also has the capacity to allow parents to switch languages, display other languages as subtitles, or both.

Communication with the child's school is crucial. If a child can read prior to entering school, the parent should meet with teachers and administrators before school begins to discuss the child's reading ability and the modifications that can be made. At this meeting, parents and teachers should review some options for appropriate assignments for their gifted reader. The child must not sit through a year's reading instruction, but must be given materials to read and challenging questions to discuss.

Emphasis should be placed on (1) open-ended questions that allow the child to think in depth about characters and options; (2) divergent questions that let the child develop numbers of possibilities; (3) questions that are not just cognitive, but are also affective, allowing the child to explore the emotional feelings of the characters and his or her own feelings in reaction to the story; and (4) questions that allow the child to compare different stories and characters, thereby accumulating a personal population of internalized models and heroes.

When to Accelerate in School

Acceleration means many things, from early entrance, to grade skipping to taking one area of content with different or older students. In essence, acceleration lets gifted students escape from artificial grade-level confines and gives them curricula that are typically given to older students. Given certain elements, such as the maturity, responsibility, and security of the student, with a well-defined and supervised program, acceleration can effectively match an appropriate curriculum to the gifted student's rapid pace and intense need to learn.

Indications of possible need for acceleration in language arts include the child's expressed dissatisfaction with the reading program, the fact that the child has already read the books assigned (possibly years earlier), the fact that the child finds the pace too slow (he or she may read a book over the weekend that is intended for 4 weeks of class), or the fact that the child is instantly ready to answer every question asked about the book in class. Other indications could be that the child already knows all of the words in the vocabulary program or can already spell all of the spelling words. In all of these situations, the child's expressed dissatisfaction is a key concern; a sufficient misalignment between the child's readiness and the school's language arts curriculum will cause the child to complain, and rightly so. It is impossible to learn what you already know, and many gifted children are doomed to learn nothing when the curriculum is not right for them.

What to Do When a Child is Reluctant to Participate or Wants to Drop Out

If a gifted child does not want to be a part of something, it is not necessarily a bad thing. A given program or activity may in fact be a poor use of the child's time. There are times when every gifted child is reluctant to participate in something or wants to drop out of something, and parents should listen carefully to their child's reasons. Is the child reluctant for healthy and positive reasons, or is the child reluctant because of simple inexperience and shyness? Certainly, there are times when a child needs gentle encouragement from the parent to join or continue a program that will soon become one of his or her favorite events. When a child is reluctant, the best thing to do is to listen and talk honestly and supportively. If you feel confident that the child should go forward, then explain your reasons and help the child in supportive ways that will aid any transition. If a child is deeply opposed, then the child's feelings should be honored.

Overinvolvement
Many gifted children are multitalented and will be excited about developing their talents; but, if parents do not exercise careful supervision, gifted

children can become involved in too many things, creating stress in both the child and the family. If the participation level becomes such that the child does not have enough personal time or time to read for pleasure, parents should help the child disengage from some activities.

Resources to Gather Information on Various Programs in the Community and Beyond

There are many resources for parents who want the best for their young gifted children. One of the best is *Parenting for High Potential*, the parents' magazine of the National Association for Gifted Children. This magazine, included with membership, is a benefit available to every parent who joins the association. Some printed resources include:

Alvino, James, *Parents Guide to Raising a Gifted Toddler: Recognizing and Developing the Potential of Your Child From Birth to Five Years.* New York: Ballantine Books, 1989.

Baskin, Barbara Holland and Gail Nelson, *Books for the Gifted Child*, vol. 1. New York: R. R. Bowker, 1980.

Halsted, Judith Wynn, *Some of My Best Friends Are Books,* 2nd ed. Scottsdale, Ariz.: Great Potential Press, 2002.

Hauser, Paul and Gail A. Nelson, *Books for the Gifted Child*, vol. 2. Westport, Conn.: Bowker-Greenwood, 1988.

Kingore, Bertie, *The Kingore Observation Inventory.* Des Moines, Iowa: Leadership Publishers, 1990.

Kurcinka, Mary Sheed, *Raising Your Spirited Child: A Guide for Parents Whose Child is More Intense, Sensitive, Perceptive, Persistent, and Energetic.* New York: Harper Perennial, 1992.

Saunders, Jacqulyn with Pamela Espeland, *Bring Out the Best: A Resource Guide for Parents of Young Gifted Children.* Minneapolis: Free Spirit, 1991.

Smutny, Joan, Sally Yahnke Walker, and Elizabeth Meckstroth, *Teaching Young Gifted Children in the Regular Classroom.* Minneapolis: Free Spirit, 1997.

The Internet also offers unprecedented opportunities for gathering information about programs for gifted children. Rather than list a series of Web site addresses that change frequently and which would probably be out of date before this book could be published, let us suggest that parents search on the Internet for various words and combinations of words: *gifted, gifted and talented, programs for gifted children, gifted preschoolers*, and so forth. This will bring up many outstanding programs and sources for information about gifted children, such as the Web site of the National Association for Gifted Children, the College of William and Mary's Center for Gifted Education, the National Research Center for the Gifted and Talented at the University of Connecticut, the Center for Talent Development at Northwestern University, the gifted education program at the University of North Carolina at Charlotte, the gifted department at Ball State University, and so forth. The Internet also offers numerous other private and institutional Web sites for parents and teachers of gifted children, the Hoagies Web site being a notable example.

Other common resources include public and university libraries, which usually have extensive information about gifted children. Parents should get to know their librarians, who will have extensive knowledge of the books and other materials available and who will be able to offer excellent reading suggestions. Many a gifted child has been profoundly influenced by a community librarian who became a supportive mentor and friend.

Parents should also seek and join their state gifted association, which often has a lending library, as well as vendors who sell materials about and for gifted children at their state conference. Through state gifted associations, parents can meet other parents of gifted children, attend conference presentations, and form networks that let them exchange reading lists, learn about local programs and summer experiences, and get ideas for communicating with school officials. State gifted associations eagerly seek committed parents who will work in the association, organize parent groups, and serve on their boards.

Finally, parents should join the National Association for Gifted Children, based in Washington, D.C. NAGC is a powerful resource in many ways, and their annual conference is an important event for all parents and teachers of gifted children. NAGC can serve as a reference for many questions and programs.

development
of mathematical
promise

by
linda jensen sheffield

Every human brain is hardwired to understand numerical quantities, and everyone has an innate ability to create mathematics.[1] Some research indicates that this inherent ability is even more basic to human nature than language.[2] Why is it, then, that so many people claim that they are incapable of understanding mathematics when virtually no one claims to be incapable of understanding language? It is not because the brain is somehow flawed or missing the "mathematics gene." Rather, it is because we have not fully developed the mathematical abilities with which we are all born. As a parent, you have the opportunity to help your child develop to his or her fullest potential as a mathematical thinker. It is an awesome responsibility, but also one full of excitement because listening to a child reason aloud as he or she struggles with a difficult mathematical question is a fascinating endeavor.

In this chapter, we will look at some of the ways that families and schools can work together with a child to fully develop this mathematical potential.

What is Mathematical Promise?

In this chapter, we will use *mathematical promise* to refer to the potential of children to become mathematically skilled, talented, creative, and even gifted. Before exploring what is meant by any of these terms, we first need to consider what it means to think like a mathematician. When we look at mathematicians from across the centuries and from around the world, we find that one aspect of "thinking like a mathematician" is that mathematicians see the world through "math-colored glasses." That is, mathematics colors their view of everything around them. They use numbers, shapes and symbols as an aid in making sense of the world. They search for patterns and use mathematics as a language to discuss their view of the physical world, as well as the mathematical worlds they create. Perhaps most importantly, they enjoy puzzles and problems and may spend years investigating questions that they raise. From Hypatia, one of the first noted female mathematicians born in Alexandria, Egypt, in 370 B.C., to more recent mathematicians such as Rear Admiral Grace Hopper, a pioneer in computer development, mathematicians enjoy prolonged investigations of problems and challenges they set for themselves. It is perhaps this passion for using mathematics to make sense of the world that is the most important factor in becoming mathematically gifted or talented

The current culture in the United States, however, often does not promote mathematical thinking. In fact, for many children (and parents), not doing mathematics is a point of pride. Children who do enjoy mathematics are often ridiculed as "geeks" or "nerds." A look at some recent history of mathematics education in the United States reveals that parents and teachers often neglect our most promising students in the area of mathematics. Parents and the community are often familiar with resources for encouraging a child's interest in and enjoyment of reading, art, music, and even science, but similar resources are often lacking or unknown to parents in the area of mathematics.

According to the 1980 National Council of Teachers of Mathematics (NCTM) report, *The Agenda for Action*, "The student most neglected, in terms of realizing full potential, is the gifted student of mathematics. Outstanding mathematical ability is a precious societal resource, sorely needed to maintain leadership in a technological world."[3] More than 20 years later, as we enter the 21st century, this issue becomes even more important. It is critical to the well-being of our society that we promote mathematical abilities in all students at the highest possible levels. We cannot be satisfied merely to identify gifted and talented mathematics students; we must create them.

In the past, gifted and talented mathematics students often have been defined as the top-scoring 3–5% of students on a standardized achievement or ability test. While helpful, this definition does not recognize the much broader concepts of mathematical ability and reasoning that are critical to the recognition and development of young mathematicians. It also does not address the fact that mathematical talent is something to be created and developed, not merely identified.

Recently, the National Council of Teachers of Mathematics appointed a task force to investigate the development of mathematically promising students. The NCTM used the term *mathematically promising*, rather than *mathematically gifted* or *talented*, to emphasize the change from the traditional definitions that tended to exclude large numbers of students, especially those from underrepresented populations such as minorities, girls, and students from lower socioeconomic groups. In the *Report of the NCTM Task Force on Mathematically Promising Students*,[4] mathematical promise is described as a function of at least four variables: ability, motivation, belief, and experience or opportunity. In this definition, none of the variables are considered to be fixed or permanent. All of the variables represent areas that need to be nurtured so that mathematical success might be maximized for a greatly increased number of promising students. Acknowledging recent research on learning and brain functioning, this definition notes that mathematical abilities are something to be developed, not just something that children are born with; that desire and motivation to learn greatly influence the amount of mathematics learned; and that students, families, and teachers all need to have confidence in a student's ability to learn. It also notes that students have a great deal of difficulty learning mathematics that they have never had the opportunity to experience on a deep, meaningful level. It is not enough to teach a child to compute rapidly with or without a calculator. Understanding mathematics on a more profound level involves being able to reason creatively and communicate effectively when solving difficult problems that may not have a single correct answer.

Parents are critical to this creation of mathematically promising children. The development of mathematical talent should begin long before children enter school and continue throughout their lives. In many ways, the development of mathematical abilities is no different than any other talent. If Tiger Woods' father had never given him a golf club, he never would have won four Masters tournaments in one year. If Venus and Serena Williams hadn't had a passion for playing tennis with their father from the time they were very young, they never would have become world champions. The same is true for mathematics: Parents can instill a love for learning and teach their children to enjoy the challenge of solving difficult mathematical problems and puzzles using simple techniques beginning when children are very young.

Just as reading with a child is an enjoyable way to help him or her develop abilities with written and spoken language, playing mathematical games, looking for patterns, organizing the world around you, and solving puzzles can be a delightful way to share your enthusiasm for mathematical reasoning. Just as the *Harry Potter* book series has encouraged millions of children to read interesting, complex literature, we need to find similar ways to encourage children to enjoy and explore the mysteries and complexities of mathematics.

The following checklist gives a number of characteristics that are often present in children or adults who have been identified as mathematically promising or precocious. It should be used to give you an idea of the breadth of traits that are components of mathematical talent. This goes far beyond being capable with addition, subtraction, multiplication, and division. In fact, many of the best mathematicians are not fast or even terribly accurate at these computations. Their strengths lie in their abilities to reason and think logically about mathematical problems.

Parents should use the checklist as a starting point for thinking about ways to help their children develop the attitudes, skills, and abilities that will enable them to become gifted or talented mathematicians. Note that the passion for exploration of problems and the enjoyment of manipulating numbers and shapes is more important to this mathematical development than the memorization of facts and formulae and the ability to compute quickly and accurately.

Checklist of Characteristics of Mathematically Promising Students[5]

I. Mathematical Frame of Mind
    A. Loves exploring numerical and spatial puzzles (e.g., enjoys jigsaw puzzles). Sees mathematics and structure in a variety of situations (e.g., sees a video game as a collection of polygons or counts everything in sight, such as steps to the front door, petals on a flower, buttons on a shirt, etc.).
    B. Recognizes, creates, and extends numerical, auditory and visual pat-

terns (e.g., designs a wallpaper border for his bedroom or creates a rhythmic drum beat using a stick and an empty plastic bucket).

C. Organizes and categorizes information (e.g., develops a database to catalog a collection of baseball cards).

D. Has a deep understanding of simple mathematical concepts including a strong number sense (e.g., explains that 7 + 8 must be 15 because it is 1 more than 7 + 7 or 1 less than 8 + 8 or because 7 + 3 is 10 and 8 is 5 more than 3, so the answer must be 5 more than 10).

II. Mathematical Creativity

A. Processes information flexibly (e.g., switches from numbers to pictures to symbols to graphs as appropriate in solving problems).

B. Reverses processes (e.g., goes from finding the sum of 4 + 3 to giving all the combinations of two single-digit numbers that give you a sum of 7).

C. Has original approaches to problem solving (e.g., solves problems in unique ways and tries unusual methods that teachers, parents, and classmates may not think of).

D. Strives for mathematical elegance and clarity in explaining reasoning (e.g., explains a solution or method to a classmate who does not understand the teacher's explanation).

III. Mathematical Formalization and Generalization

A. Generalizes the structure of a problem, often from only a few examples (e.g., accurately multiplies or divides three- and four-digit numbers after the teacher has demonstrated a few examples with two-digit numbers).

B. Uses proportional reasoning (e.g., makes an accurate scale drawing of a room with a consistent scale of 1 inch = 1 foot or finds the price of 5 cans of corn when given the price for 3 cans).

C. Thinks logically and symbolically with quantitative and spatial relations (e.g. recognizes that it does not matter which number you start with when adding two numbers and writes # + * = * + # to explain this).

D. Develops proofs and other convincing arguments (e.g., figures out why a math trick works, such as why when you multiply any single digit by 9 you can find the answer by subtracting 1 from that digit to get the number in the tens place in the answer and then subtracting the number in the tens place from 9 to get the number in the ones place—8 x 9: 8 – 1 gives you a 7 in the tens place and 9 – 7 gives you a 2 in the ones place; therefore 8 x 9 = 72).

IV. Mathematical Curiosity and Perseverance

    A. Is curious about mathematical connections and relationships (e.g., asks "Why?" and "What if?").

    B. Has energy and persistence in solving difficult problems (e.g., works on a question or problem on and off for days or relates new information to a question or problem that was investigated weeks or even months before).

    C. Digs beyond the surface of a problem (e.g., continues to explore after the initial problem has been solved).

The following characteristics may be useful in a mathematics class, but are not necessary for a child to be mathematically promising:

- speed and accuracy with computation (addition, subtraction, multiplication, and division);
- memory for formulae and facts; and
- spatial ability.

What Might Families Do at Home to Create Mathematical Promise?

Developing a Mathematical Frame of Mind

The human mind naturally views the world mathematically, and parents need only follow the child's lead to develop this ability. Studies have shown that children only a few weeks old can distinguish between one, two and three objects,[6] and these ideas lead naturally to the development of the concepts of counting and assigning a number to a set of objects. Children are also naturally curious about combining and separating groups of objects, and even very young infants know to expect to see two objects when a single object joins another single object or when one object is taken away from a group of three objects. This leads naturally to the development of the concepts of addition and subtraction, building later to concepts of multiplication and division.

When reading to your infant or child, be sure to include lots of bright, colorful books about numbers and shapes. Bookstores are full of counting and shape books, and those by Mitsumasa Anno, David Schwartz, Tana Hoban, Paul Giganti, Ruby Dee, Rod Clement, Eric Carle, Maurice Sendak, and Dr. Seuss are just a few to begin with. Don't restrict your child's learning about shapes and numbers to books, however. We all learn by using all of our senses, and, for children, the active involvement of the total body is critical. Be sure to actively involve your baby in "mathematizing" the world. Encourage your child to count the stairs as he or she climbs them, feel the shape of the round orange before eating it, and play peek-a-boo by hiding two or three objects under a handkerchief and listening to you name the number as he or she looks at them.

This ability to quickly see small numbers of objects without counting them is called *subitizing*. The human brain is designed to distinguish automatically between one, two, or three objects and to tell which of two disparate sets is larger than the other without having to count the number of objects in each set. Some authors, such as Glenn and Janet Doman, even recommend using large cards with 1–100 red dots for use with very young children.[7] Part of their recommended program consists of saying the names of the numbers of dots as the cards are shown to the child, beginning with cards showing from 1–10 dots and gradually increasing to the cards with 90–100 dots. Most brain researchers argue that humans of any age have trouble recognizing more than four objects without counting, but the Domans claim to have success with young children able to distinguish between a card with 58 dots and one card with 60 dots. (I must admit to having used these cards on a limited basis with my own son beginning when he was about 18 months old, and he later breezed through calculus in high school at the age of 15 and received a perfect score on the SAT II Advanced Mathematics test. I would not claim any direct cause and effect from the Doman program, however.)

It may be extreme to expect a toddler to distinguish 73 dots from 75 dots, but simple games that involve subitizing should be encouraged. Games where children roll dice to determine the number of spaces to move on a game board give children the opportunity to recognize small numbers and to associate those numbers with a physical action of moving a matching number of spaces. In a like manner, domino games are quite useful in helping children recognize and match patterns and add and subtract small numbers of objects. For young children, it is important that working with numbers, patterns, and shapes should be a fun way to explore the world.

A mathematical frame of mind consists of much more than counting and computing, however. Seeing the world mathematically also includes the desire to organize and understand the world around us and to make sense of patterns. Learning to think mathematically should arise from everyday activities such as organizing your home. You should set up areas in your home that encourage children to be involved in its organization and structure. This might include placing low shelves or baskets in the children's bedrooms where they can organize their collections of stuffed animals or blocks or setting up drawers and shelves in the kitchen that the child can reach to put away silverware and pots and pans in some organized fashion. Include children as you straighten up your home or sort your laundry and talk to them about what you are doing. For example, you might say, "I put this stuffed bear on the bottom shelf because that is where the rest of the bears are. Where should we put the blocks?" Encourage your child to give you reasons for sorting objects. You might find that he or she wants to put a ball on the shelf with the bears because her bear likes to play ball. Don't force the child to follow a structure that is set by you, but rather encourage independent thinking and reasoning.

Mathematics is sometimes defined as the study of patterns, which the human brain is uniquely suited for recognizing. We even have a brain wave, the P-300 wave, whose function is to look for patterns. Children should be encouraged to recognize, extend, and create patterns in their everyday world. This can be as simple as helping a child recognize that setting the table follows a pattern of napkin, fork, plate, knife, spoon or that his or her bedtime routine follows a pattern of take a bath, have a snack, brush your teeth, read a bedtime story, and go to sleep. Songs and storybooks where phrases are repeated in a predictable pattern, such as "The Farmer in the Dell" or the Russian folk tale "The Turnip," give children a chance to "read" along by anticipating patterns as they complete the songs or stories to fit the patterns they notice. Encourage children to make up additional verses or story endings that follow the same patterns.

Recognizing how shapes fit together in two- or three-dimensional space is also a very important aspect of "mathematizing" one's world. Simple activities such as putting together jigsaw puzzles or constructing a building with blocks can help young children develop these spatial abilities. Participating actively in sports also helps children with this development by giving them a better sense of their own position in relation to the world around them. Some research indicates that adolescent girls often do not perform as well as adolescent boys on tests of spatial abilities, especially in instances where they are required to predict outcomes of rotations of three-dimensional objects or to recognize a two-dimensional outline that could be folded to make a certain three-dimensional figure. Girls who have more experience building with blocks, solving spatial puzzles, and participating in sports seem to do better on these tasks, however. Not surprisingly, as with many other abilities, children who have more experience with a certain activity perform better on tests that measure abilities used in that activity. Be sure to encourage your daughters, as well as your sons, in activities involving building, sports, electronics, and other areas that utilize mathematics, science, and engineering. It is critical that we give all children the opportunities necessary to increase their mathematical competence and confidence.

Developing Mathematical Creativity

When we think of creativity, we often think of creative writing and arts such as music, drawing, and dance. We seldom think of mathematics as a creative subject. This is a real mistake. Memorization of mathematical facts and formulae and learning the algorithms (steps for solving) for traditional computation exercises are only a very small part of mathematics. The enjoyment and beauty of mathematics derives from using your own creative methods to solve problems that were previously unknown to you. Children need to experience this joy that comes from using their own techniques to answer difficult questions. As parents, it is sometimes annoying that our children are always asking us "Why?" or "Why not?," and we may be tempted to just say, "Because that's the way it is." However, this would deprive the child of discovering that mathematics is built on logic and patterns that he or she can create. You might encourage young children to begin by exploring well-known properties such as the commutative property that tells us that it does not matter what order you add or multiply numbers (3 + 5 is the same as 5 + 3 and 4 x 2 is the same as 2 x 4) and that this does not work for subtraction or division. A 4- or 5-year-old who discovers this for him- or herself while playing around with counting sets of objects is far more likely to remember this than an older child who is taught this as a rule in first or second grade. In addition, children who learn to trust their own instincts and abilities for discovering such rules are more likely to become confident, inquiring mathematicians.

A model that I like to use with children in mathematical investigations is the following one,[8] which encourages children to take time to explore the depth and complexities of problems, patterns, and connections. Parents can use this model to help older children think about interesting mathematics that they would like to explore. This should not be a formal model that you use in a step-by-step process; rather, it should give you some guidelines of the types of questions and investigations that you might encourage children to explore.

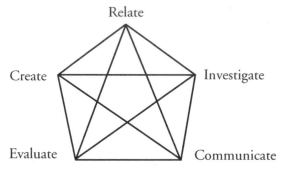

In this model, children learn that, in mathematics, not only do you want to answer the questions, but you should also question the answers. In fact, the real mathematical learning frequently begins after the original question has been answered. The problem-solving method illustrated above is not a linear one, since students may begin their mathematical explorations at any step and proceed in a variety of ways. For example, a child may begin with a question that puzzles her. She then may relate this problem to others that she has previously encountered and begin to investigate possible solutions. In the course of working on the problem, other questions and problems, as well as a variety of solutions, may be created. As these are evaluated for accuracy and interest, the resulting solutions and new problems should be communicated to other children or adults. Input from others may then suggest the creation of new lines of investigation, and the process begins again.

For example, you might have a child who is interested in exploring all the ways that addition facts can be used to show five. The child might get out a big pile of pennies and arrange them as follows:

If the child has learned to write equations, she might record this as:

$$0 + 5 = 5 \quad 1 + 4 = 5 \quad 2 + 3 = 5 \quad 3 + 2 = 5 \quad 4 + 1 = 5 \quad 5 + 0 = 5$$

The child might then realize that he could find six different ways to get the number 5 and wonder what would happen if she tried to find the number of ways to get 6 or 7. Relating this exploration to the one just completed using pennies to find the combinations for the number 5, the child might find that there are seven ways to get the number 6 and eight ways to make the number 7. The child might predict that there is always one more way to make the number than the number itself. This could lead to further explorations of other numbers to evaluate whether this always works. The child might then want to talk to someone about why this might be true. In the discussion, the question might arise as to how many ways there would be if 2 + 3 and 3 + 2 were considered to be the same. The child might find at this point there are only 3 ways (0 + 5, 1 + 4, and 2 + 3) and begin a new exploration to determine if there is a general rule for the number of ways to make a number when pairs of numbers are considered the same even if the order is different.

As a parent, you will want to encourage your child's explorations by asking questions such as Why does that work? Will that always work? Will that ever work? What is the largest answer you can get? What is the smallest answer you can get? Do you see a pattern? Can you show me your answer with a picture or a model? Is there another way to find that? In mathematics, even though a problem may have one right answer, there are usually several ways to arrive at that answer. Encourage your child to use methods that make sense to him or her, rather than trying to impose methods that make sense to you as an adult. There are certainly times when your child will want you to demonstrate methods that you use in problem solving, but generally those methods should be delayed until the child has an opportunity to explore the problem on his or her own.

Developing Mathematical Formalization and Generalization

It is not necessary for young children to learn formal methods of mathematical proofs, but children can be encouraged to generalize their solutions and give reasons for why they believe that their methods are correct. It is good to ask a child to give you reasons for the way things work. For example, if a child tells you that, whenever you multiply two numbers together, you always get a larger number, ask why that happens. The child might be able to tell you that when you multiply, you are taking several groups of the same size and adding them together. This gives you a group that is larger than when you started. For older children, you might ask what would happen if you took half of a group, rather than 2 or more of the group. Would this still be multiplication? (Note that 12 ÷ 2 and 1/2 x 12 both represent methods of taking 1/2 of 12.) That is an example of multiplying that gives you an answer smaller than the group you started with. Are there other times that this would happen?

Puzzles involving patterns also give children an opportunity to generalize their solutions. For example, ask the child to write his first name repeatedly, for example

J O H N J O H N J O H N J O H N

Ask the child to tell you what letter is the 4th letter in the pattern; what is the 10th letter, and so forth? Then, ask if the pattern continues to tell you what the 40th letter would be. Ask, "How do you know?" Try similar questions with other patterns of letters, colors, or shapes.

You might also try this with toothpicks with a problem such as the following:

Make squares in a row by using toothpicks as shown below.

How many toothpicks does it take to make four squares? Five squares? Twenty-five squares? What pattern do you notice? Can you predict the number of toothpicks that it would take to make any number of squares? Explain your prediction.

Children might tell you that the first square takes 4 toothpicks and every square after that only takes 3 toothpicks, so 25 squares would take 4 + 3 x 24, or 76 toothpicks. Or, she might say that there would be 25 toothpicks on the top, 25 on the bottom, and 26 standing up in the middle for 76 toothpicks, or 3 toothpicks each for 25 squares plus one on the end to close up the last square. Again, encourage the child to give you a variety of methods for solving the problem and reasons for the method she has chosen.

Developing Mathematical Curiosity and Perseverance

You have probably noticed the previously discussed problems and conversations that go along with encouraging mathematical creativity and generalizations also encourage curiosity and perseverance in mathematical problem solving. In some schools, children measure their mathematical expertise by how quickly they complete their mathematics assignments. They believe that they must be good at mathematics if they can finish their work faster than anyone else and move on to something else. This view of mathematics as something to get over as quickly as possible destroys a child's natural curiosity and desire to understand why things work. It may be desirable in some instances to complete a computation exercise quickly, but mathematics should be much more than this. There should be numerous opportunities to explore mathematics in depth, searching for the beauty and complexity behind the original question. Be sure that your child has numerous opportunities both at home and in school for these in-depth explorations.

What Resources Are There for Families?

This brings us to the question of where families might find interesting problems, questions, games, books, and other resources for student exploration. Fortunately, in this electronic age, some resources are as near as the nearest Internet connection. Whether you have Internet access at home, at work, or in your local library, you should take advantage of some of the resources you might find there for challenging your children. The following are just a few places to get you started.

Resources for Families

- Ask Dr. Math (http://mathforum.org/dr.math)
- Eisenhower National Clearinghouse (http://www.enc.org)
- Figure This! Math Challenges for Families (http://www.figurethis.org)
- Gifted Resources Home Page (http://www.eskimo.com/~user/kids.html)

- Help Series: Helping Your Child Learn Math (http://www.ed.gov/pubs/parents/hyc.html)
- Illuminations (http://Illuminations.nctm.org/index2.html)
- Marco Polo (http://marcopolo-education.org)
- Math Forum (http://mathforum.org)
- Lanius Mathematics Lessons (http://math.rice.edu/~lanius/Lessons)
- National Association for Gifted Children (http://www.nagc.org)
- National Council of Teachers of Mathematics (http://www.nctm.org)
- What Should I Look for in a Math Classroom (http://www.learner.org)

Problems for Children

- AIMS puzzle page (http://www.aimsedu.org/Puzzle/PuzzleList.html)
- Cool Math (http://www.coolmath.com)
- Coolmath4kids (http://www.coolmath4kids.com)
- Funbrain (http://www.funbrain.com)
- Interactive Mathematics Miscellany and Puzzles (http://www.cut-the-knot.com)
- Math Applets (http://www.albertaonline.ab.ca/resources/MathApplets.htm)
- Math Brain Teasers (http://www.eduplace.com/math/brain)
- Mathematics Problems for Japanese Sixth Graders (http://www.japanese-online.com/math/index.htm)
- Mathematics Problems of the Week Contest Page (http://www.olemiss.edu/mathed/contest/contests.htm)
- The Mathman (http://www.shout.net/~mathman)
- Math Word Problems for Children (http://www.mathstories.com)
- Mega Mathematics (http://www.c3.lanl.gov/mega-math/index.html)
- National Security Agency Kids Page (http://www.nsa.gov/programs/kids)
- NRICH Online Maths Club, University of Cambridge, England (http://www.nrich.maths.org.uk)
- Shack's Math Problems (http://www.thewizardofodds.com/math)
- Word Problems for Kids (http://www.stfx.ca/special/mathproblems/welcome.html)

Math Competitions

- American Mathematics Competitions (http://www.unl.edu/amc)

- MATHCOUNTS, National Society of Professional Engineers Information Center (http://www.mathcounts.org)
- Mathematical Olympiads for Elementary and Middle Schools (http://www.moems.org)
- Odyssey of the Mind (http://www.odysseyofthemind.com)
- ThinkQuest (http://www.thinkquest.org)
- Toshiba/NSTA ExploraVision Awards (http://www.toshiba.com/tai/exploravision)

These Web sites give you resources ranging from research on whether you should allow your child to use a calculator, to math games children can play with you or other children, to mathematics competitions for children of all ages. All the sites attempt to show parents and children just how much fun doing math can be.

Games are another great way to encourage your child's development of mathematics. Simple card, dice, and board games that help children recognize numbers and associate numbers with moves are useful in building early number concepts, but you should also look for games that build spatial perception such as Battleship or Towers of Hanoi, card games that build number skills such as 24 or 1–2–3–OY!, and strategy games such as SET, chess, and checkers that help children build their logical, sequential reasoning skills. Mathematical games and puzzles are important for children and adults of all ages. Just as your child should see you enjoying reading in your spare time, so should your child see that you enjoy solving mathematical puzzles and playing games that involve logical reasoning and mathematics. In addition, as your children get older, be sure they have lots of opportunities to join mathematics clubs and competitions at school. If mathematics clubs and competitions are not currently offered at your local school, offer to help the school get started. Several of the Web sites noted above give you resources to do this. Perhaps you can find someone in the mathematics education department at your local college or university that will help you get started.

If you have a computer in your home, you might be wondering how young (or how old) children should be when they start to use a computer. As with any other electronic device (television, music, calculators, etc.), there are good points and bad points about using a computer. You want to be sure that you look at any software that your child might use and determine whether it is interesting and challenging. Also, even if this is the best software on the market, you don't want your child to play computer games to the neglect of everything else. If you want to see what others say about the games you are considering purchasing, you might look at SuperKids (http://www.superkids.com), a Web site where you will find noncomputer games to play with your child, research on children's learning, and a review of some of the most popular educational software. There are lots of games where children can challenge themselves to solve interesting problems or just practice computation in an enjoyable fashion. Some of these are even designed for infants and toddlers as young as 8 months old. You will have to decide for yourself whether you want your infants staring at a computer screen; but, for toddlers, the software can be fun, challenging, and enriching when used in a reasonable manner. Even hand-held electronic games such as Tetris can be very beneficial to building spatial abilities in children.

A related question might be whether you should allow your child to use a calculator. The views of the National Council of Teachers of Mathematics may be found at http://standards.nctm.org. It seems to be the case from research around the world for nearly 30 years that, when used properly, calculators not only do not harm children's computation abilities, but can greatly help their problem-solving skills. Be sure to challenge your child to compute mentally as much as possible and to find ways to "beat the calculator." Children enjoy games where they are asked to see if they can find answers faster than you can put the equation into a calculator. It is always faster to mentally answer 5 + 3 than it is to punch 5 + 3 into a calculator. With some practice, children often can learn to answer 15 x 13 or 102 − 86 faster than the calculator, too. Some calculators such as the TI-15 are designed to quiz children on computation with addition, subtraction, multiplication, and division of one-, two-, or three-digit numbers in addition to performing as a regular calculator. Many children will play with these for hours, honing their computation skills until they are much better than the average adult.

How Might Schools and Families Work Together?

When your child enters school, perhaps able to add and subtract two-digit numbers mentally, you may question whether the school program can offer adequate challenge. This especially may be true if the school's mathematics program seems to consist of giving your child simplistic worksheets where he or she is asked to write the number of objects in the picture day after day. You should be able to expect that your child's teacher recognizes the following:

- All students have the right to learn something new every day.
- All students have the right to experience the joy of mastering difficult problems.
- All students have the right to work with teachers and peers who will challenge, enrich, and motivate them.

This means that you should expect the school to challenge your child at an appropriate level just as any other child should be able to expect appropriate challenges. The school should not expect your child to tutor other children just because he or she can answer mathematics questions quickly, and he or she should not be given extra "busy work" while other children finish their work. He or she should not be told to go "read a book" or do something else fun as soon as low-level mathematics worksheets are finished. Neither should he or she be given the math book for the next grade level and told to work on his or her own. Math should be an enjoyable challenge, and the same resources that are useful to parents at home can be shared with teachers so they might appropriately challenge their top students at school.

If your child consistently completes all his or her mathematics homework during school or on the bus ride home, this is probably an indication that more challenge is needed. This does not mean that the teacher should assign more low-level problems or give additional work on top of the homework expected of other children. Mathematics homework for students who have already mastered the homework topics assigned to others should be a replacement for other assignments, not an addition to them.

In contrast, if your child spends up to an hour struggling with challenging mathematics problems, this may not be a sign that the mathematics is too difficult. Rather, the child may simply be intrigued by the challenge and want to spend time digging more deeply in the concepts. Encourage your child and his or her teacher to continue to find challenging problems that may be explored in some depth.

Adding Depth

Traditionally, discussions of serving the needs of promising students have centered on a debate of whether to accelerate or enrich the curricula for talented students. You should look for a mathematics program that is at least three-dimensional, as in the following model.[9]

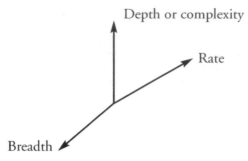

This model is an attempt to illustrate that educational services for our most promising mathematics students should not only look at changing the rate of presentation or the number of topics, but more importantly must also look at changing the depth or complexities of the questions, projects, investigations, and means of assessment. Promising students should be encouraged to take time to explore in depth issues and problems, their patterns and generalizations, and connections among them. If teachers use interesting problems, the same problems might challenge children on a variety of levels. For example, a first-grade teacher might ask his or her students to make a booklet that would help other children learn their addition facts. Some children might simply choose to draw pictures of objects to illustrate facts such as showing two apples and three more apples to illustrate $2 + 3 = 5$. Your gifted child might choose to explore properties of numbers that would help children learn facts (e.g., knowing the commutative property means that any child who knows $8 + 3$ already knows $3 + 8$, or knowing doubles means that a child who knows $6 + 6$ can answer $6 + 7$ by adding one to the sum of $6 + 6$). A bright child might be encouraged to find dozens of such tips to help other children learn facts while at the same time strengthening his or her own knowledge of operations.

In 1999–2000, the U.S. Department of Education published *Exemplary and Promising Mathematics Programs Reports*, which is available online at http://www.enc.org. These reports were developed by an Expert Panel on Mathematics established to develop a high-quality, research-based process for selecting programs and use that selection process to identify exemplary and promising programs. These programs were judged to have challenging learning goals, to meet national standards, and to be successful at engaging and motivating students to learn at high levels. In addition, The American Association for the Advancement of Science's Project 2061 (available at http://project2061.org/tools/textbook/matheval) recently conducted an independent evaluation of algebra and middle grades mathematics textbooks. You should compare the mathematics programs used in your child's school to those listed in these reports to aid in determining if your child is being properly challenged at school in a manner consistent with the latest research and national recommendations.

Accelerating

Parents often wonder whether they should move their child to a higher grade level for mathematics. There is no simple answer to this. The National Council of Teachers of Mathematics' (NCTM) *Report of the Task Force on Mathematically Promising Students*[10] lists a number of questions that should be raised if you are considering this option. One of the most important questions is "Are curriculum, instruction, and assessment qualitatively different and designed to meet the differing needs of promising students? Is the curriculum more challenging with provisions for individualization, faster pace, more higher level thinking, and higher standards than remaining in the regular classroom?" Often, moving a child to a higher grade level still does not provide needed challenge. Questions raised by the NCTM Task Force might assist you in determining what provisions can be made regarding whether the child remains in the regular classroom or moves to an accelerated placement. These questions include:

- Are there resources, projects, problems, and means of assessment that allow for differences in the level of depth of understanding and engagement?
- Do teachers have the pedagogical techniques to work with student populations with diverse learning needs and from diverse backgrounds?
- Are there teachers who have been adequately prepared to work in the role of a facilitator with mathematically promising students?
- Does the teacher have a contingency plan to determine when students have mastered mathematical concepts and skills so that they do not unnecessarily repeat material?
- Are there opportunities for promising students to explore interesting problems with others of like interests and abilities?

If these questions are answered satisfactorily, adding challenge within the context of the regular classroom might be the best placement for the child. This might be supplemented by other opportunities, including:

- summer and after-school programs;
- mathematics contest;
- games and puzzles that deepen mathematical and logical reasoning;
- mentoring by an older student or adult with similar mathematical interests;
- utilizing resources on the Internet; and
- mathematics clubs where children can explore problems in greater depth.

No one answer is best suited to the needs of all gifted and talented mathematics students. Even in this top range, if you have two students who are scoring at the 99th percentile on a standardized mathematics test, they could still be quite different from each other in mathematical abilities and understanding. A child who is in the top 0.1 of 1% or higher (that child who scores higher than 1 child out of 1,000) may need provisions quite different than the child who scores above the top 1–2% of his or her peer group. These highly prodigious children need to find mentors who can guide their development to an even higher level than the average mathematics teacher or parent. Just as the parent of a piano prodigy or outstanding tennis player might seek out a teacher or coach from across the country, so might a parent of a mathematical prodigy need to seek guidance from a mathematical mentor. The best situation for your child needs to be determined with input from the family, the teachers, the school counselor, and the child him- or herself.

Schools might assist you in determining if your child's test scores are in this prodigious range by administering tests that were designed for older students. For example, there are several regional talent searches for academically talented students. These might administer a test designed for eighth graders such as the Explore from the American College Testing Program to students as young as third or fourth grade, or they may administer a test to seventh graders that was designed for college-bound high school students, such as the ACT or SAT. Students who perform at a level comparable to talented students who are much older qualify for special regional and national programs where they can be challenged with other highly prodigious mathematics students. For more information, see the Gifted Resources: Talent Search page at http://www.eskimo.com/~user/ztsearch.html.

Thinking Ahead

Many parents wonder whether middle grades students should be studying high school curricula, especially whether their sixth- or seventh-grade student should be taking Algebra I. Again, there is not a simple answer to this question. One issue is whether it is appropriate to teach algebra separately from geometry and probability and statistics. In most other countries in the world, these topics are taught in integrated mathematics courses throughout high school. In the United States, these topics are often integrated in middle school and then separated in high school. If that is the case in your district, you need to find out what mathematical topics your child might not study in sixth or seventh grade mathematics (such as fractions, decimals, geometry, probability, and statistics) if he or she decides to take algebra in place of the typical mathematics course. If you would like to compare the curriculum offered in your school district to the recommendations of the National Council of Teachers of Mathematics, look at the NCTM Principles and Standards for School Mathematics at http://standards.nctm.org. Here you will find recommendations for all students from preschool through high school in addition to the recommendations for those students desiring deeper and more complex mathematics preparation in high school. At all levels, it is recommended that students study number and operations, algebra, geometry, measurement, data analysis, and probability. At no level should any of these areas be omitted. Therefore, primary students should investigate algebraic concepts just as concepts of data analysis and probability should be strengthened in high school.

The school needs to ensure that your child will not run out of mathematics course options before his or her senior year. If your child takes calculus earlier than the last year of high school, be sure that the high school will make provisions for him or her to continue taking college-level mathematics during the final years of high school. This might be accomplished through enrollment in advanced mathematics courses in a near-by university or by taking distance-learning classes offered over the Internet. It is critical that all students preparing for college take mathematics every year in high school. Remember that mathematics is not a race to be completed as quickly as possible. It should be an enjoyable area of study that prepares a student for a lifetime of exploration.

Every high school should offer challenging mathematics courses for as many students as possible. This means that every high school should offer Advanced Placement or International Baccalaureate courses (or their equivalent) in mathematics and computer science (AP Calculus AB, AP Calculus BC, and AP Statistics or IB Mathematics). Beginning in middle school, large numbers of students (in addition to the mathematically gifted) should be preparing to enter these classes in high school. Students attending high schools without these courses are often at a disadvantage for many majors when they attend college. When your child is still in elementary school, you should find out if these advanced classes are available at your high school. If not, encourage the teachers at the high school and middle school to set up vertical (across grades) teams of teachers who will work together to ensure a continuum of classes from elementary school on that will prepare students to enter these high-level classes. It often takes a couple of years to add Advanced Placement classes in high school because students must be prepared for these classes much earlier in their school programs. You should also talk to the counselors, the principal, and mathematics teachers at the high school to determine what is available for students who exhaust all the mathematics courses offered. Many schools can arrange for students to take classes for dual credit at a local university or can arrange distance-learning classes based on the Internet or interactive television, where the instructor may be anywhere in the world teaching a class of students based in their home schools. Many states offer students the opportunity to take courses through a "virtual high school" in this manner. (Some of these distance-learning opportunities may be found at http://www.eskimo.com/~user/zdist.html.) These high school offerings may determine how quickly to encourage your child to continue through a mathematics sequence beginning in middle school or even earlier.

Final Thoughts

With new information coming out every day about the potential of the human brain, this is an exciting time to be raising a child. Children who develop a passion for learning mathematics at a young age should be able to achieve higher levels of mathematical competence than we have ever seen in U.S. schools. Already, Advanced Placement Calculus is being offered to more students every year. Forty years ago, it was rare to see anyone learning calculus in high school, and now some schools are offering this to as many as one-third or even one-half or more of their high school students. Unfortunately, there are still far too many schools where such courses are not available to even a single student. Parents can be a strong force in making sure that all students have the opportunity to learn as much mathematics as possible in every public and private school in the United States. In this way, with proper guidance beginning at an early age, all children will be able to become the mathematical leaders of our increasingly technological world.

Resources

Fielker, David, *Extending Mathematical Ability Through Whole Class Teaching*. London: Hodder and Stoughton, 1997.

House, Peggy A., ed. *Providing Opportunities for the Mathematically Gifted K–12*. Reston, Va.: National Council of Teachers of Mathematics, 1987.

Sheffield, Linda J., ed., *Developing Mathematically Promising Students*. Reston, Va.: National Council of Teachers of Mathematics, 1999,

Sheffield, Linda J., "Creating and Developing Promising Young Mathematicians," *Teaching Children Mathematics*, 6 no. 6 (February 2000): 416–419, 426.

Sheffield, Linda J. *Extending the Challenge in Mathematics: Developing Mathematical Promise in K–8 Students*. Thousand Oaks, Calif.: Corwin Press, 2002.

Sheffield, Linda J., C. Greenes, C. Findel, and M. K. Gavin, *Awesome Math Problems for Creative Thinking*. Alsip, Ill.: Creative Publications, 2000.

5

musical talent

nurturing potential and guiding development

by
joanne haroutounian

"Of all the gifts with which individuals may be endowed,
none emerges earlier than musical talent."
—Howard Gardner

Fingers work feverishly through the final passage. With a dramatic sweep of the bow, the poised violinist gratefully acknowledges the immediate standing ovation and calls of "bravo" that greet her performance. She is a competition winner with an amazing talent.

The church resounds with the sweet, rich voice of the gospel choir soloist, weaving an improvised version of the hymn with eyes closed, caught up in the emotion of the music. Parishioners wipe away tears as they are captured by this naturally talented singer.

Down in the basement, a guitarist adjusts the amplifier, sequencer, microphones, and tracking device as he works diligently to capture composed ideas on tape. Although he cannot read music, he has already produced several CDs of promising musical works.

These three aspiring musicians have chosen different routes to express themselves through music. If we backtrack 10 or more years, we may have spied youngsters marching around the house to music while playing toy drums or singing as naturally as talking in play, fascinated with the quality of sounds that surround them. From the start, parents play a decided role in nurturing a child's musical potential. Questions quickly arise: What are the first signs of musical talent? We are not musicians—what can we do to help our child? When should we start lessons? As training progresses, parents are faced with issues of balancing practice and academic demands. What role should competition play in a talented young musician's training? Should lessons discontinue if my child is not planning to pursue music as a career? The musical journey is a long one that begins in the home and relies on the ongoing support and understanding of parents who wish to see their child's musical potential blossom.

The First Signs of Musical Development

Infants listen before they are born. They are aware of their mother's heartbeat, voice, and different environmental sounds filtering into their cozy womb. Hundreds of prenatal studies have measured movements and startle reflexes to show that the perception of music and sound is in place prior to birth. Newborns can distinguish their mother's voice from other female voices. Songs and stories that were heard prior to birth are recognized by newborn infants through excited sucking responses, versus relative inactivity when hearing an unfamiliar story or song.[1]

Once a child enters the world, parents communicate through speech that is slow, high-pitched, with broad fluctuation—"baby talk" or "infant-directed speech." This creates a heightened response from infants. A rising voice captures an infant's attention, a falling voice is soothing, and bell-shaped contours communicate approval. Interestingly, these same vocal patterns occur globally in parent-infant conversations, regardless of native language.[2] Singing a lullaby while rocking a baby to sleep combines the gentle tone of voice, slow tempo, rhythmic movement, and soothing melody to transform infant-directed speech into musical communication. The aural sensing (hearing) that is basic to musical talent is stimulated by these intimate musical experiences between parent and child.

Infants are not only listening, but learning to communicate through sound, creating "cooing" sounds at 2 months, followed by "vocal play" at 4–6 months. During vocal play, infants simply use their voice as a toy, discovering how to make new sounds. Vocal play develops into babbling ("mama," "da-da") by 9 months, gradually developing into bits and pieces of songs in a limited vocal range by the age of 2½. A majority of the studies mark the 6-year-old framework as the normal age when children can sing an entire song with stabilized pitch (i.e. sing in tune).[3] Parents should take notice of youngsters who have mastered singing relatively in tune before the age of 5, realizing that children who naturally sing while playing from an early age will be more prone to develop this ability.

Rhythmic awareness begins with bobbing and swaying to music as soon as a child can sit upright. Children by the age of two learn to match the movements of others, naturally "coalescing" or merging together to establish a single rhythm as a group. By the age of 3, children can make broad distinctions between fast and slow, but usually the ability to maintain a steady beat is not established until beyond the age of 6.[4] Again, children who show a natural "feel" of the beat in music through fluid rhythmic movement earlier than normal may demonstrate potential musical talent.

The most obvious early sign of musical potential is the fascination of listening to music, playing through music, and showing curiosity about sound. For example, singing and dancing become a natural part of play for potentially talented youngsters. Creating nonsense songs indicates early signs of musical invention. Preschoolers who recognize particular instrument sounds on a CD or call attention to subtle environmental sounds unnoticed by adults show the perceptive listening capacity that is at the heart of music aptitude.

This brief overview of the development of early childhood musical abilities highlights the importance of parental and environmental influences in the growth of musical potential. Although there may be some biological givens ("nature") inherent to musical talent, music psychologists on both sides of the "nature-nurture" debate agree that early environmental influences ("nurture") play a decidedly important role in nurturing the earliest stages of musical potential. Studies show that many parents of talented musicians were not musically trained themselves, but did enjoy sharing musical activities with their children.[5] A child will naturally play through music if music is a part of the everyday home environment. Musical communication between parent and child does not rely on the quality of a parent's voice, but simply on its desire to express emotion through music. Playing through song with a child surely invites musical creativity in the future.

Basic Underpinnings of Musical Talent

So often we equate musical talent with visions of a young Mozart or other prodigy easily performing difficult music by the age of 5 or 6. This type of exceptional talent is rare and does not describe the typical development of potential musical talent. An examination of biographic studies of concert pianists and talented teenage musicians indicates that these talented musicians did not necessarily display precocious or exceptional musical abilities at a young age.[6] However, their parents did take note of certain behaviors that decidedly pointed to a strong inclination to music from an early age. These basic musical talent behaviors include *musical awareness and discrimination, creative interpretation, the dynamic of performance,* and *commitment.*[7]

Musical Awareness and Discrimination

The basic musical behaviors of listening attentively, reacting to a rhythmic pulse or beat, and remembering and repeating songs describe a child's *musical awareness and discrimination.* As noted earlier, these abilities are noticeable from the initial stages of musical development. Music psychologists describe these basic sensory capacities as *music aptitude.* They are also the fundamental elements of *musical intelligence,* described in Howard Gardner's theory of multiple intelligences (see Chapter 1).

Most young children enjoy listening, clapping, and moving to music. A musically talented child obviously "tunes in" while listening. This child may continually ask, "What is that sound? Where does it come from?" A radio

Ways to Nurture Musical Potential

- Make music a natural part of the home environment.
- Communicate with your baby through "infant-directed" speech.
- Stimulate rhythmic awareness through physical movement with your child while responding to music.
- Sing—often, any old way, sharing the joy of song with your child.
- Encourage your child's musical play: listening to CDs, playing with early childhood percussion instruments (rattles, jingle bells, drums), moving to music and other creative musical activities.
- Seek out family or "tiny tot" musical performances available in your community.
- Consider enrolling your child in an early childhood music program.

playing outside may draw listening attention more than surrounding conversation. This child actually listens to background music.

A musically talented child shows a physical connection with the music through fluid rhythmic body movement. Many preschool classes include rhythm games where children clap and step while singing or chanting, keeping the beat as best they can. The musically talented child will show adept awareness of the rhythmic pulse of the music and may be able to coordinate hand and foot movements more easily than other children. When observing a group of youngsters moving to music, this child will stand out as one who is clearly involved in this movement.

Vocal skills are only at the budding stage prior to school age, so singing in tune is not always an accurate measure of future musical talent. However, the ability to remember and repeat complete songs prior to the age of 5 is notable. The musically talented child will most likely enjoy repeating favorite songs and use song as a natural part of creative play. Youngsters who enjoy experimenting and picking out tunes on an available keyboard or other instrument also show a definite strong sense of pitch or ability to discriminate different musical pitches. Take special note of the child who can pick out pitches of a song while singing.

Creative Interpretation

How does a young child "personalize" a musical statement? Most young children, when seated at a piano keyboard, will either pound or poke for a few minutes at the most, with no real purpose. A creatively interpretive youngster will sit and rework simple ideas, discover how a single note can be played soft to loud, and possibly link notes together into a simple musical statement that is remembered. You may notice a child exploring the sounds of a number of simple percussion instruments, creating a musical story from this experimentation. There is an obvious sensory and mental engagement in this kind of musical play.

The term *metaperception* is used to describe this type of musical thinking and decision making in the arts. In young children, this process is basically intuitive (i.e., untaught and unlearned), growing more sensitive and selective through maturity and training. The musical decision-making process requires the ability to listen carefully and inwardly sense sounds. Musicians then "play" with these perceptions both internally and externally until they discover how to interpret what they want to express through the medium of music.[8]

Metaperception is at play when a young child simply plays with sound, creating unique variations to a favorite tune. It is at work when a student musician repeatedly practices a musical section, listening for technical improvement and experimenting with ways to create sounds that express a certain mood. A concert artist refines the metaperceptive process by developing subtle sound colors and technical flamboyance that creates a unique artistic interpretation.

Dynamic of Performance

When observing a group of preschoolers in a musical performance, you smile over their adorable enthusiasm. However, you may catch yourself noticing several children who seem to truly *express themselves* through this music. In any performance, there is a dynamic created between the musician and the audience. An expressive performance communicates the musician's abilities of discriminative musical awareness and creative interpretation to the audience.

A talented child's naturally expressive performance will create this type of dynamic with the listener, whether it is a mother listening to a child singing a lullaby to a rag doll or an audience enjoying an early recital performance experience. As musical abilities grow, children must hurdle technical obstacles that may impede this natural expressive dynamic. However, it is not unusual for seasoned judges at festivals or competitions to note this dynamic in a performance that may be technically flawed by occasional wrong notes, but still exudes that expressive "spark" of musical talent.

Commitment

There are a number of motivating factors displayed by musically talented children that play an essential role in their musical development. Although these behaviors are not music-specific, they often predict a child's success in long-term talent development. Talented children show a concentrated focus of attention while engaged in musical tasks. This *artistic focus* may be short-lived in young children, but it is a sure sign of metaperceptive decision making at work. With maturity and development, this focus expands to one of "deliberate practice," characterized by intensive concentration while solving technical and musical problems.[9]

It is not unusual for musically talented children to work persistently in musical play. They may rework ideas and experiment with different sounds for relatively long periods of time. They often enjoy working alone in these musical tasks, which shows the first signs of self-motivation and discipline that depict the normal working style of a musician. As parents notice this task commitment to music, they may seek advice on the best way to begin some type of musical instruction for their child.

Early Childhood Musical Experiences

Research findings over the past decade emphasizing the value of musical learning in early childhood have spawned numerous options for parents seeking organized musical experiences for their preschool children. Early childhood musical curricula have been developed for use from birth through school age. These curricula begin with instruction of parent-infant interaction to stimulate perceptive awareness, vocal play between parent and child, and musical activities to extend to the home environment. As children grow, activities include simple songs, rhythm games, percussion activities, creativity, and finger play.

Specialists in early childhood music have developed programs available nationally that essentially introduce small groups of young children to the basic skills of music making. Most programs have pro-

Musical Talent Characteristics

Musical Awareness and Discrimination
- Awareness of sound: listens carefully, noticing details
- Rhythmic sense: fluidly responds to rhythm, keeping a steady beat
- Sense of pitch: Remembers and repeats melodies or songs

Creative Interpretation
- Experiments and "plays" with sounds.
- Performs and reacts to music with personal expression.
- Recognizes aesthetic qualities of music—mood, sounds of different instruments, loud and soft dynamics, change of tempo or speed.

Dynamic of Performance
- Performs expressively, showing signs of creative interpretation.
- Performs naturally, with ease.
- Enjoys performance experiences.

Commitment
- Perseveres in musical activities.
- Works on musical tasks with focused concentration.
- Reworks and refines musical ideas.

gressive levels as children grow, with parental involvement gradually distancing to one of observer at the end of classes to ensure continued musical activities in the home. A list of early childhood programs is included in the resource list at the end of the chapter. Parents may wish to observe a class in session to gauge its suitability for their child.

A child who shows evidence of small motor coordination and a genuine interest in music lessons may be ready for early instrumental training. Early training is available mostly in piano and strings. Options include the Suzuki or Yamaha approaches to early instrumental instruction, stemming from Japanese music curricula, or lessons with independent music teachers who may specialize in preschool private and class instruction.

Suzuki instrumental training requires the parent and student to take lessons together. The teaching techniques emphasize modeling by the teacher, rote learning, and ear-training with children playing entirely by ear, rather than reading music, to instill listening abilities. The Yamaha curriculum offers group keyboard instruction beginning at age 4, and also includes composition and training in ways to improvise or make up music by ear.

There has been a dramatic increase in the publication of materials for preschool keyboard instruction over the past 5 years. Many independent teachers are including preschool keyboard instruction in their studios. This instruction may be done in groups or in a combination of short private lessons plus group activities. Studios often include computer music games in this instruction. Preschool keyboard instruction essentially familiarizes a child with the keyboard and basic understanding of rhythm symbols and helps develop finger coordination and listening skills.

Many parents may question the rationale behind seeking formal music instruction at such a tender age. Although the renewed interest in early musical training stems from generalized research findings in spatial reasoning and other areas, the field of music psychology has long held that early instruction benefits a child's development of music aptitude. Music aptitude tests, developed over the past 40 years, measure listening capacities of musical awareness that are "a product of both innate potential and early environmental experiences."[10] Test developers believe that music aptitude is developmental up to the age of 9 or 10, when it becomes stabilized, basically plateauing in the ability to discriminate sounds and rhythms. "The younger a child is when he or she begins to receive early informal and formal instruction in music, the more he or she can profit from such instruction and the higher the level at which his or her music aptitude will eventually stabilize."[11]

School Offerings for the Young Talented Musician

Early childhood musical activities naturally lead to elementary music classes in school, which expand group musical experiences in complexity as children develop physically and socially. Many schools combine the basic music education curricula of folk songs and listening activities with experiences in Orff, Dalcroze, and Kodály activities. These imported European curricula allow children to improvise with movement and percussion instruments and learn to "sign" as they sing different pitches.

A typical Orff classroom will have youngsters performing together on different xylophone-type instruments, enjoying free improvisation on instruments that are tuned to a scale that essentially has no wrong notes. A glimpse into a Dalcroze class will find children moving freely to music, using their full bodies to show the rhythmic beat and expressing the mood of the music with their arms and hands. A Kodály class will have students using hand signals to show the different levels of the scale (do re mi) as they sing.

Few schools specifically identify musically talented children as part of the gifted identification process. A study of gifted identification procedures sent from 1,200 locations in the United States showed that only 14 locations included any procedures for talent identification in music or the arts, providing clear evidence of the lack of attention to the arts in talent identification nationally.[11] Identification basically relies on individual teachers noticing students who quickly grasp musical concepts in class and offering them more individualized musical performance and creative opportunities within music class.

The national profile of music programs across the country shows quite a range of musical offerings for elementary-age children. Some schools may offer rich creative experiences through general music classes, leading to string and instrumental instruction as early as fourth grade. These programs may even include specialized advanced performance groups for talented students.

Unfortunately, many areas across the country offer minimal if any music education for children in this crucial period of musical development. If an elementary school has no music specialist, music learning rests on the capabilities and interests of the classroom teacher. Studies show that these circumstances often lead to educators dismissing music instruction as "dispensable entertainment."[13] This scenario does not bode well for any child's development of essential musical skills, let alone the child who shows potential talent. Often, parent-teacher organizations play a key role in altering the educational climate in their community. School music programs and gifted/talented options for promising young music students may be developed in local schools through organized parental action.

The young musically talented student requires more individualized, challenging musical experiences than most schools can offer at the elementary level. An astute classroom or music teacher may suggest private music instruction for this child. Studies show that musical talent development largely relies on musical study beyond typical school offerings.[14]

Beginning Private Lessons

Anyone who has taken music lessons remembers that very first lesson, when books are slick and new and every maneuver learned on the instrument is an adventure. The talented youngster literally takes off full speed ahead in this adventure. The journey can be exciting and rewarding, if the match of teacher and student "clicks." The decision to begin private lessons rests on the child's readiness for these lessons, as well as finding a teacher who can best mesh with the child's personality and learning style. This single link may last for many years, with private music teachers forming the third side of the triangle of parent-child-teacher that molds a child's musical training.

How do parents know when to begin private instruction for their child? The following guidelines may prove helpful in this decision:

- *The child must show a strong interest in the lessons.* If lessons are the choice of the parent, with minimal interest evidenced by the young child, they will most likely be an unsuccessful and unpleasant experience that will mar any chance of future musical training. Watch for noted commitment and persistence to musical tasks when your child is playing.

- *The child must have developed the physical coordination and capability to play the instrument.* Small muscle coordination requires independence of the fingers and the ability to do several things at once. If children begin lessons before they are physically ready, the experience is very frustrating. Piano and string instruction may begin in primary grades. Band instrumental instruction normally begins around fourth to fifth grade. (Vocal lessons do not begin until the voice is mature in the secondary grades.) An informal session with a private teacher may be helpful in determining readiness for a particular instrument.

- *The child and parent must realize that music lessons require practice.* Consistent practice is an essential part of private instruction. Encourage your child to "practice" on creative musical things in play. Working toward an informal performance for parents of these reworked ideas affords an excellent opportunity for parents to gauge practice-readiness.

Choosing a Teacher

The first music teacher is important in establishing the basic habits and love of music in the child. This teacher does not necessarily need to have the credentials of a master teacher, but does need the experience of working with young children to help them enjoy working and achieving through music. Parents of talented youngsters should realize that, since their child may learn quickly, he or she will require a teacher who is nurturing in character, but knowledgeable in establishing a strong musical foundation with appropriate pacing for a quick learner. Unlike other talents where acceleration may be limited by school parameters, a musically talented child working one on one with an astute private teacher can quickly excel to an appropriate level of challenging musical work.

Locating the most appropriate private music teacher for your child will require a bit of research. The independent music teacher profession does not readily advertise in the yellow pages. Parents may seek advice from a music store that stocks instructional music for teachers or ask for personal referrals from parents of music students who seem to be performing well. A university or college music department is a prime source when seeking a teacher who may specialize in teaching musically talented students.

Private teachers may have a studio in their home or work through a music store or community music school. What type of private studio can enhance talent development from the start?

- *A studio that has a variety of age and developmental levels* will provide both peer dynamics and older role models for the child. It also indicates a teacher who has a breadth of teaching experience and who may recognize the pacing needs of a talented child.
- *A studio that offers a combination of private instruction plus performance and music theory classes* encourages short-term performance goals in a

comfortable peer setting. In music theory, students learn the structure of music and how to write and compose, expanding musical learning beyond learning pieces, scales, and technical exercises.

- *A studio that includes multiple performance experiences*, from informal classes to periodic recitals, provides assessment of student progress and a sense of studio accountability. Astute listening from year to year by parents shows how students are progressing in the studio and presents a real-world formal recital experience for students.
- *A studio that includes activities offered by professional music organizations* encourages assessment of performance, theory work, or technical progress by outside judges. Many teachers belong to music organizations that offer activities (judged and nonjudged) in structured progressive levels that foster motivation to achieve short-term and long-term goals through musical development.
- *A studio that includes theory, improvisation, composition, and other creative and critical listening activities* nurtures a talented student's ability to work across different musical dimensions. These activities enhance metaperceptive decision making and provide tools for creating music.[15]

Monitoring Practice

The young talented student requires a comfortable challenge in learning. The learning environment of positive encouragement and stimulation from home nurtures these first years of training. Talented young musicians are quick learners, requiring a constant check by the teacher to secure understanding and accuracy beneath the flow of notes that speed by in those first few years of instruction.

The commitment to practice begins in the first year of lessons. There is no sure way to make practice fun for young children; but, again, there are some pointers that may guide parents in making practice a positive experience:

- Practice should be in a quiet space where the child can work without disturbance. Very young children will need guided supervision by parents. Teachers often have parents observe lessons and advise them on ways to assist practice.
- Consistent practice sessions as a young child will establish long-lasting habits. When a child personally completes practice rosters with checks or stickers, there is an immediate self-assessment and mini-reward for work done.

- Practice requires learning how to solve problems to achieve musical skills. Teachers will guide practice procedures of repetitive drills of problem areas, leading to larger working areas toward a full performance of the piece. Parents should discourage children from playing pieces all the way through, mistakes and all. Instead, children should be encouraged to set small subgoals for themselves, mastering problem areas one at a time. Establishing good practice habits from the start fosters learning patterns that are generalizable to academic areas.
- Parents should encourage periodic informal performances of pieces children have mastered. Performing for interested parents inspires goal-oriented work and affords an attentive, appreciative audience for a young performer.

During the first few years of private instruction, the parent plays a pivotal role in establishing the basic habits of a young musician. Talented young beginners already sense that they are "special" because they can do something that is unique from their peers. Parents are the guiding force in encouraging ongoing practice, supporting frustrating moments when technical hurdles develop, and nurturing the idea that being a young talented musician is, indeed, something "special."

Stages of Musical Development

Musical talent development consists of three basic stages, similar to talent development in sports, math, science, and art. During the early playful years of instruction, a child enjoys the encouragement of his or her teacher and stimulation by his or her parents. Musical work encourages creativity and freedom as basic technical skills take shape. The intermediate stage of training emphasizes technical precision, accuracy in performance, and disciplined practice. In the final stage, the advancing student seeks individuality in interpretation and in-depth analysis and understanding reflecting the attitudes of a professional musician.[16]

Throughout this process, there is a delicate balance between the parent, child, and teacher in guiding the healthy development of a talented musician. In our prior sketch of musical learning from early childhood through the elementary school years, we emphasized the importance of parental interest, stimulation, and positive guidance through the first stage of musical talent development. A talented young child who learns rapidly may quickly arrive at the intermediate stage prior to secondary school, requiring parents to monitor the proper balance of musical discipline and the creative play still required for a child.

Intermediate Stage

Somewhere between the age of 10 and 13 young talented musicians begin to crave accuracy. The notes that whizzed by, just for fun, are now bothersome if they are not clean and precise. During this phase, students are intent on musical details, notice flaws in their playing, and seek out knowledgeable criticism from peers and teachers. Lessons change in character, with more emphasis on technical skills to acquire the physical coordination required for more mature musical interpretations. This intermediate stage of development relies heavily on the student's commitment to practice and the development of self-regulated work habits or "metaskills" necessary for working independently through musical problems.[17]

This middle stage often calls for a change of private studio, depending on the experience and scope of the initial teacher's studio. Several studies show that a series of transitions and learning environments is common for talented students. Parents and students seek teachers with more musical expertise and challenging student expectations. Many initial teachers encourage this change of studio, realizing this need for more demanding instruction.[18]

Performance experiences during this stage emphasize assessment of technical proficiency and growing musical understanding. Talented musicians, guided by their teachers, seek out opportunities for critiques by knowledgeable judges through competitive events at various levels. Recitals beyond the studio level and school music activities provide more opportunities for performance experience. A progressive step-wise process, from comfortable peer performance settings, to studio recitals, leading to competitive settings allows students to gain poise and confidence in performance.

The role of competition in talent development is a hot topic of controversy within the music profession. Is this experience healthy or detrimental to the sensitive musician in these adolescent years? An interview with winners of a prestigious national competition for teenagers a decade after the event elicited some interesting viewpoints from young aspiring musical artists. They felt that the competition had been valuable not because they had won, but because of the intense preparation, the satisfaction of achieving a goal, and the musical growth they had experienced through competing.[19]

Competitions also present the outside pressure of parents and teachers, whose career image or personal initiatives may seek that first-place spot for the child. At a stage when students should be exploring a variety of pieces in different styles and by different composers, competition-oriented studios may limit choices to those that will impress the judges. More than any time in the development of talent, this tenuous stage of personal and musical development presents psychological concerns for a young musician greatly influenced by the dominating influences of parent and teacher. Parents may need to take the helm in balancing the needs for competitive challenge and self-assessment of a blossoming musician with the pangs of a self-conscious adolescent.

This transitional stage separates the music makers from the musicians, in a sense. The age of play is complete, and the "work" of musical learning now takes precedence. Parents who have been an active presence in monitoring practice must now determine how to encourage their child's own monitoring of consistent practice while taking a decided step backward to avoid conflict. Students who are unable to acquire the necessary "metaskills" to handle disciplined practice during this stage will most likely drop lessons at this point.

Advanced Stage

Although parents of talented elementary-age children cannot project what may occur after many years of musical training, a glance at possibilities and problems that may arise in this final stage of musical development may be helpful. Let's present possible scenarios of development for our three opening musicians.

Our competition-experienced violinist has reached high school with a set of highly individualized skills in music far above her peers in the normal high school orchestra. She continues to be part of her school orchestra to lend support to the music program and share music with her friends. However, her parents also sought more challenging musical opportunities when she entered middle school, having her join a selective youth orchestra program in the community. They now travel each weekend for lessons, theory, and chamber music classes at a conservatory in a major city an hour away. She is considering an independent study in music performance for her senior year, where she can develop her own curriculum by performing a solo recital. The independent study also provides service to the community through performance at nursing homes and teaching music to underprivileged children. Her practice, rehearsal, and performance schedule easily extends beyond 30 hours a week. She is debating on either majoring in music or medicine in college, currently holding a 4.0 academic average.

Parents of this violinist met with difficult decisions in encouraging their daughter to continue advanced musical study through high school. Academic demands greatly strained musical practice. Discussions with her master teacher on practice schedules resulted in the decision of an independent study, rather than homeschooling or early conservatory entry, which is often an option for a highly talented musical teenager. The dilemma of continuing in the school music program has been ongoing, with school music teachers heavily reliant on the few talented performers that can strengthen performances of their orchestra or band in festivals and competitions. Their daughter obviously is not challenged, and often this extra time in rehearsal and festivals greatly impacts her study and practice schedule. Realizing their child is multiply talented, they chose to seek ways to allow her to continue her musical studies by careful time management for academic work. As they sit in the audience at the opening recital, they realize the decision to provide their daughter the opportunity to study music reaching an artistic level through high school was a wise one.

Our gospel singer developed voice primarily through performing in church and school choir, reaching the intermediate level of development in middle school. An astute choral director realized her potential talent and worked individually on helping her learn to read music through sight reading and ear training. Her church choir director prepared her for solos with the gospel choir every week. When she reached high school, her choral director suggested that she take private lessons, but her family could not afford them. This teacher nominated her for the Governors School for the Arts in her junior year, which afforded her a summer experience sharing music with other talented students in the arts. Now a senior, she plans to audition for a scholarship to a local college as a voice major.

Our singer's family has been actively engaged in church gospel music for generations. Through her natural musical development, they sought advice from church and school music teachers on ways to nurture their child's "God-given gift." They were pleased that the Governor's School acceptance was based primarily on artistic talent, rather than having a threshold of academic test scores that would have eliminated their daughter. They see their mature high school student now busily engaged in both academic studies and musical work, preparing for a possible college education, something they were not able to do themselves.

Ways to Guide Musical Development

Initial Stage: Playful years of early childhood programs and beginning instruction.

- Join in musical activities through early childhood programs, continuing these musical experiences in the home.
- Encourage creative musical expression in play and practice.
- Seek out a private teacher who will nurture the love of music and is also knowledgeable of the instructional needs of a young talented child.
- Provide guidance in establishing positive, productive practice habits.
- Show interest in musical accomplishments by being an attentive audience for informal performances.

Intermediate Stage: Emphasis on precision and discipline in musical training.

- Determine the suitability of the private teacher for instruction that will require the expertise to challenge your child.
- Encourage your child to self-monitor consistent practice, providing guidance in establishing self-disciplined metaskills.
- Monitor the role of competitions in your child's training, realizing the value of the dynamic of performance above winning.
- Assess your child's ability and commitment to work through future musical training.

Advanced Stage: Emphasis on the development of refined interpretation, analysis, and artistry

- Guide your child in establishing priorities and time management to allow time to continue advanced musical study.
- Seek challenging community resources to augment school musical offerings.
- Determine the suitability of possible schooling at a specialized high school for the performing arts or courses at conservatories or colleges.
- Discuss future options of music realistically, allowing room for pursuing music and academic interests in college.

Our guitarist is unknown to school choir, band, or orchestra directors at his high school. He picked up the instrument from some informal lessons with his uncle in elementary school. By sixth grade, he had formed his own band with a few friends, copying what they could pick up from their favorite CDs. He spent most of his free time listening to guitar greats in his room, systematically absorbing ideas that he would work out on his instrument for hours. His fascination with sound manipulation began after a visit to a recording studio. After years of developing his musical interests through informal lessons with performers and observing studio work, he discovered the High School for the Performing Arts in his city, which had courses in composing, computer music, and sound engineering. Not an unusually strong student academically, he has now found a niche where he feels his talents are appreciated, and he is thriving in school.

Our guitarist's family realized their son was absorbed by music and sound from an early age. He constantly invented sound machines and listened to all kinds of music when he was in elementary school. A brief try at formal lessons with a piano teacher failed after a few months because their son used his ear to learn, rather than learning to read music. They supported their son's unwavering interest, but there were many conflicts concerning his lack of commitment to academic work. They realize how fortunate they are to live in a major city that has an impressive specialized high school for the performing arts. It has made all the difference for their talented son. They now see a disciplined young man who is studying academic and musical work in an atmosphere with creatively artistic peers that seems to make the difference—he is special, rather than different.

These profiles are composites of possibilities at the advanced stage of musical development. If we ponder on these three teenagers, we wonder which one may ultimately be a success in the musical world. They all will decidedly have music as a vital part of their adult life, regardless of their career choice. Again, parents play a crucial role as advisors in guiding their teenager through the myriad of possibilities available to a dynamic teenager while holding onto a talent that has been nurtured since that first day in a preschool music class.[20]

The elementary years of musical development establish healthy habits of discipline and commitment that last a lifetime, within music and generalized to other areas. Parents of musically talented children realize the joy these musical experiences bring to their child. They will work through the ups and downs of this long journey of musical talent development, seeing their child grow artistically through the process. You will surely recognize them. They are sitting in the audience, glowing with pride, realizing the value of raising a musically talented child.

Resources

Books for Parents

Cutietta, Robert A., *Raising Musical Kids.* New York: Oxford University Press, 2001.

Haroutounian, Joanne, *Kindling the Spark: Recognizing and Developing Musical Talent.* New York: Oxford University Press, 2001.

Machover, W. and M. Uszler, *Sound Choices: Guiding Your Child's Musical Experiences.* New York: Oxford University Press, 1996.

Early Instrumental Instruction

Suzuki Association of the Americas, Inc.
P.O. Box 17310
Boulder, Colo. 80308
(303) 444-0948
http://www.suzukiassociation.org

Yamaha Corporation of America
Music Education System
P.O. Box 6600
Buena Park, Calif. 90622-6600
(800) 722-8856
http://www.yamaha.com

Early Childhood Music Programs

Kindermusik International
Box 26575
Greensboro, N.C. 27415
(800) 628-5687
http://www.kindermusik.com

Music Together
66 Witherspoon St.
Princeton, N.J. 08542
(800) 728-2692, ext. 13
http://www.MusicTogether.com

Musikgarten
P.O. Box 10846
Greensboro, N.C. 27404-0846
(800) 216-6864
musgarten@aol.com
http://www.musikgarten.org

Resources for Locating Independent Music Teachers

American String Teachers Association (ASTA)
1806 Robert Fulton Dr.
Reston, Va. 22091
(703) 476-1316
http://www.astaweb.com

Music Teacher National Association (MTNA)
The Carew Tower, Ste. 505, 441 Vine St.
Cincinnati, Ohio 45202-2814
(888) 512-5278
http://www.mtna.org

National Association of Teachers of Singing (NATS)
2800 North University Blvd.
Jacksonville, Fla. 32211
(904) 744-9022
http://www.nats.org

National Federation of Music Clubs
1336 N. Delaware St.
Indianapolis, Ind. 46202-2481
(317) 638-4003
http://www.nfmc-music.org

6

identifying and nurturing abilities in the dramatic arts

by

julie k. fishell,
lynn johnson
and
maria chrysanthou

This chapter provides information intended to assist parents, teachers and interested individuals in the process of identifying and cultivating dramatic abilities in young children. We will share scholarly research and practical experience to assist adults as they guide children who are gifted and talented in dramatic arts. Our investigation has revealed very few statistical studies devoted to identifying such children. The sources we cite range from accepted acting theory and educational research, to psychological studies. Our teaching and directing experiences range from public, private, and homeschooled instruction, to professional theater experiences.

This chapter will provide the following:

- working definitions of what it means to be gifted and talented in drama;
- profiles of children, from preschool to elementary-age, with dramatic abilities;
- a list of indicators of dramatic talent;
- creative options to nurture children who are gifted in drama;
- other ways, besides acting, to be involved in dramatic arts; and
- suggested books, journals, and Web sites for further exploration.

Prologue: Defining "Gifted in Drama"

Madeleine L'Engle has inspired this chapter with her comments on creativity. L'Engle, a well-known children's author, cited statistics from Finley Eversole's *The Politics of Creativity*:

> In our society, at the age of five, 90 percent of the population measures "high creativity." By the age of seven, the figure has dropped to 10 percent. And the percentage of adults with high creativity is only two percent! Our creativity is destroyed not through the use of outside force, but through criticism, innuendo . . . by the dirty devices of this world.[1]

These statistics especially resonate with those of us who regularly observe and work with early elementary-age children. We believe that a room full of young children is a room full of creators and that this creativity can be retained and developed throughout a lifetime.

Our student profiles are meant to illustrate characteristics of potential giftedness in both preschool and elementary-age students. As educators and nurturers in drama, we hope readers will use this information to identify, rather than attempt to create, gifted children in drama. We know of no method to identify ultimate abilities in drama, but we hope to provide some reliable indicators.

Indicators of ability in drama for the preschool-age child include a broad range of characteristics. We would encourage adults working with children younger than 7 to allow students a carte blanche or improvisatory attitude in drama activities. Dorothy Heathcote, a legendary force in drama education, described this attitude as:

- a respect for children and what they bring to the learning situation;
- a will to accept and use what they offer in class (home) situations; and
- self-identification as a member of a team—older, more experienced, as a rule, able to keep the team together.[2]

Educator Michael Grinder believes that primary students first learn kinesthetically or through body experience: "They enter kindergarten/first grade as primarily kinesthetic creatures."[3] At this age, children learn by doing. From third to fourth grade, intermediate students are switching from kinesthetic to primarily auditory learning. Chapter books with fewer illustrations are often introduced at this point, and other demands for visual reception are increased in the school curriculum. Instructors often encourage reading aloud to large groups so children can develop the ability to express themselves in front of others.

The authors of this chapter all agree that, by 8 or 9 years of age, a child can more easily be identified as gifted in drama. The following indicators may suggest exceptional dramatic abilities or indicate strengths in other creative arts:

- observation;
- focus and concentration;
- an attention to detail; and
- willingness to take risks.

Young acting students who display all four of these traits in a balanced way may achieve the much-desired state of "personal point of view," in other words, being comfortable with themselves and open to sharing their contributions with others.

Nellie McCaslin, New York University professor of educational drama, has developed a useful checklist of skills as a way of assessing progress for individual students in drama. This checklist of detailed abilities fits nicely under the umbrella of our four indicators. It may also be used to more specifically assess the strengths of student work. McCaslin ranks student growth in each area from 1 (rudimentary) to 4 (exceptional):[4]

- listening (hearing instructions, discussing topics, responding to questions);
- concentration (the ability to hold an idea long enough to respond thoughtfully or creatively);
- response (can be varied, most importantly note ability to physically, verbally, or emotionally respond to a challenge);
- imagination (the element that distinguishes a response as original, creative, or interesting);
- verbal activity (increased vocabulary and initiation in speaking);
- cooperation (the ability to offer ideas and to accept the ideas of others easily and graciously);

- organization (planning, seeing relationships between parts, making choices);
- attitude (the feeling or disposition toward the work and the other members of the class); and
- understanding (the ability to use the material; knowing what it is and how to handle it, going beyond comprehension of meaning, becoming engaged physically, emotionally and intellectually).

Act I: Identifying the Child Gifted in Drama

Act I, Scene i: A Preschool-Age Profile

Dillon is a 4-year-old boy who participated in the summer musical at my (Julie Fishell's) church. The play focused on the biblical story of Noah and his family. All preschool-age children within our church were invited to be animals on the ark and to dance and sing during a specific song. They were given a number of masks, and each child was encouraged to choose the animal he or she wanted to play. Two of each type of animal would be represented.

Dillon and his friend Blake chose tiger masks and rehearsed for several weeks. Dillon immediately made specific choices about the behavior of his tiger. During rehearsals, he shared a picture from one of his favorite animal books and vocally and physically imitated the tiger he had seen on a recent trip to the zoo. His mother shared with me that Dillon was the tiger at the grocery store, the dinner table, and all points in between. At every rehearsal, Dillon continued to fulfill his part, clarify his movement, and gain confidence in his work.

In contrast, Blake had fun with her friends, but was inconsistent in her focus and her vocal and physical choices as the tiger. As rehearsals progressed, she grew more nervous and needed special attention. The floor was too cold to crawl on or she constantly asked to go to the bathroom. On the day of performance, Blake forgot her tiger mask. She was crying and unwilling to participate without her mask. Dillon comforted Blake and, without a prompt from his friend, a parent, or me, suggested that Blake use his mask. He then asked me if I had any make-up. Dillon coached me through the design of his new mask with great confidence and was the envy of every other animal.

Dillon is a good example of a very young child who already shows signs of the indicators of dramatic giftedness mentioned earlier. When presented with a dramatic exercise (be a tiger), he showed himself to be a good observer of tigers. For weeks, Dillon focused and concentrated on tigers, both in rehearsals and at home, showing an attention to detail in the movements and voice characteristics. Dillon also was willing to take risks on the day of the performance, investigating an alternate way (with makeup, rather than a mask) to portray his character visually.

Dillon's story also shows how central imaginative play is to a young child with dramatic ability. Like Viola Spolin, a pioneer in educating through theater games, we believe that, through play, young children develop a sense of purpose. Spolin wrote:

> Outside of play there are few places where children can contribute to the world in which they find themselves. Their world, controlled by adults who tell them what to do and when to do it, offers them little opportunity to act or to accept community responsibility.[5]

Adam Blatner, psychiatrist and coauthor of *The Art of Play: Helping Adults Reclaim Imagination and Spontaneity*, eloquently described play as something that is spontaneous or is the opposite of habit.[6] Play is a natural activity for all young children; however, we believe there are specific indicators of extremely creative play that may eventually lead to dramatic ability. Indicators of this "predramatic" play observable even in preschool children are that the child:

- feels comfortable in a leadership role;
- takes charge;
- suggests ideas while considering the ideas of others;
- is kinesthetically agile and spatially aware;
- invites an audience ("Watch me, Mommy");
- invents his or her own games with imaginative logic;
- mimics people, animals, and things, including speech and movement patterns (according to Gerald Tyler, "To let one's dolls talk to one another and to hold conversations with them holds the beginnings of characterization"); and
- shows mutual respect for the feelings and experiences of both the self and others.[7]

We feel that this last characteristic is an especially important indicator among younger children (ages 5–7), where "egocentricism" eventually gives way toward what drama educator of the very young, Donald Baker calls "decentralized attention."[8] Early sensitivity to others matters here.

Act I, Scene ii: Two Elementary Student Profiles

Owen is an extremely gifted and talented 9-year-old theater student. He stands out among my (Lynn Johnson's) "geniuses"—a very short list from over a decade of teaching. I met Owen when he was 5, and I immediately knew I was working with someone special. In our classes, we create original plays in which the children craft their own characters, and then a story is fashioned around those characters.

Whereas most of the children tend to stick with similar types of characters based on their general interests, Owen has played a castle guard (named Guard–a-Boo-Boo), the King, an intergalactic space hero's sidekick, and a drunken soldier. All from his own imagination, he has challenged himself to explore various aspects of his personality and has seen our plays as his outlet for that exploration. He is a subtle and understated little leader who is often heard saying, "I have an idea about what we can do." At the same time, he is a caring and generous ensemble member who is able to play with the group, perform unison movement and text, and focus in on our group activities.

Like Dillon, Owen exhibits notable abilities to observe in detail, focus on the task, and take risks. Owen's prolific cast of characters was the creative by-product of impressive *observation* skills. His characters began as generic types: a guard, a soldier, a hero. But, through careful observation, he realized that they must be individuals: a *castle* guard, a *drunken* soldier, and an *intergalactic space* hero's *sidekick*! Another indicator of observational skills is his attitude or temperament; rather than attempting to force himself on the situation, Owen observes and responds to it.

Owen also showed a special ability to be fully *focused* on his task. The treasured ability to be fully focused is achieved through relaxation and hinges on sensory awareness. When the senses are engaged, the student often appears without tensions and can undertake tasks with ease and effortlessness. For example, the professional baseball player approaching the plate to swing a bat in a tied game must stay loose—feel the bat and the breeze, smell the air, relate to internal muscles for just the right placement of body and bat.

It is through the five basic senses that we begin to learn everything that we know. There is no other way. If we were to shut eyes and ears, stop feeling and taste and smell, the world would become a blank, and we ourselves would only be alive through remembered sensation.[9]

Owen used a base of sensory awareness to observe others and allow these perceptions to move him to create detailed realities for the exercise.

Finally, children and adults alike can relate to the vulnerability of sharing a personal idea. Students with exceptional abilities in drama often feel the desire to protect their ideas, but find a way to overcome this internal obstacle. A burning desire to share and express often fuels their willingness to *take risks*. Owen seems to have a natural ability to risk with the group when he says, "I have an idea about what we can do."

Helping a talented student accomplish these three key tasks—detailed observation, relaxed focus on the task, and risk taking—can release the student to function at his or her fullest potential. Rose was a 10-year-old student when she sang a Broadway song and performed a memorized speech from the screenplay *Annie* for an audition. She presented me (Julie Fishell) with a typed resume that included a list of community theater productions, naming role, director, and theater, along with a current black-and-white photo stapled to the back. Her audition was meticulously rehearsed.

Following her song and speech, I asked her to have a seat and read a short speech from the upcoming production. "Deer in the headlights" quite accurately describes her response. Sensing her distress, I offered another idea and suggested we explore her memorized speech from *Annie*. Her response: "Wasn't it perfect?" Her face revealed a presence that was mature and thoughtful.

I very genuinely responded that her outstanding audition had prompted my requests. Then I said, "Let's just see what happens if we have some fun and try the words in a new way." With Rose's next breath, her face relaxed and she seemed intrigued by the idea. I asked her if she liked ice cream, and she said, "Yes! Vanilla!" Then I said, "What if the words were *vanilla ice cream*—what would you do? How might they sound?" She proceeded to say each word of her speech with genuine enjoyment and ownership. She was off and running and we both had a great time. Her voice was free and her smiles were genuine. This incident revealed that I probably had a real budding actress on my hands complete with great instincts, an immediate ability to relate through a suggestible imagination, and a real dose of perfectionism.

Unlike Owen, Rose in her initial audition was focused on my assessment of her work, rather than on the work itself. Her desire to control the audition—rather than focus on embodying the words and feelings of her pieces—created sensory shutdown. Instead of paying attention to the details of her characterization with a sense of joy, Rose was encouraged to pay excessive attention to the details of her résumé, picture, and demeanor. Though Rose is certainly talented, she was on the cusp of losing the "gift of seeing and feeling keenly."[10] Rose's focus and attention were centered on what Virginia Tanner has called "false artistic values," values that keep children from experiencing "the real beauty of self expression."[11] Young drama students who are pushed too hard and too soon to appear poised and professional may be encouraged to look at drama as a "job" meant to please others.

When the instructor prompted Rose's imagination with the supposition "What if the words were vanilla ice cream?," there was an immediate change in focus and observation. This coaching encouraged Rose to focus on her sensory awareness. In an almost domino-like effect, Rose began to relax and showed an ability to risk improvised work willingly. The "Magic If," a concept coined by the seminal force in modern acting theory, Constantin Stanislavski, helps prompt a response that is personal to the actor, avoiding hollow playing or cliché.[12]

Act II: How to Nurture Your Child's Dramatic Talents

Act II, Scene i: The Role of the Parent

Theater should be a family affair. In the case of "Owen," he is homeschooled. As a result, his talents and interests are supported by his day-to-day contact with his mother. Although homeschooling is not a viable option for all families, its process of child-centered, family-directed education provides a model for how to encourage growth in the area of drama. Because drama is not often explored in many of our public schools, you, as a parent of a gifted child, will most likely be the key link between your child and valuable dramatic experiences.

The most important thing you can do in that role is to experience theater with your children, both as an audience member and as a player. Take them to plays for young audiences, as well as more sophisticated plays. (Classics are often appropriate. We have listed some suggested plays in Appendix A at the end of the chapter.) Many theaters, especially children's theaters, have opportunities to meet and ask questions of the actors and technicians. In addition, most communities have opportunities for parents and children to work together on the production of a play, both on- and off-stage. But, you don't have to be in a theater or constantly surround your child with professionals in order to expose them to positive experiences. There are some activities you can do at home with your child that are simple and fun and will help enhance your child's dramatic gifts (see Appendix B).

Finally, if you, like Rose's parents, are dealing with a perfectionist, help your child to engage in activities where there are few apparent rules and there are no seeming rights and wrongs. Make a stepping stone—who is to say what color marbles to use or what the stone should say; finger paint; play on the playground; visit an art museum and take time to interpret individually a painting or photograph; ask your child what they like most about a certain food, song, or activity. Encourage your child's unique, delightful, individual point of view. Model learning for them in as relaxed a manner as possible. Heidi Priesnitz put it this way:

> Kids learn a lot by watching their parents. If you actively pursue your own learning, your children will pick up on it. Teach by example. Let your kids know that you are also learning new things. Kids should not be given the impression that learning only takes place at school, or between the ages of five and 21. By being curious yourself, and by asking questions in front of your kids, you will show them that learning is a constant and natural process. Kids who understand this will be much more relaxed and open to the idea of learning.[13]

Act II, Scene ii: The Role of the School

Some students are fortunate enough to attend schools with drama programs. Still, even in schools that teach and value the arts, talent can be missed. The Youth Talent Identification Program (YTP) sponsored by ArtsConnection, a not-for-profit organization for arts in education, studied third- and fourth-grade students in an elementary school in New York City. The researchers related:

> The process is a full class activity, not voluntary or based on teacher recommendations, as are many such selection processes in school. With the official sanction of the teacher and school, and the participation of the whole class, students who might have been reluctant to attend an arts audition found it easy to demonstrate their talents . . . many of the students selected for the advanced talent develop-

ment program were surprises to their teachers, parents, and some-times even themselves. "He is so shy. I know he likes music, but I never thought he was any good at it."[14]

We feel that a strong commitment to expose elementary-age children to dramatic arts within a school curriculum is extremely important. In a class-room, there is the ability for students to learn about their own abilities while simultaneously recognizing new skills among their peers. While private classes or community-based activities are of equal value, in our opinion, it is optimal for schools to promote study in dramatic arts. Availability of arts education in public school settings levels out the economic playing field for all children. As Oreck, Baum, and McCartney stated, "Most models of talent develop-ment are based on studies of people born into a family who both valued their talents and had the financial means to support their development."[15]

According to a study of arts in education conducted by the President's Committee on the Arts and the Humanities and the Arts Education Partnership, the most critical factor in sustaining arts education in their schools is "the active involvement of influential segments of the community in shaping and implementing the policies and programs of the district."[16] The study goes on to define community as parents and political and busi-ness leaders. Most school districts that lack a strong level of community arts advocacy will eventually suffer from a lack of arts programming, which can have a negative effect on your gifted child's education.

As a parent, there are choices you can make and ways you can work with your child's school to ensure a quality arts education.

- Enroll your child in a public or a private school that has arts educa-tion as its core philosophy. In North Carolina, for example, The A+ Schools Program (http://www.aplus-schools.org) is "an approach to teaching and learning grounded in the belief that the arts can play a central role in how children learn."[17] This network of public schools employs certified arts integration specialists to work with the teach-ing faculty to integrate the artistic process in the teaching of all sub-jects. There are similar projects throughout the United States.
- Enroll your child in an after-school program. These programs are often tuition-based, but they allow students to study a variety of subjects not offered during the school day. Local college students or area professionals often teach drama classes.

- Run for the school board. If you have the time and the energy to take on a leadership position in your community, being a member of the school board will ensure that you are taking an active role in the decisions that are being made in your child's school.
- Volunteer your time in the school. This can be especially valuable if you have a younger child in a preschool or kindergarten with a high population. Sometimes, these teachers need an extra set of hands in order to implement all the creative projects they would like. You could volunteer to read stories with the kids or organize a class play.
- Volunteer your time with the Parent-Teacher Association. Being a member of the PTA can give you a voice in what types of activities come to your school. Local PTAs raise money to hire traveling performance troupes to perform in-school assemblies. Also, PTA members have the opportunity to work with local arts councils to find artists to work in residence in the schools. Artist residencies can provide a large number of students with unique and exciting performance experiences that would not normally be offered.
- Donate money to the school especially earmarked for drama programming. Most schools complain that lack of funds prohibits arts programming. So, give them some.
- Maintain active communication with your child's teachers.[18] Both you and the teacher should be effective participants in your child's education. Being able to share effectively successes and frustrations will provide your gifted child with the tools he or she needs to succeed.

Act II, Scene iii: The Role of the Community

Higher education and conservatory training in the dramatic arts have greatly increased the connection between the artistic aims and merits of classroom drama and outside or community drama. Nellie McCaslin reported in *Creative Drama in the Classroom and Beyond* that, between 1974 and 1998, community arts agencies in the United States grew from approximately 200 to 4,000.[19]

Drama programs that include participatory programs such as workshops are held in a variety of venues and may be funded as community outreach projects. Use the following as a guide to places where drama activities may be offered in your community. This list, based on a model from Nellie McCaslin, may serve as a catalyst to encourage community models of such programs.[20]

First, investigate the resources offered by your local cultural institutions:

- Museums may offer interactive programs featuring a tour, performance, and question-and-answer session with the actors. The Abigail Adams Smith Museum in New York City is one such institution.
- Parks, such as the Wolf Trap Farm Park for the Performing Arts in Virginia, offer summer drama classes for adults and children.
- Libraries often include puppetry workshops to enhance story enjoyment.

Both businesses and not-for-profit institutions offer a variety of activities in drama. These activities can include drama camps, community theater, dramatic productions by religious communities, and professional theater.

Drama Camps. Camps in drama are offered from Maine to California. An Internet search will turn up a cornucopia of options for summer and year-round drama programs. Another great way to find a camp is by word-of-mouth or recommendation from others. Contacting universities, conservatories, local professional and nonprofessional theaters, or arts councils may also help you locate opportunities for your child. Investigate any community opportunity and especially camps by attending a final presentation and meet some of the faculty and staff prior to enrollment.

Most camps for elementary-age children will be nonresidential and will include activities that expose children to various creative arts. Drawing, dance, music, and drama are usually explored, giving shape to an eclectic "performance" of the camp's activities. A tip: Don't overestimate the value of the camp facilities, bells and whistles, or assurances of a "professional" product. According to McCaslin,

> Without discrediting academic preparation, what seems most important are those personal attributes that make a good teacher . . . sympathetic leadership, imagination, and respect for the ideas of others . . . familiarity with techniques is an invaluable asset, but imaginative leaders will, in the end, create their own methods.[21]

Residential drama camps usually cater to the child 9 or above. For example, The People's Light & Theatre Company located in Malvern, Pennsylvania, offers three- and four-week camps, Monday through Friday, as a part of their Summerstage. The camp's curriculum is focused by theme (fairy tales, mythology, sports) and culminates in a student-created original performance. A staff of professional theater artists, including directors, actors, playwrights, musicians, and designers, lead the camps.

Community Theater. Community theaters often produce musicals or lighter fare that include young performers. Performances are usually limited, and rehearsal can be accommodated in the early evening. Even in a nonprofessional situation, the child needs to be prepped on proper conduct and agree to certain circumstances. These include willingness to:

- rehearse the same story/scenes over an extended period of time;
- take direction and be part of an ensemble regardless of the size of part; and
- take the commitment seriously and forgo other conflicting activities (sports, social engagements).

Religious Communities. Religious communities can also be terrific places for children to participate in drama activities.

- Children's Choir pieces may include speaking and singing parts. Publishing companies devote exclusive attention to such works. Performance rights are minimal, and scripts are easily purchased through an Education Fund.
- Secular works may also prove appropriate for production via some religious communities; an example might be the dramatic work based on *The Diary of Anne Frank.*
- Intergenerational faith exploration is possible through drama, and the authors of this chapter strongly support this activity. Most published faith-based dramas include music and text and can be cast for multiple participants of varying ages. Publishers include Baker's Plays (http://www.bakersplays.com).

Professional Theater. Professional theater also occasionally offers opportunities for young children to work onstage. This can be a wonderful opportunity for the child *and parent* who are ready for the following:

- An extended and intense performance schedule. Most regional theaters perform a given play from 5–10 weeks. Professional productions occur on average 6 days a week, with Monday being the day off. There are often matinee performances in addition to a typical 8 p.m. curtain nightly.

- A high rejection factor. You and your child must be prepared to audition, interview, or both without expectation. The truth is that personality and looks will often weigh heavily on the director's decision and equal the value of talent. "Whatever else acting might be, it is a job, and a job within one of America's biggest enterprises: the entertainment industry. . . .You can't ever forget: The industry's goal is to make money, and your value to the industry is determined precisely (and often solely) by how much money you can make it."[22]

Theaters will often accommodate young performers and their families by double-casting roles. This can be wise and give each child needed rest and "down time" from production.

Act III: How to Find
Good Drama Teachers and Programs

Act III, Scene i: Finding an Outstanding Instructor

Flexibility is a key characteristic that often sets outstanding drama teachers/leaders apart from the merely adequate. This characteristic makes so many things possible for the young drama student. A flexible drama teacher:

- sets overall benchmark goals with the class clearly;
- shares thoughts and ideas easily without coercing outcomes;
- respects each child and establishes the importance of peer respect; and
- knows when to be silent and let the students lead exploration, trusting that "brainstorming" works.

Brainstorming with gifted children on what kinds of projects they could do may also generate ideas teachers may never have thought of on their own. In 1987, Morgan and Saxton devised a "categorization of identification" to help teachers to recognize levels of role play.[23] These levels include:

- dramatic playing (being oneself in a make-believe situation);
- mantle of the expert (being oneself, but looking at the situation through special eyes);
- characterizing (representing an individual lifestyle that is somewhat or markedly different from the student's own); and
- acting (selecting symbols, movements, gestures and voices to represent a particular individual to others; acting can be in the form of [a] presenting or [b] performing).

We are especially fond of the group vitality that "mantle of the expert" often produces. A savvy and daring teacher will often encourage a child who is noticeably shy or distanced from the group to assume this role, allowing the teacher to "place children in the role of the expert. When an adult takes on a low-status role and the children are required to be helpers and the solvers of problems, we elevate their role into that of being the 'one who knows.'"[10]

Finally, appropriate certification, education, or comparable experience is important when trusting a teacher/Instructor. As suggested earlier, contact institutions of higher learning or arts councils. References from an established organization can serve as a safety net here. It is not necessary that a teacher be trained at a top-flight institution. In fact, many summer camps in drama hire a lead teacher who is an experienced undergraduate or graduate student studying drama. Each teacher is assisted by a middle school student who may be an alumnus/alumna of the camp. This tier of experience is wonderful for youngsters and often provides children with role models who serve to inspire openness and ease.

Act III, Scene ii: Questions to Ask Before Enrolling Your Child
The following list of questions can serve as a guide when investigating a program, class, or camp:

- What is the total cost of the program? This should include all "hidden" costs, including costumes and so forth.
- How will "casting" or performance assignments be given? If you have reservations about the program hinging on auditions prior to the class, you may want to avoid the program. Will your child only commit to a leading part or will he or she be bored if cast in a small role? We suggest that children invariably shine when encouraged to create as an ensemble. Some teachers will ask students to write

down or privately relate what role they wish to play. This is an excellent mechanism for casting.

- Are parents allowed to observe rehearsals and classes? Will you be comfortable allowing your child to be in a closed session with the instructor? Frankly, we feel that this autonomy is often necessary for students to excel. Perhaps you can observe a bit of a class in which your child does not participate.

- How much homework or "outside time" is my child expected to devote to coursework? Remember that you are committing both yourself and your child to this course and will most likely be asked to assist your child. Practicing dance steps, working on text, creating a costume—these are just a sampling of potential home activities. Still, remember that a great camp or class for a young person may have little or no mandatory homework.

Epilogue: Beyond Acting—Essential Collaborators in Drama

As students develop their abilities, you may notice an uncanny tendency for them to develop competence in a variety of skills. Your emergent theater artist may play piano, golf, or tennis; cook; or engage in any number of activities with success. Our guess is that no one activity will satisfy the ever moving and self-challenging drama kid. As the parent, you shouldn't hesitate to encourage these skills and interests even when they seem to be "off track." Successful practitioners in the field often possess a variety of talents that allow them to be employable in many different areas. As your gifted child advances in drama, he or she will most likely become interested in experimenting with some of the other roles in the theater. Keep in mind that some of the finest playwrights, directors, and designers all began as actors.

The playwright creates the story. The whole process of creating theater really begins with the vision of this person. Playwrights are able to express their views of and hopes for humanity through the art of dialogue and characterization. The budding playwright will likely:

- have an interest in English, foreign languages, and history;
- keep a journal or a diary;

- love to read and often question what he or she reads;
- stay interested in a concentrated task over a period of time;
- have strong sensory awareness;
- *not* be interested in being on stage or the center of attention;
- have an advanced vocabulary and command of parts of speech; and
- be able to read his or her writing aloud in a supportive environment.

The director serves as the ultimate interpreter of the playwright's text. This individual considers each area of production and communicates a consistent vision or goal for the production. The director must work with every other member of the creative team. The budding director will likely:

- have the ability to inspire others and motivate a group;
- love to read and be able to imagine and describe what he or she reads in three-dimensional terms;
- be organized;
- be comfortable in a leadership role;
- be concerned with the scope of human experience; and
- enjoy researching a variety of topics.

Designers create a theater production's external environment, either realistic or stylized, including *sets*, *costumes*, *lights*, and even *sound*. The budding designer will likely:

- love to manipulate three-dimensional objects such as blocks, crayons, clay, and fabric;
- be an illustrator of his or her own stories, having to always put pictures to the text;
- be fascinated with sound effects and music;
- emerge with particular sensitivity to shade and intensity of color; and
- have a strong interest in computers and other forms of technology.

Appendix A:
Some Favorite Plays to Experience With Your Child

Please investigate the following publishers. Most large companies offer free catalogues in which you will find titles, description of the play, size of the cast, and sometimes age appropriateness. Please refer to the following Web sites to access plays for all ages:

- http://www.dramaticpublishing.com
- http://www.bakersplays.com
- http://usaplays4kids.drury.edu
- http://www.edta.org/connections/script_sources.asp

Plays for Beginners

Fairy tales, myths, favorite books, and poems all make terrific material for improved or adapted plays. Keep in mind that a portion of any set play may be performed.

Plays for the Intermediate Student

Swortzell, Lowell, ed., *All the World's a Stage: Modern Plays for Young People*. New York: Delacorte Press, 1975.

Shakespeare, William, *A Midsummer Night's Dream*. England: Oxford School University Press, 2001. (Note: The Oxford School Shakespeare series appeals to the young with "cool" graphics, footnotes, and accessible commentary.)

Haubold, Cleve, *The Wishin' Tree*. New York: Samuel French, 1973.

Plays for the Advanced Student

Classics, classics, and more classics!

Allen, Woody, *Don't Drink the Water*. New York: Random House, 1967.

Hansberry, Lorraine, *A Raisin in the Sun*. New York: Samuel French, 1989.

Nash, R. Richard, *Rainmaker*. New York: Random House, 1955.

Shakespeare, William, *Romeo and Juliet* and *Macbeth*. London: Oxford School University Press, 2001.

Sills, Paul, *Story Theatre*. New York: Samuel French, 1990.

Wilson, August, *Fences*. New York: New American Library, 1986.

Appendix B:
Drama Activities to Try

The dramatic activities included below are developmental in nature and are examples of how parents, teachers, and other adults can nurture dramatic talent in young children. There is no clear-cut or correct way of doing these exercises; therefore, outcomes will vary. Our exercises were designed using the principles of educational drama described by Richard Courtney in his book *Dictionary of Developmental Drama*. He identifies four core objectives as aims of educational drama. "Intrinsic aims: reinforcing methods for a student to learn; Social aims: social and cultural awareness; Extrinsic aims: Learning subject matter through dramatic activity; and Aesthetic aims: teaching choice, expressing feelings and opinions."[25]

From the example of Dillon, the 4-year-old gifted child, you can see that your preschooler should be encouraged to engage his body and his voice fully to portray animals, other people, and even inanimate objects.

The first exercise below is a simply organized play that you and your young child can do together. This type of exercise also introduces your young child to the concept of research, learning as much as possible about his or her favorite animals and applying that knowledge to his or her performance skills. Even though this is a very basic exercise and perfect for preschoolers, it is strikingly similar to a required exercise from my (Lynn Johnson's) first year of acting class at Northwestern University. I studied and performed African elephants, which taught me valuable lessons about movement and power on stage and about my strengths and limitations as a performer.

Exercise One: Be the Tiger

Go to a zoo or a farm and observe the animals. Take note of the animals to which your child is most attracted. Together, the two of you should imitate the animals, how they walk, and what sounds they make. Ask the experts questions about what kinds of foods the animals eat, what environments they thrive in, how often they sleep. Then, find a book or a folktale or create your own story that features one of your child's favorite animals. Narrate the story while your child acts it out. Make an event out of it by including other children to join in the play and inviting friends and other family members to watch your performance. This exercise can be repeated multiple times, following the rhythms of your child's interests. Instead of portraying animals, try fire trucks, mermaids, or robots. The bold physical choices created through this exercise help drama kids learn the power of external silhouette and movement to create character.

Exercise Two: The Senses

This exercise is so effective because it can be done anywhere and it fosters the skills of observation and attention to detail that are so important to maintain in children while they are still young. This exercise is appropriate for children of all ages, from preschool through elementary school.

Take a trip to somewhere special or not so special. You could choose a trip to the garden, the bowling alley, or even your office. Tell the child to close his or her eyes and recognize the smells in the room. Then, ask the student to imagine something that he or she smells as a color, a taste, a sound, and a fabric or surface ("Does it smell blue?" "Does it smell soothing like ocean waves or does it smell harsh like a million trumpets?"). Give him or her the option to write or verbally share his or her impressions. Listen or read the responses and encourage his or her impressions positively. When appropriate, search their meanings with:

- "I never would have thought of that!"
- "Tell me more!"
- "Fascinating!"

Feel free to continue this activity with a focus on the other senses. Maybe you want to focus on all the sounds on a bus or all the textures in a bookstore. It is best to *encourage their responses as completely valid.* You will reinforce ownership of their experiences by dislodging the need to be "right" or produce an answer meant to please their peers or you.

This activity is fun for all ages and particularly sparks the interest of elementary-age students.

Exercise Three: Learn From the Masters

Try hosting a movie night complete with popcorn and treat your young thespian to some raucous research of the talents of Charlie Chaplin, Buster Keaton, the Marx Brothers, or the Three Stooges. Studying silent film or even turning down the sound on some films can confirm the power of physical presence and how it tells us as much or more than words. Create characters of your own using exaggerated movements. Think about how you would walk or eat or dance if you were a sad hobo, or a snobby mayor, or a young girl in love. Gifted elementary-age students possess the skills of focus and discipline. They are able to engage the process of creation, collaboration, and revision necessary in drama. This exercise reinforces these elements.

Exercise Four: The Story—Make it Your Own

Photocopy a passage of text from a favorite book, or write one. Do not use narration—find a short paragraph that is one character's speech. It is best that you choose a passage with a clear dilemma. Provide a pencil and a dictionary for each child. Ask them to find the verbs in each sentence and circle them. Continue by drawing a box around the subjects. Then, ask them to write down any words they don't know and define them. (It is important that you are there to encourage and also help when necessary. We want the students to enjoy making the text their own. Different color highlighters or pencils may be used for the identified parts of speech.) If an actual text is being used, always encourage the child to memorize it as written. *However, encourage personal paraphrase!* Let them tell you the story in their own words. Children with natural dramatic ability will very quickly paraphrase their parts.

Come away from the table. Ask each child to choose a circled verb and explore a whole body gesture that "means" that word. By using verbs, we will ensure something active. For example, the word *grab* obviously involves the hands; however, encourage each child to "grab with the whole body." Involve the voice, as well (it is a physical instrument), and encourage the student to say the word along with the gesture exploration.

Repeat the above exercises using subjects instead of verbs.

Appendix C:
Related Reading

The following resources provide a range of information for both teachers and parents on nurturing and supporting dramatic talent in the young child. A short annotated bibliography of related articles can also be found at this Web site: http://scs.une.edu.au/TalentEd/ResMat/ABDrama.htm.

The Education and Development of the Drama Student

Heathcote, Dorothy, *Dorothy Heathcote: Collected Writings on Drama and Education*, ed. Liz Johnson and Cecily O'Neill. London: Hutchinson, 1984.

Hendy, Lesley and Lucy Toon, *Supporting Drama and Imaginative Play in the Early Years*. Buckingham, England: Open University, 2001.

McCaslin, Nellie, *Children and Drama*. New York: Longman, 1981.

Slade, Peter, *Child Play: Its Importance for Human Development*. London: Jessica Kingsley, 1995.

Schwartz, Dorothy and Dorothy Aldrich, *Give Them Roots and Wings*. Washington D.C.: American Theatre Association, 1972.

Vygotsky, Lev, *Mind and Society: Development of Higher Psychological Processes*. Cambridge, Mass.: Harvard University Press, 1978.

Ward, Winifred, *Playmaking With Children from Kindergarten to High School Acting*. New York: D. Appleton, Century Company, 1947.

Theater Craft and Exercises

Archer, Stephen M., *How Theatre Happens*. New York: Macmillan, 1983.

Barker, Clive, *Theatre Games: A New Approach to Drama Training*. London: Eyre Methuen, 1977.

Cohen, Robert, *Acting Professionally: Raw Facts About Careers in Acting*. Mountain View, Calif.: Mayfield, 1990.

Hagen, Uta, *Respect for Acting*. New York: Macmillan, 1973.

O'Neil, Brian, *Acting as a Business*. Portsmouth, N.H.: Heinemann, 1999.

Polsky, Milton E., *Let's Improvise: Becoming Creative, Expressive & Spontaneous Through Drama*. Englewood Cliffs, N.J.: Prentice-Hall, 1980.

Spolin, Viola, *Improvisations for the Theatre: A Handbook of Teaching and Directing Techniques*. Evanston, Ill: Northwestern University Press, 1986.

Spolin, Viola, *Theatre Games for the Classroom: A Teacher's Handbook*. Evanston, Ill: Northwestern University Press, 1986.

7

recognizing
and developing
early talent
in the visual arts

by

sandra kay

To be chosen for the elite membership of an Academy of Art is the pinnacle of acceptance as a significant artist for adults in Europe. Although he is more renowned as a pioneer of abstract expressionism, Willem de Kooning (1904–1997) was a full-fledged member of the Academy in Holland at the age of 12. Like de Kooning, many well-known artists show signs of their talent —including advanced technical skills and an intense emotional response to art[1]— during early childhood.

However, strong interest in the visual arts is also quite frequently seen in intellectually or academically gifted students.[2] The joy and challenge of developing technical proficiency is not limited to artistically gifted individuals. Both the artistically gifted and the academically gifted need good art instruction: "What is clearly apparent from practice is that bright students respond quickly and adeptly to art instruction. On the other hand, those with artistic gifts often need to be challenged to use their image-making abilities to think about and explore the world of ideas which reside in the history of art and in the realm of aesthetics."[3]

Knowing more about the visual arts and how talent in these areas develops can help parents determine the guidance and resources their child will need to develop as a young artist. This chapter will look at ways to recognize early talent in visual art, what we know about developing artistic talent, and the roles typically played by family, community, and school in this area of talent development.

What are the visual arts? We will use a comprehensive definition that includes:

- the skills and products related to the fine arts (e.g., drawing, painting, sculpture, printmaking, photography);
- the crafts (e.g., ceramics, wood, metal, fibers);
- the applied design fields (architecture, environmental and industrial design, graphic design and illustration); and
- the various forms of multimedia (e.g., collage, assemblage, conceptual art, performance art, and video).[4]

Recognizing Early Talent

Some time ago, a 6-year-old boy arrived at my office carrying a folder of his work in one hand while holding his mother's hand in the other. Drawings of cowboys dominated the subject matter of the dozen or so samples. I asked him to tell me about his drawings. With a critical eye, he told me how he has improved since these were done and that the inspiration for these drawings came from watching the movie *The Magnificent Seven*. The work that covered my desk at that moment was later evaluated by six art educators. Asked to estimate the age of the young artist, they all concluded that the work had been done by a middle school student.

When I asked this 6-year-old if he remembered when he started drawing, he answered, "I was very young. I think 4 or 5. No, I must have been 3 [mother nodded confirmation]. I wasn't as good as now. I get better." Asked why he needed to draw so much (20–50 drawings a week), the response was "Because I love it. I just love it!"

The rest of the interview went as follows:

"How do you choose what to draw?"

"Oh, I pick which picture would look good as a drawing."

"What do you mean? Where are these pictures you pick from?"

"In my head. I pick which one I would like to see as a drawing."

"Are there many to choose from?"

"Oh, yes!"

Art making, like play, provides intense joy. It is an activity that appeals to young gifted children as a form of expression. Oftentimes, young children find that drawing and sculpting give them ways to record detailed observations of their world. Most very young children begin by exploring mark making as a kinesthetic activity, recording their arm movements on the page. Eventually, however, they begin to develop meanings associated with each of their drawn symbols. When meaning is communicated through their artwork, a "visual language" begins to take shape. Sometimes, children become so interested in developing this visual language that they do not have an interest in developing verbal or written language skills (much to the chagrin of parents and educators).

Like verbal language, visual language develops predictably and sequentially. Victor Lowenfeld's research on creative and mental growth has given us benchmarks for identifying the developmental stages of a fundamental area of the visual arts: drawing.[5] For the artistically gifted, however, acceleration through the developmental stages of drawing may be so fast that stages appear to be skipped.

Lowenfeld described five stages of self-expression that begin with the *scribbling stage* from approximately ages 2–4. Random mark making or disordered scribbling moves to controlled scribbling when children discover a connection between their motions and the marks on the paper. Gaining control over the motion and developing coordination between visual and manual activity may be reflected in scribbles that form horizontal, vertical, or circular lines. The child will begin lifting the crayon off the page to start again elsewhere or may experiment with using more than one color. Once scribbles are given names or titles, another level of development within the scribbling stage has become evident.

The *pre-schematic stage* usually occurs between the ages of 4 and 7. Usually, the child will begin to draw representational symbols of a person. The circle (head) with two vertical lines (feet) is a common representation of a person by a 5-year-old. Geometric shapes are used for many objects. Size and placement on the page are not important in this self-communication stage. Most children begin with circles and can copy a square at about 4 years of age and a triangle at 5.

A few words of caution are in order here: The art of children follows the same developmental patterns and variations as any other aspect of growth. Developmental differences can be tremendous at this age. The general trends and predictability of development can be marked by both growth spurts and regressing to an earlier stage.

With that caveat, when drawings begin to show concepts and reflect an active knowledge of the environment, the child has entered the *schematic stage*—usually at ages 7–9. In the schematic stage, a schema (meaningful symbol) is used to represent a person, but arms and legs will show volume and are usually correctly placed. Objects are often placed on a baseline reflecting location in the environment in a two-dimensional (flat) representation. Proportions depend more on emotional values than physical accuracy.

The gang age (9–12 years old) reflects the *dawning realism* characteristic of this stage. Drawings tend to demonstrate attention to details and the interrelationship between objects, and there is an overlapping of objects and attempts at showing depth through size of objects. The age of reasoning, or *pseudo-naturalistic stage*, typically occurs between the ages of 12 and 14. Common characteristics include cartooning, variations of facial expressions, and attention focused on only important details for personally meaningful representations. Adolescent art (*the period of decision*) most often occurs between the ages of 14 and 17. At this level, conscious development of artistic skills such as perspective, use of light and shade, and mastery of a variety of materials compliment exaggerated or satirical subject matter.

High ability in the technical aspects of artwork is necessary to develop as a mature artist, but *technical skills* are not all that an artist needs. Other important characteristics that have been identified include *extended concentration; visual fluency*[6]; *problem-defining skills*[7]; *motivation; perceptual acuity*; a sense of *aesthetic intelligence*; and *creative imagination.*[8] Regular practice by a motivated young artist will sharpen these attributes into developed artistic talent. These characteristics, which are found in professional artists, are sometimes found in very young children who have artistic potential. Some of these characteristics can be recognized by parents; others may require the expertise of an art educator who has seen the work of thousands of students. Most art educators use some form of these three main criteria to evaluate students' art: the degree of explorations with varied media (such as painting, drawing, sculpture, etc.), the level of technical skills, and the perceptual aptitude used to capture the real-life subjects the child has chosen from his or her imagination or environment.

As in the instance of the 6-year-old who entered my office door, subject themes, such as the cowboys, may emerge as a result of *extended concentration*. Extended concentration is reflected in the ability to stay with an artistic problem because there are many possibilities to explore. Although, like this child, artistically gifted children are often very prolific—that is, they produce many pieces of artwork—they may have more ideas than they can find time to work on. Artistically gifted children's degree of *visual fluency* (number of ideas or variations) can equal that of professional artists.

Perceptual acuity is a super-accurate sensibility or ability to perceive information from the senses. Two extreme examples of this trait were demonstrated by the young child described above. First, when he was seeking technical advice, he asked me for a better white to use with his ink drawings because the white of the paper was not correct. When I provided three choices of white pencils, only one satisfied his need. The second instance was even more dramatic. In one of his drawings in which he was copying a photograph from a printed brochure, images of a flag with Russian lettering were depicted in the drawing, but these were not visible to my eye or his mother's on the brochure. A magnifying glass (10x) provided us with the raw sensory material that the child saw and depicted in his drawing. This perceptual "overexcitability"[9] (i.e. extreme sensitivity to perceptual images) and extreme accuracy in reading images are characteristic of a talented young artist, but can interfere with an artist's performance on a timed test of figural reasoning such as a nonverbal IQ test.[10]

Like professional artists, gifted young artists may possess highly focused *problem-defining skills.*[11] These skills are used to specialize and narrow the many available artistic options in order to concentrate on exploring a particular problem, topic, or theme. Expert artists tend to define the parameters (i.e., medium, etc.) in which they choose to work whereas a novice or beginning artist may have more of a discovery-oriented approach to learning, with a desire to sample many different possibilities.[12] The professional artist uses whatever art materials it takes to best address the issue or problem at hand. This might involve learning how to use familiar materials in a new way or learning how to use totally new materials.

In the process of defining the artistic problems they want to work on, young artists often concentrate on a particular challenge. For instance, a student might decide to work only on a certain subject or only with certain art materials (i.e., only pencil or only one type of black marker). Our 6-year-old had chosen to focus his artistic energies on drawing cowboys. His choices of drawing materials, inspirational material, and working conditions were also acutely specific. These decisions reflect well-developed problem-defining skills. While art teachers may include subjective criteria such as "art spirit" when evaluating children's work, it is rare for them to accurately assess this problem-defining characteristic in a young artist.

In addition, the development of *personal aesthetic preferences* appears to evolve from such self-directed challenges.[13] A child's strong sense of what is elegant, beautiful, or personally correct is a behavior similar to that of professional artists.[14] Historically, problem finding and an aesthetic sensitivity have been associated with creative thought in science, mathematics, and the arts.

Although *creative imagination* is also an active ingredient in artistic talent, creativity can look very different in each child. Random improvisation may be characteristic of the doodles that children produce. Gifted children will frequently improvise with shapes, patterns, and lines.[15] Artistic children may demonstrate an awareness of the spaces between lines and the subtle effects of a line's quality. However, children who continue to develop their visual vocabulary may at times exhibit behaviors we would not typically associate with creativity. For example, there are times when a child may feel the need to develop a technique or solve a problem (like the accuracy of shading or perspective) that has no apparent relationship to creative thought. Fulfilling this need may even involve copying the work of others. Similarly, artistically talented children may at times approach new problems with extreme caution as a way of protecting themselves from ridicule or embarrassment in front of peers or adults with high expectations. The recognition and success received from extensive practice is not easily given up to try something unfamiliar.

The young child described earlier is a good example of many of the behavioral characteristics identified in the research on the artistically gifted. Not all artistically gifted children show such unusually advanced skills for their age, but it is characteristic for these students to begin their artistic development before entering school. Artistically gifted children also tend to display a high level of self-motivation and independence regarding their art. This trait has been described as "self-directedness" by Hurwitz and Day in their book *Children and Their Art*[16] and as "a rage to master" by Ellen Winner.[17]

Developing Early Talent

The intense emotional aspect of creative work leads many to assume that, because art is expressive, it is not intellectual. This misperception has been fueled by the fact that artistic performance and standard IQ tests are generally not "correlated"; that is, talented school-age artists do not necessarily also have high scores on IQ tests. Research on the problem-solving behaviors of adult artists may provide new evidence about this issue.[18] Artists prefer to identify their own problems, rather than solve problems that are presented to them. This type of thinking, sometimes called *creative thinking* or *abductive reasoning*,[19] can interfere with the deductive reasoning that is measured by most standardized tests used by schools and is reflected in most school tasks and assignments.

Research on identification of artistically gifted elementary children for music or dance programs has found that the children identified with strengths in the creativity criteria could easily be taught specific musical or dance skills, but those children with advanced technical skills had far more difficulty developing their skills in creativity.[20] The visual arts follow this same pattern. Perhaps it is this complex combination of creative, intellectual, and emotional capacities that prevents the development of a standardized measure of artistic talent.

Role of the Family

Many artistically gifted children are immersed in acquiring the power to render a realistic image of a subject that is of interest to them. Some young artists are engrossed in translating their emotions through art making. The prolific making of images, whether they are drawings, paintings, sculptures, or buildings made from building blocks, holds the key to what parents can do to assist their child in developing this talent. Parents do not need to draw alongside their child or engage in the actual art making (unless it is pleasurable) to cultivate their child's talent. The important roles a parent must play are those of appreciator, curator, and advocate.

Appreciator. Most importantly, savor the joy together. Biographies of famous artists suggest that often they benefited from the support and encouragement of their families.[21] The value of showing sincere appreciation of your child's artwork is immeasurable. Young artists need dialogue and feedback. For example, when a 2-year-old presents you with an indescribable scribble, give specific comments such as "I see you used lots of colors," or "I really like the colors you chose, tell me about this," or "Your line gives me the feeling of fast movements. What else do you want me to see here?" Direct, emotional reaction to the work also can provide a young artist with information on how successfully an idea, thought, or feeling has been communicated.

Curator. Nurturing artistic development can also take a curatorial form. Parents show their children how much they value their art when they care for the artwork itself. Also, it is very helpful if an accurate record is made including dating the work and recording conversations about it. Even unfinished explorations can later serve as a record of development. A rotating date stamp (found in office supply stores) helps to keep track of the order of the volumes of work that is produced by developing artists. Very young artists can be taught to use the stamp on the back of the work they complete each week, to file the work in a portfolio (a box with a lid or two cardboard rectangles tied or taped together), and to select one or two favorites to display in a frame (plastic, magnetic, or box frames without glass are available). If a child produces sculptures or other three-dimensional structures, instant or digital photographs may offer an alternative means of documentation. Another useful strategy is to keep a journal of events, comments, or behaviors that strike you as unusual, meaningful, or relevant anecdotes to your child's artistic development. Journal entries can provide insight into the idiocentric nature of a child's artistic development. For example, discussions of favorite works along with display choices might have value later. One should also include a record of contests entered, exhibits, and other achievements. Engaging young artists in these record-keeping activities can develop important organizational and critical thinking skills. Cultivating these skills is effortless when developed in an atmosphere of attentiveness to the child and his or her artistic productions.

Advocate. Like every parent of a gifted child in any domain, parents of a child talented in the visual arts need persistent advocacy skills. Advocacy involves pursuing the optimum match between child and learning environment. This may mean attending to weaknesses, as well as seeking ways to nurture the child's strengths. The mother who escorted her talented young son to my door had pursued many avenues and will continue to seek opportunities to match her child's needs. Her quest began when her son's reading skills were not developing within a standard developmental sequence. To develop exceptional abilities, parents need the help of others, especially when no family member is involved in the field and can offer specific advice. Seeking out resources (human and otherwise) requires time and effort, yet can help identify a clear path for finding the appropriate level of challenge and opportunities for a particular child. Fortunately, there are many resources in most communities.

How to Find Good Art Instruction

In order to choose opportunities that will best enhance a young artist's repertoire of experiences, parents must look and listen attentively to what the child is exploring. Encouraging a child to discuss his or her own work or what he or she sees in the work of others (keeping a log of these encounters) will provide some insights. Other insights are available from those directly involved in the field.

A good art program must develop more than technical skills. If you think of art as a language using figures (images) instead of words, it may be easier to understand that figural language requires a vocabulary and grammatical rules that are at least as complex as verbal language. The traditional approach to studying art involved apprenticing with a master artist or copying the work of several master artists in order to understand the art "grammar" and "vocabulary" that these artists articulated so well. The childhood work of Pablo Picasso includes drawings and paintings in styles reminiscent of Renoir and other Impressionists. Picasso's early studies provide the "introductory language" necessary to create the new language that makes a Picasso look like a Picasso. It also provides fertile ground for studying the important ideas that renowned artists chose to "discuss" (through their sculptures or paintings) among their peers and express to their viewers.

Another way of developing critical and creative thinking skills in concert with technical skills is to use elegant problems for instruction.[22] An elegant problem is an assignment or challenge that encourages personal interpretation by providing an open-ended task that promotes creative thought. An elegant problem provides flexibility of problem space, fluency of responses, room for elaboration, opportunity for original answers, and a problem that is worthy (for the individual or the field) of the required effort. Elegant problems elicit elegant solutions. Art schools, museum education classes and sophisticated public school programs tend to provide this type of experience, but are often unavailable to very young art students.

Parents should seek out instructors who can provide this type of art instruction for their artistically gifted child. Ask potential art instructors about the kinds of assignments and challenges they give their students and pay attention to how your child reacts to assignments from a current art instructor. Good art teachers present students with problems that

- fascinate the student, stimulating curiosity and a sense of wonder;
- are personally meaningful to the student;
- address issues that are of technical, intellectual, and emotional importance; and
- help students make connections, see similarities, and transfer knowledge to other domains. For instance, principles of design can be thought of as the "grammar" of images; making this connection

can help a student who already understands English grammar understand how design principles work.

No two artists think and feel alike. Therefore, no two artists approach a problem in the same way, choose the exact same problem, or take the same journey in their artistic development. This is also true of artistically gifted children as they begin their journey in art. Child prodigies such as Picasso or Wang Yani come from families with art backgrounds. Their development was carefully orchestrated with attentively selected exposure and instruction. Parents who cannot provide this kind of instruction themselves—and most cannot—should consider all the resources and services that may be available in their local schools and communities.

School Services: Possibilities and Limitations

Art educators are frequently the most knowledgeable and "resourceful" people available to children with advanced artistic talent. Art educators are familiar with both age-appropriate and "exceptional" development, whereas professional artists without training in art education tend to compare children's work to their own or professional adult standards—an inappropriate and useless comparison. Positive, constructive feedback during an evaluation of the artwork provided by an art educator can be a pivotal experience for a budding artist.

A competent art educator also has a pulse on opportunities available, including the limitations of the private instructors in the community and connections to the most appropriate next level of art instruction. This knowledge can yield older students as mentors, greater connections to advanced training, or even a potential letter of recommendation to eliminate age requirements for a class because of the child's unusually advanced accomplishments and seriousness of purpose.

Several factors make it unlikely that artistically gifted students would get this kind of mentoring unless parents initiate contact with the instructor. First of all, many artistically talented children do not perform at the same level of accomplishment at school, which limits the teacher's knowledge of the extent of their ability or level of their talent. The sparse 40-minute art class per week that is the norm in elementary schools or the child's desire to be more like classmates are two potentially good reasons for an enormous difference between work done at home and work done in school. The kindergartener who draws like a middle school student at home might demonstrate the skills of a third grader on his school projects. Understanding that disbelief is a logical reaction by an art teacher when schoolwork and work done at home are not congruent should help frame the parent's conversation with the teacher. Had I not videotaped the young child in his endeavors at home, few would have believed his mother.

Second, elementary schools may not be prepared to address the needs of artistically talented children. A developmentally appropriate curriculum is *by definition* not a good match for a *developmentally advanced* student. The distaste for art instruction in elementary school cited by artists[23] is easily understood under these circumstances. National art education policy defines quality art education as providing art experiences that reflect the national standards of a comprehensive art program and are grounded in age-appropriate developmental practices.[24] Opportunities such as contests or competitions that may find a student's artwork superior to other students are considered "undesirable," especially at the elementary level.[25] Without instructional and curricular modifications that challenge and interest the artistically talented student, the elementary art room is merely a place to learn what their future appreciators like and understand. But, outside the classroom is another story, one that is waiting to be heard and told.

In addition to the art educator (who may teach 500–900 students per week), many schools may have parent-teacher organizations, librarians, or classroom teachers eager to encourage artistic endeavors. The National PTA sponsors a contest each year that encourages artistic expression on an annual theme in a variety of forms. Everyone is encouraged to participate, each school finds volunteer judges, and top choices are sent on to the state competition. All of these special opportunities depend on volunteers to conduct the event. In a similar vein, the child with cultivated social graces in addition to talent may experience a synergistic effort among school personnel (such as librarians, clerks, and teachers) to locate resources and opportunities for artistic development, including exhibit spaces, mentor possibilities, and special events.

Community Resources

Interest in drawing, painting, sculpture, or built environments (architecture) can be fueled through visits to a public library or any museum to look for visual images or high-quality art books written for young children. Museum shops tend to offer outstanding examples of books for children. Inviting the child to choose a book may be the best way to match learning with current needs or desires. Biographies that discuss the childhood of a famous artist are vital for making connections to what the life of an emerging artist might entail. Visits to art galleries and museums (online or in person) provide a wealth of other information, too. But, keep in mind that prints or anything other than an original work of art cannot provide most of the technical answers these learners are seeking.

The ideal situation for young artists is an opportunity to meet someone else who works with similar ideas in art. Going to gallery openings, seeking out and interviewing the local instructors of art classes, and getting to know the local arts councils are all good places to begin to search for a suitable match between a child's interests and a learning opportunity. Museum-sponsored art classes tend to be geared toward serious learners. A carefully selected sample of five to seven current pieces of the child's work helps potential instructors understand the nature and level of his or her development. Opportunities to hear responses to one's work are learning moments for the young artist, as well.

Of course, all of these pursuits are suggestions for art students seeking more stimulation or direct contact. Not all students will want outside assistance at all times. Careful listening and observation provide clues as to the appropriateness of this alternative.

The same advice is useful for decisions regarding participation in art shows, competitions, or contests. Parents should be alert to the real (though small) potential for exploitation. Most sponsors tend to be quite ethical in their approach and procedures. However, careful reading and discussion of all the fine print is highly recommended before participating. For example, some contests or competitions (quite ethically) state that the winning entries become the property of the sponsor. A child unwilling to part with the work submitted would have a traumatic experience if the entry were selected. Some sponsors are seeking a particular look to compliment their product, which may have very little to do with the quality of the work that is chosen.

If a child is emotionally ready to have his or her work judged by others, these experiences can be constructive. An award is an external (someone else's view) validation of the work *in the context of that assignment.* The child must be just as prepared emotionally to not have the artwork chosen. Although creating a product to meet the specific demands of a contest is challenging and an important way to learn healthy competition skills, most competitions do not provide an explanation or any feedback to unselected entries. It is very important for parents to stress these facts prior to entering these activities. It is also critical for parents to emphasize that understanding ways to improve on one's work is far more constructive than comparing it to others. Like an athlete, it is one's personal best that is the focus of improvement.

Conclusion

Significant influences on the making of an artist are, in a scientific sense, unknown. Although retrospective accounts and other biographical research provide rich hypotheses and patterns for rigorous research, there is no known recipe for development in any talent domain. In fact, the only reasonable observation that can be suggested from the empirical research on adult artists is that a recipe is unlikely.[26] Different catalysts affect different learners at different times. Parents seeking to encourage artistic talent need to concentrate their efforts in developing their skills as an appreciator, curator, and advocate.

Why identify and nurture talent in the visual arts if you are not convinced a child will become an artist? Just as not every student who learns to write well will become a writer, not every student who learns to draw or sculpt will become an artist. The importance of reading visual information or images, as well as a facility with nonverbal reasoning, is just beginning to be realized. The ability to think equally well in images, words, and numbers provides gifted students with the multilingual skills utilized by the most creative producers of ideas in every field.

Resources

The National Gallery of Art (http://www.nga.gov)
The Louvre Online (http://www.Louvre.fr/louvrea.htm)
ARTSEDGE (http://artsedge.kennedy-center.org/teaching_materials/artsedge.html)

Author Note

The first two paragraphs of this chapter previously appeared in Sandra I. Kay, "Identifying and Nurturing Talent in the Visual Arts," *Duke Gifted Newsletter 1*, no. 4 (Summer 2001): 1–2.

developing
athletic talent
through
participation
in youth sports

by
karen l. drill

Over the years, I have spoken with many mothers and fathers of young athletes searching for answers to their questions about how to nurture their child's athletic ability. This chapter is written with the needs of parents in mind as a way to address some of the concerns they may have about their child's athletic ability. Often, parents of children with highly advanced abilities in specific areas feel lost or confused about what to do once their child's talent has been recognized and defined. Making decisions about the next steps can be difficult and challenging, particularly if the child's interest lies in a sport that feels foreign to the parent. At times, parents may even wonder what motivates their child to pursue athletic activities so doggedly.

This chapter is not a step-by-step guide on how to develop and create an Olympic Gold Medallist. Instead, it will provide information about the various elements that comprise superior athletic talent and guide you toward resources that will help your family make decisions about the next step in the process. Primarily, you will be given enough information to quell any initial confusion that may stem from the realization that your child possesses athletic potential.

To illustrate the elements that make up the full picture of athletic talent (ability, motivation, concentration, and a nurturing environment), we will follow the athletic path of Stephanie Fox, a five-time U.S. Girls' National Table Tennis champion and five-time Junior Olympic Gold Medallist.

During Stephanie's 8-year table tennis career, she won dozens of medals, competed both nationally and internationally, and trained for a short period at the U.S. Olympic Training Facility in Colorado.*

By witnessing Stephanie's developmental path, you will have the opportunity to see heavily researched concepts come to life in an athlete who displayed very advanced physical and cognitive abilities at an early age. Some aspects of Stephanie's experience may ring true for you and your child; other aspects may not. Nonetheless, her athletic development demonstrates how talent emerges and evolves when all of the right conditions are in place.

Developing Athletic Ability

The development of athletic talent depends on the integration of several elements, including ability, achievement orientation (the desire to excel), motivation, concentration, competitiveness, and the training environment. None of the these elements stands alone to create a successful athlete; rather, talented young athletes develop in a context where they have room to grow in all of the areas.

Early athletic ability is the easiest to observe. Once children become more mobile (toddling, walking, running, etc.), you may begin to notice that your son or daughter has a strong interest in playing physical games. You may begin to see signs of advanced motor skills, hand-eye coordination, focus, concentration, and physical grace and ease, or you may simply be aware that your child is deriving fun and pleasure in sports or games. For example, if your 3-year-old is drawn to the Nerf basketball hoop in the basement, wants to continue shooting, and exhibits joy during the process, he or she may be cueing into the positive physical and emotional feelings that can stem from physical play.

Increasingly, you may notice that your child continues to exhibit more advanced, fluid coordination than peers. He or she may have fun participating in athletic games at recess, in physical education class, in the backyard, or during recreational sports. When you begin to notice signs of athletic potential, the key is to provide your child with access to activities and athletic equipment

---

* Interviews with Stephanie Fox and her father, Michael Fox, were conducted in October 2001.

that will help him or her discover which sports bring the most enjoyment. As early as age 5, athletically inclined children often long to try basketball, football, soccer, softball, or even lower profile sports such as bowling, archery, or table tennis (sometimes all at once!). Whatever the case, encourage your child's exploration of sports, particularly if the motivation is coming from within. You may have different ideas about what type of athlete you would like your child to be; however, for the child to be motivated, he or she needs the freedom to try an array of sports until just the right one comes along.

For example, you might be keen on tennis, but your child really wants to play ice hockey. Although you may prefer tennis (less physical contact, more socially acceptable, more opportunities to compete, etc.), your child will most likely be a better hockey player than tennis player if his or her inner sense of excitement and enthusiasm piques at the mention of the word *hockey*. In such cases, consider putting your emotions aside and giving your child a chance at the sport that he or she yearns to try. Maybe after a few weeks on the ice, your child will realize that hockey is not what he or she expected. Conversely, the sport could be exactly what was wanted and anticipated, and, the next thing you know, you have an aspiring hockey player on your hands!

Many adults shy away from participating in sports because their early athletic experiences were not validated by coaches, teachers, parents, or peers. The child who dropped a routine fly ball during physical education class in first grade may be discouraged by feedback that "anyone could have caught that" or if he or she does not learn the proper catching technique. Opportunities for learning happen in many places, including recreational leagues, school, and home.

Example

Stephanie was first introduced to table tennis at age 7 after her father bought a ping-pong table for the family's basement. When describing the beginning of her table tennis career, Stephanie remarked,

> At the time, [table tennis] was just for recreation, and we were playing the game of ping-pong, not table tennis. After 1 or 2 years, I started getting to the point where I could beat my dad. When I was 8, I competed in a local tournament in St. Louis, and I did well. I remember that somebody went up to my dad and told him that I had great potential, but that I needed to change my paddle, my grip, and my strokes. That's when I began learning the sport of table tennis.

According to Stephanie's father, she began walking when she was about 9 months old, which was the first sign of her advanced physical ability. After watching her play ball with her older sister, Stephanie's father said that "it was very easy to see that her skills were way ahead of any of the other kids in the neighborhood."

For Parents

Stephanie's first experience with table tennis proved to be positive. She clearly possessed natural athletic ability, and her initial motivation stemmed from the positive feelings of improving and winning. Stephanie was provided access to table tennis equipment at home and in the community, and her father acted as a partner for her skill development. Once Stephanie's skill level surpassed her father's, he sought opportunities where Stephanie could compete and be challenged. An observer who validated her potential and made suggestions for positive change helped Stephanie advance in her table tennis career.

What is Achievement Orientation?

The second variable in athletic excellence is achievement orientation. Athletes are motivated by a variety of factors and are inclined toward different types of achievement. One theory about achievement focuses on two types of achievement: task and ego. With task involvement, athletes are motivated by a desire to strive toward personal mastery or excellence. In this case, talent develops by exerting maximum effort. Alternately, in an ego, or performance, state of involvement, the athlete believes ability is demonstrated only when his or her performance exceeds that of others.[1]

Whether an athlete is inclined toward task or ego involvement depends on the athlete's prior sport experiences, the current athletic context, and personality. Researchers Walling, Duda, and Chi found that athletes involved in a mastery-oriented climate where coaches stress that effort leads to success are more likely to attribute hard work and persistence to their success.[2] Athletes in a performance-oriented climate where they are encouraged to excel in relation to their teammates are more likely to possess concerns about failing and about the adequacy of their performance.

In a 1998 study of female basketball players ages 10–18, researchers found that the basketball players in environments that stressed individual effort were more likely to believe that their effort caused their success. Additionally, basketball players in this environment expressed satisfaction from the effort-based experience, as well as their perception of social approval from their teammates. On the other hand, when the coaching environment was perceived as performance-based, players were more likely to believe that high ability rather than effort, would lead to more success. In the performance climate, players felt satisfaction by outperforming others; in the long run, a performance-oriented environment may lead to motivational difficulties if winning consistently becomes a more difficult challenge for the athlete. In all, the perception of the coaching environment does affect whether an athlete attributes success to effort or to ability. Thus, the athlete's own achievement orientation, combined with the environment, can influence the athlete's chances for success.[3]

Example

Stephanie's achievement orientation during her early years on the table tennis circuit can be described as mastery-oriented, where her aim was to display mastery during competition. Stephanie describes her motivation as stemming from her "competitive nature," motivating her to "continue to play hard and to improve." Stephanie commented, "I love the feeling of winning, especially when I was younger," and described feeling very upset when she lost, particularly if she felt she had "played badly." Stephanie's mastery oriented nature pushed her to work toward perfecting her skills. When she lost matches, though, she felt that she had not fulfilled her own expectations about what her level of performance should be based on her mastery nature.

For Parents

When you observe your child's participation in either training or competition, take note of whether his or her achievement orientation seems to be task- or ego-driven. If, like Stephanie, your child has a strong internal push to master skills, according to the research, the likelihood of maintaining success down the road increases. If your child seems more performance-oriented, you may run into motivational and interest struggles later if the focus is primarily on comparing his or her skill level to that of others.

Motivation

The third variable in athletic success, motivation, has been classified as either primarily intrinsic or extrinsic and is related to achievement orientation. Intrinsic motivation stems from within (i.e., an inner desire to improve where personal satisfaction is the reward) and is generally believed to be a crucial motive toward success in sports. When motivation is extrinsic, children are stimulated by external rewards such as money, applause, and medals. In addition to intrinsic and extrinsic motivation, athletes can be motivated by other factors. Generally, children (and adults) are motivated to improve and master their skills in areas where they perceive they have high ability.[4] Klint and Weiss noticed motivational differences between athletic children who believed they were physically competent and those who saw themselves as socially competent.[5] The athletes with physical ability were primarily athletically motivated by the desire to improve their skills; those with social competence were motivated by a desire to connect with their teammates. Braathen and Sveback took motivation research one step further by examining gender and found that skilled male athletes were more likely to be motivated by a strong desire to compete physically, whereas female athletes were more likely to be motivated by the connection with their teammates.[6] Gill, Gross, and Haddelston found that girls play sports to improve and to learn skills, to have fun, to be physically fit, and to challenge themselves.[7] Boys tend to participate in sports for similar reasons, although improving skill, personal challenge, and competition precede fun in order of importance.

What keeps athletes playing? Highly skilled athletes are motivated by competition, they strive to deliver high quality performances, and their talented teammates encourage them to even greater feats.

Motivation can also wane, thus leading the athlete to quit sports participation. The following aspects may contribute to an adolescent leaving organized athletics: a lack of playing time; the competitive emphasis of the program that does not match the participant's sense of competition; dislike of the coach; burnout; sport injustices; lack of improvement in performance; and the need for more time for schoolwork. Braathen and Sveback found that 35% of athletes quit competitive sports between the ages of 16–18.[8]

Example

Stephanie's motivation to play table tennis at an elite training level was primarily intrinsically motivated. She describes being motivated not by winning, but by the desire to "play well (as a team or individual), to always improve, and for the mental and physical exercise." Stephanie defines her motivation during her elite table tennis career with words like "excitement, fun, competition, the thrill of winning, and the rush of adrenaline I got (and still get) from playing." This intrinsic motivation propelled Stephanie to the top of her sport and pushed her to always improve her game.

After 8 years of training and competition, Stephanie stopped playing table tennis when she was given the option to train in Iowa. At that point, Stephanie assessed whether she wanted to take her game to the next level of competition. After serious reflection, Stephanie decided that she did not want to "devote my life to table tennis." She felt that she "did not have enough time to continue at that pace." She played several sports, enjoyed them all, and "was not willing to give them up."

For Parents

Parents motivate their athletic children in many ways, and some methods are better than others. Intrinsically motivated athletes are easiest to encourage because their drive to participate in sports stems from within. Often, parents attempt to reward their child extrinsically for good performance. One parent motivated his daughter by paying her $5 for every basket she made during her high school basketball games. This athlete took many more shots than necessary, and her motivation gradually shifted from a love of the game to playing for external reward and validation; her promising athletic career was short-lived.

Striking a balance between intrinsic and extrinsic motivation can be difficult. Be aware of what motivates your child to play and avoid excessive external rewards to encourage better performance. Ideally, the game itself should be payment enough; too much external reward can kill the inner desire to play.

The Mental Side of Sports

Concentration is an essential quality to encourage in young athletes and is a vital prerequisite for success in sports since competition is almost entirely an exercise in balancing both the mental and physical elements of sport.[9] Winter and Martin have written that, "without good concentration, no amount of skill, fitness, or motivation is going to get you to your peak."[10]

Concentration is the ability to selectively pay attention to the appropriate cues critical in most athletic situations.[11] To truly be in a state of concentration, the athlete must be able to focus his or her attention on the task at hand and to remain unaffected by irrelevant external and psychological cues.[12] Concentration also requires the ability to adapt and to refocus depending on the situation.[13] In athletic competition, selective attention becomes central to accomplishing the task at hand. Moran's study of gymnasts and wrestlers found that those who were successful had a greater ability to pay attention to the right cues while discarding the irrelevant ones.[14] Distracted wrestlers thought about previous losses, speculated about future encounters, were excessively aware of officials, and had a tendency toward external distraction. The "mental side" of sports can influence both success and defeat.

Expertise results from the growth of particular knowledge and skills through experience.[15] Each sport has its own specific set of skills to be mastered, and experts and novices differ in the mental aspects of their game. Experts can rely on a richer knowledge base and a more extensive repertoire of refined skills than novices. Additionally, experts are able to respond to the right cues and possess well-developed strategies to "organize, interpret, and utilize the information the sport provides."[16] For example, Abernathy found that top tennis players use advanced cues from the server's racquet and ball toss to make predictions about the likely flight and destination of the ball.[17]

Moran stresses that achieving a level of expertise takes at least 10 years and depends on a long and systematic process of training and development.[18] Beginners must learn to sort and reject information. Expertise also implies differences in knowledge gained over time, rather than simply physical factors; experts are able to perceive, recall, and retain information much more readily than novices. Because of their substantial knowledge base, experts are able to assess what is left to learn and what is already known. In fast ball sports, experts are able to attend to the ball and advanced cues earlier than novices and are prepared earlier to initiate responses.[19] For example, an expert hitter will be more likely to follow and predict the path of a pitched ball based on whether the pitch is thrown inside, outside, high, or low. Novice hitters, on the other hand, will concentrate solely on making contact with the ball, regardless of where the ball is placed. The expert, based on years of practice and mental and physical training, will have an edge over the novice because he or she is able to focus on the elements of the pitch that the novice cannot.

Mental training, often practiced in elite sport preparation, is a form of visualization in which the athlete visualizes his actions in a pregame situation.[20] During mental training, the athlete envisions him- or herself performing an aspect of the game and then continues to rework the image until it matches the ideal performance. For example, a tennis player may be struggling with her backhand and has a personal goal of being able to hit a backhand down the line to her opponent. In competition, though, she has struggled with this shot. During mental training, the athlete can close her eyes and envision what it would feel like to hit the line shot just right: where she should step, where she should make contact with the ball, and how she should follow through. After reworking the image in her mind until she feels that the kinks in her backhand are gone, the athlete can then try it on the court and, ideally, her shot will have improved. Another example of early forms of mental training can include the child verbalizing situations. Young baseball enthusiasts often place themselves in game situations and see themselves making the big play during an imaginary tie game in the bottom of the ninth with bases loaded. The goal of mental training, which may only work with people able to produce images in their mind, is to improve physical performance as a part of the long-term learning process. Experts, more so than novices, are able to connect to both the mental and physical elements of the imagery.

Example

Stephanie's mental training and process were demonstrated in her pregame preparation:

> During pregame warm-up, I tried to get a sense of my opponent and to get a feel for how much and what type of spin his or her paddle produced. I would try to figure out his or her weaknesses or strengths. The game itself is extremely mental, and, as I got older, I learned how to let people beat themselves and how to play smarter than the other person.

Because Stephanie's knowledge and performance were at the expert level, she was better able to assess her opponent's strengths, weaknesses, and spin and then use that information to her advantage.

For Parents

Reaching the highest cognitive level takes years of training and preparation and is a significant part of the process of athletic talent development. Generally, a good foundation of physical skill needs to be in place in order to begin work on the finer shades of the mental game. A young pitcher may know some strategy regarding where to pitch based on the hitter's stance, strengths, weaknesses, and situation on the field, but if he cannot throw an accurate fastball, then he is not quite ready to be in tune with the subtleties of the game. The mental aspect can be fine-tuned and improved after your child has the basics down in his or her sport. As parents, do not expect that your child will reach the mental aspect of expertise overnight. In time, both the mental and physical elements will come together. Athletes who have reached a level where they are working on the mental side of their sport should work with an expert who can help enhance their performance.

Predicting Success

Predicting athletic success is nearly impossible, but some athletes may possess qualities more likely to lead to success. Self-concept (the way an athlete perceives his- or herself) appears to be a trait that predicts successful athletic performance. If an athlete feels comfortable on the balance beam, on the field, or on the court, he or she will be more likely to perform well in competition. Physical ability helps an athlete develop a positive self-concept, which translates into confidence, independence, and satisfaction.[21] An athlete's sense that he or she controls the situation has also been associated with successful performance. All athletes can feel anxious when performing in front of crowds (a potentially threatening situation), but anxiety has been found to be significantly lower in highly successful athletes prior to competition than in moderately successful athletes. One study of gymnasts showed that positive self-concept, belief in control over the circumstances, and low anxiety predicted success.[22]

Peak performance, the psychological process that combines psychological, cognitive, and personality factors during optimal athletic performance, is another aspect of well-honed skills. During peak performance, the athlete is able to be fully focused on the game while still aware of the self.[23] Peak performance has been characterized by many factors, including sharp focus during competition; intense, exciting feelings during performance; and a sense of fulfillment and play. In contrast, a failing performance may be characterized by a lack of fulfillment, feelings of uncertainty, disinterest in socializing with teammates, an inability to focus, feelings of confusion, and a sense of powerlessness. During a peak performance experience, the athlete feels fully engrossed in the competition, both mentally and physically, and his or her concentration is keen as he or she is fully focused in the experience. This intense experience has been described as being "in the zone." Other aspects of peak performance include exceptional concentration, a trance-like state, abundant energy, the sense that time has slowed down, and a general feeling that the athlete has and can exert complete mastery over the situation.[24]

Example

Stephanie describes her moments of peak performance in the following manner:

> Sometimes, I would get into a "zone" where I just couldn't do anything wrong. I would have so much confidence in the "zone," which made me play even better. It's an incredible feeling to feel like you can do anything, make any shot, and win any point.

For Parents

Most athletes do not reach the peak performance (or "flow") state without a strong foundation of physical skill and knowledge of the game. Your child may not reach moments of peak athletic performance. If it happens, you will know that he or she has experienced one of the optimal, most advanced states of athletic development.

A Nurturing Environment

The fourth element of athletic giftedness, practice, training, and parental involvement, is where parents can make the most difference in a child's success.

The right amount of practice and training can help your child continue to develop and improve his or her skills. Practice brings players together with coaches and other players who can provide good drills, healthy competition, and feedback on performance. Practicing is essential to improving; however, it can be overdone.

Many coaches regard training as the single most important factor in performance improvement.[25] Over the past several decades, the amount of training athletes undertake has increased significantly; but, in some cases, intensified training can hamper performance. Athletes respond in different ways to a training regimen; a schedule helpful to one athlete may be detrimental to another. During training, we know that elite athletes need supplemental forms of training, such as access to specialized training facilities and coaches, in order to achieve the highest level of performance. However, some athletes may overtrain, which can lead to future problems with performance.

Athletes who have trained too much may experience staleness (a disinterest in the sport and preparing for competition). When staleness persists for more than several weeks, you will see a chronic decrease in performance that does not improve with reduced training or a brief rest. In stale athletes, mood disturbances such as depression become more chronic. To combat staleness, the athlete should take a prolonged rest ranging from 2 weeks to 2 months, using that time to recuperate and recover. At times, convincing an athlete to rest may be difficult simply because athletes have often internalized the concept of "pushing it to the limit" to improve.

Staleness is only one symptoms of overtraining. Other symptoms can be psychological, cognitive, or performance related. Psychological symptoms include a decrease in energy and self-esteem along with an increase in fatigue, anger, tension, or depression. Cognitive changes include increased confusion and decreased concentration. Performance difficulties are marked by decreased athletic performance, an inability to meet previous performance levels, a prolonged recovery from workouts, and a decrease in maximum work capacity. At the extreme, we see burnout: a negative emotional reaction to sport participation that is characterized by a disinterest in a sport once loved.[26]

For Parents

Parents, along with coaches, play the most significant role in the athlete's progress and are essential to talent development. As parents, you may begin to see signs of burnout in your child, particularly if he or she is involved in a rigorous schedule with an elite traveling team. At the time, participation in traveling teams or international competition can seem crucially important; however, if your child exhibits signs of disinterest or burnout, traveling more will not help to reduce the symptoms or to improve the caliber of play. If your child seems tired of the sport, suggest rest, even if only for a week, to help renew the flame; otherwise, a young athlete may end up hating a sport that had been equated with joy and pleasure.

Parental Involvement

Parents play an enormous role in both providing access to athletic opportunities and helping their children evolve and grow as athletes. Several studies have addressed the role of the parents of young athletes. One study found that 9–11-year-old girls who were involved in sports believed that they received greater encouragement from family members than boys who were highly involved in sports.[27] Lewko and Ewing suggest that girls may be more aware of parental support because parents are able to buffer any negative stereotyping the girls may encounter.[28] Negative stereotyping of female athletes has waned since Lewko and Ewing's study; however, some negative stereotypes may still exist, including the idea that female athletes are more "masculine" than their peers. Girls with parental support also perceived themselves to be more highly skilled than athletes with less-involved parents.

Parents involved in their own athletic endeavors act as role models for their children regarding sporting activity and behavior attributes. Boys reported playing a greater range of sports outside of school than girls and said their fathers were more involved than their mothers. With girls, researchers found a relationship between the sports participation of one or both parents and that of daughters. Researchers also found that no boys played girls' sports, while 20% of girls played boys' sports, suggesting that boys may be more rigidly sex-typed than girls. This stereotyping increases with age and is not as powerful in the third grade as in adulthood, where very few women play men's sports.[29]

Boys and girls have also been found to respond differently to parental support. For young males, encouraging fathers provided a role model for them to emulate.[30] For young women, the mother's influence was significant, and the father's influence was only slightly greater than the mother's. These studies show rather strongly that the perceived availability of parental support can buffer uncertainty and that support from both parents increases the likelihood that children will cope effectively with stressors that confront them when they play sports.[31]

Gender and Athletics

Historically, sports have been a male domain, and, even though gender equality has made headway since Title IX passed in 1972 , equality in sports is still a distant reality. Part of this inequality can be linked to sex-role social-ization, widely regarded as encouraging athletic participation in boys but discouraging it in girls.[32] Sports generate and reinforce patterns of social stratification, including those based on gender, that parallel the larger cul-ture.[33] Sage notes that sport opportunities for males still significantly out-weigh those presented to girls at all levels.[34] Children become aware of social separations at an early age; children as young as 4 have very explicit percep-tions about what they deem to be gender-appropriate behavior and are aware that boys often make decisions about which girls, if any, can participate in athletic games with them.[35]

Soloman and Bredemeier examined children's reasoning about gender and sport and found that children do recognize sport as a gender-based activ-ity; children from ages 6–11 interpret sport as a domain that favors males because of their "superior athletic prowess."[36] Such assumptions lead to the generalization that men are more naturally talented due to emphasis on physical strength and that women are less physically skilled and therefore less deserving of opportunities to participate in sports.[37] Coaches and parents can help dispel the myth that an athlete's ability is determined by gender by modeling sport involvement by both genders.

Example

When Stephanie began playing table tennis, she joined a club comprised of 50 adult men who played regularly. Soon, she was able to win most games with them, and her father, by supporting her participation, was able to mit-igate any gender issues Stephanie may have faced.

For Parents

You can confront gender issues in sports by allowing each child to par-ticipate in sports based on his or her interests. If your child chooses a sport where he or she may be socially stigmatized based on gender, then provide a supportive environment for your child and stand fully behind his or her par-ticipation. Also, provide your child with the emotional tools, particularly empathy, support, and encouragement, to cope with any difficulties that will be encountered.

Stephanie's parents were able to give her everything that she needed in order to succeed in her sport. Stephanie describes her parents' involvement as crucial to her athletic success.

> My parents were always very encouraging and supportive of me in all my sports and they never tried to influence any of my decisions. Over the years, I have seen and dealt with many parents who criticize, yell at, and are outwardly disappointed in their child if he or she doesn't play perfectly. I am grateful that my parents were not like that. They never gave negative feedback, never yelled, and didn't really care if I won, lost, or even played well. They always wanted me to do well because they knew that would make me happy, but they did not ever push me to do anything that I didn't want to do. My dad was my practice partner, and my coach. Without his support, encouragement, and the time commitment that he gave, I would not have been able to accomplish nearly as much in table tennis.

Stephanie's father had a significant effect on her table tennis career through his involvement and contribution to Stephanie's athletic development:

> For the better part of 10 years, all of my nonworking hours were dedicated to Steph—watching, practicing, coaching, driving her to events in soccer, softball, basketball, and table tennis. It's a tremendous thrill watching your child compete and excel while listening to the parents of other children. I was always very proud of her and still am.

Stephanie's father illustrates the time commitment and parental involvement necessary to foster and nurture your child's athletic potential. As your child becomes better at his or her sport, the more time and money you will have to invest to continue skill development and to provide the right level of competition, be it on the national or international level.

As parents, your positive involvement in your child's athletic endeavors will contribute monumentally to his or her growth as both an athlete and a person. Walking the line between support and overinvolvement can be a challenge. Minimally, provide your child with opportunities that line up with his or her inner drive without letting your child's interests become your own. Parents sometimes attempt to live their unfulfilled wishes and dreams through their children. Be aware of this possibility, and, if you see this tendency emerge in yourself, take a step back and assess what might be happening. Remember that, although your child is a part of you, he is not you. Give your child access to opportunity and the chance to thrive in a safe, contained athletic environment.

Selecting and Working With a Coach

Your child's coach can and will have an enormous impact on your child's experience as an athlete. Because of this, he or she should be very carefully chosen. Parents should address the following aspects of coaching when choosing the right coach: level of expertise in the sport, success as a coach, coaching style, years coaching, ages of players coached, and parent references.

First, parents should inquire about the coach's background in the sport. What was the highest level of competition reached? Was he a successful athlete? Why has she chosen to coach? The coach's level of expertise is critical for conveying the correct information about the game, form, and technique and properly guiding players. Many coaches will act as if they know the game, but end up dispensing erroneous information that ultimately ends up needing to be corrected down the road. Be sure that your child's coach possesses the technical competence to continue to raise your child's level of play.

Second, you should investigate how successful the coach has been with other players. Does she have a winning record? Have her players continued to achieve in the sport? Do current players speak positively about the coach? A coach who has been consistently successful will most likely possess the ability not only to instruct, but also to motivate her players.

Another key ingredient to ensure that your child and coach are well matched is the coach's style. Some players perform better with a nurturing coach; others are more successful with an authoritarian coach. Each coach conveys information and instructs in a different manner. Before signing on with a coach and team, observe the coach running a few practices or teaching a lesson. By watching his style, you will get a good idea about how he will approach working with your child.

You also should look into how many years the coach has been coaching and with what ages he has spent most of his years working. Someone who has recently switched from coaching high school to little league may not be aware of the developmental differences of the two groups. The more experience the coach has with your child's age group, the better.

Finally, be sure to talk with several parents whose children have worked with the coach. Other parents are some of the best resources for an honest appraisal. They will be able to provide insight into the coach's style, demeanor, success rate, strengths, and weaknesses. Most importantly, your child should be coached by the person who is best suited in manner and expertise to your child's level of competition and personality.

Participating in Athletic Camps

Athletic camps are a great way for young athletes to meet others who share a similar passion for a sport. Attending camps has many benefits. Camps are an organized way to bring athletes together to focus on specific skills and to meet other people. Athletic camps come in many forms, from weekend day camps to multiweek residential camps. Young athletes most often participate in one-day clinics put on by park district leagues or universities. As athletes become older and more experienced, they can attend multiweek, overnight camps where they work with experts in the sport and have an opportunity to be seen by college scouts.

Camps can be an excellent way for athletes to enhance their skills, and they can provide access to some of the top-notch instructors in the sport. Like searching for a coach, parents should make sure of the camp's credibility by talking with other parents, inquiring about how long the camp has been in existence, and checking into the coaches' backgrounds.

Final Words

Helping children develop and expand on their natural abilities can feel like an enormous responsibility, especially negotiating when and how much to direct them toward the right opportunities. You may occasionally feel overwhelmed by the many practices, games, and tournaments that crop up in your child's life. As you navigate your child's athletic career, remember that, while athletics can be great for both physical and social development, too much stress and pressure can lead to burnout. Take time to enjoy witnessing and being a part of your child's development in all areas and you will feel the rewards for many years to come.

Resources

Youth Sports USA (http://www.ysusa.com)
American Youth Soccer Organization (http://www.soccer.org)
US Youth Soccer Organization (http://www.usysa.org)
AAU Girls Basketball (http://www.aaugirlsbasketball.org)
AAU Boys Basketball (http://www.aauboysbasketball.org)
I-Glow: for girls who play (http://www.I-Glow.com)
The Female Athlete (http://www.thefemaleathlete.com)

9

relationships between families and schools

partnership and collaboration

by
vicki b. stocking

During the elementary years, children spend a great deal of time in school. Students thrive when parents and school personnel work together to develop educational opportunities.[1] This is especially important during the elementary years, when a close connection between home and school can help establish a sound beginning for a gifted student's educational progress.

One way to think about the relationships between family members (particularly parents) and school personnel is in terms of *partnerships* and *collaboration.* In a collaboration, "families and school personnel work together to develop shared goals and find common ground on which to work toward those goals."[2] We will begin this chapter with introductory information about schools and gifted education. After that, I will discuss developing family-school partnerships to promote the well-being of gifted children during the elementary years. I will draw from research literature, work with parents and school personnel, and experience with my own two early elementary children in school, mainly my son, who has had two more years of school experience than his sister.

General Information: What Parents Should Know

Learning about a gifted child's educational opportunities can be daunting. Here's a basic overview of some of the things parents should know.

The Big Picture: States and School Districts

A gifted child's experience in school will be impacted on a number of levels. Parents should try to find out as much as they can about local policies and practices related to serving gifted children. Most states define "gifted students," and some provide guidance about the provision of special educational opportunities, although the terminology varies widely.[3] For example, although many state definitions of gifted students include high intelligence, creative artistic abilities, and demonstrated high achievement, fewer address critical thinking or motor skills. A few states leave the decisions to local school districts and do not define gifted students at all. The state gifted association (ask the gifted coordinator at your school or district), as well as the school district administrative offices, should be able to provide relevant information to parents.

The state's guidelines are interpreted and implemented by policies and practices set by the school district. The district's policies are then put into practice by a school's principal, the instructional leader of the school. The principal's expectations are enacted in the classroom by the teacher or a team of teachers. Schools that serve gifted students most effectively have clear policies about the identification of gifted students and assignment to special programs. Parents should become familiar with the guidelines for educating gifted children at each step of the way.

State Guidelines → School and Principal → Teacher

Parents should explore the district and school and get to know everyone involved in the child's education. In particular, parents should develop a working relationship with the teacher by spending time at school. They should learn what programs are available, how students are selected into special programs, who is responsible for which part of the process, and what role parents can play. Parents have expectations about their children's schooling; for gifted children, these expectations are not often met in the schools without some involvement/intervention on the part of the parents.[4]

Types of School-Based Programs

Parents who are exploring their children's educational opportunities may benefit from learning basic terminology related to how schools serve gifted students. Most school programs designed to serve talented children are largely based on combinations of three basic strategies related to instruction and curriculum: acceleration, enrichment, and differentiation. No method is necessarily better or worse than another; each is based on and supported by empirical research.[5] It is important that a teacher and school be flexible enough to provide strategies to meet the needs of each gifted child.[6] In *Stand Up for Your Gifted Child*, Joan Smutny explains these techniques in more detail and provides examples of each of these methods.[7]

Acceleration includes strategies designed to provide flexible pacing for gifted students, such as skipping a grade in a subject or testing out of instruction on a topic because the child has already mastered the material. Effective acceleration is more than just going faster; it also includes efficient organization and compacting of material (e.g., reduction of already mastered material or repetition) to allow inclusion of enrichment activities.

Enrichment strategies focus on engaging the student in higher level thinking (e.g., evaluation as opposed to memorization) and creative activities such as pull-out programs in which students work in small groups outside the regular classroom with an enrichment specialist for several hours a week. They are literally "pulled out" of the regular classroom activities for this special instruction. These kinds of activities typically allow in-depth exploration of topics of high interest to an individual student. Effective enrichment activities are not simply added on to the standard curriculum, but are integrated into the instructional goals of the program.

Differentiation includes instructional practices by which gifted students are served in the regular classroom by varying content (what is learned), process of learning (how it is learned), pace (rate of instruction), and product (e.g., paper, poster, report, drawing). The most effective differentiated classrooms include increased acceleration, complexity, novelty, and depth of material for gifted children. If teachers have sufficient support to develop or adopt differentiated curricula, this can be an effective way to serve students with varying levels of ability in the same class.[8]

Identification and Placement

Learn how the district and school identify gifted students and select them for special programming. Some districts and schools use a combination of strategies, sometimes adapted for particular programs.[9] Many districts rely on *group-administered intelligence tests* or *standardized achievement tests*, which generally compare students to others at their grade level; students who achieve at a particular level beyond what is expected for their grade may be considered for special programming. This is an efficient way to identify students who are adept at the kind of learning on which schools focus.

Depending on how often and at what ages these tests are administered, students might have one chance in a year (or even less) to be selected. Therefore, a great deal could be riding on a child's performance. However, a number of factors can influence how well these tests work for a gifted child.

- Tests only cover particular topics and skills that may or may not reflect a child's exceptional talents or areas of talent.
- A child's score could be impacted by tiredness, illness, anxiety, language, or cultural issues (e.g., not being familiar with a particular holiday or custom).
- The child may have a learning difficulty that has affected test performance.
- If the test provides one single number, sometimes called a *global score*, it may not identify students who are gifted in only one area, such as math.
- The test may not have a high enough "ceiling," meaning that it does not have enough difficult items to distinguish very gifted children from those who are simply good at schoolwork.
- These tests are generally not administered during the very early years of elementary school, so gifted children in preschool through second grade (depending on the state or district) will not be recognized by this method.

Because of some of these issues with group standardized testing, some students with special abilities are simply missed. Some schools supplement this approach with others to allow for more individual expression of talents, like portfolio assessment, which involves a collection of the student's work. This complex issue often requires a great deal of parent awareness and involvement to ensure the adequate identification of students with special abilities.

Sometimes *teachers* recommend students for gifted services. Teachers might complete a standard form, often a checklist of characteristics commonly believed to indicate giftedness; other districts rely on a teacher's experience with a range of children to identify students more informally for special services. Teachers are familiar with a student's work habits and school-related abilities and can often determine which students could benefit from additional services. However, one disadvantage to this method is that many teachers do not have a solid foundation in gifted education and may not be able to identify gifted students in their classes, often possibly missing students who are performing at a level below their abilities. Another difficulty with teacher recommendations is that these ratings are subjective and may be affected by a child's behavior or personality, either of which might prevent the teacher from truly appreciating the child's talents. Sometimes, students misbehave in class because they are bored[10] and are therefore not chosen for the very programs that might engage them.

Parents may or may not be involved in the process of identifying talented students or informed of the outcome. My son was part of a small group that was pulled out of his first-grade class on a regular basis to work with another teacher. He mentioned this to us in passing; because my husband worked with the school district, we happened to know that the teacher was the school's enrichment specialist. My son's teacher had recognized that he could benefit from an enriched curriculum, and she arranged for this on his behalf. For this district, serving students with diverse needs was "business as usual."

A parent whose child was not selected for special services based on standardized group tests or teacher recommendations, but believes that his or her child needs these services to stay motivated in school, must produce information the teacher and school can use to serve the child. In this case, *individual testing* may provide helpful information.

Begin at the school or district with a *school psychologist*. He or she may be able to identify patterns of abilities that are not apparent from the group test or characteristics of an individual child that could prevent the full expression of abilities on a test. Individualized testing can be especially helpful if a child has an array of talents along with learning difficulties that may impact performance on group tests. For example, a school psychologist might pinpoint a learning difficulty that is clouding a child's performance on a test. Gifted children are adept at compensating for any weaknesses in their skills (e.g. relying on memory or context to read unfamiliar words); sometimes, only a trained evaluator can detect problems that may have far-reaching consequences for the child's learning if left unattended. The school psychologist will explain the results of the evaluation and prepare a report about the child with recommendations for appropriate educational services. If the school district does not have a school psychologist available to perform this evaluation or if the district's psychologist is not available to assist your child, parents may need to go to a *private consultant* for this service. Consultants often have specialized training in working with gifted students, but they can be costly and difficult to find.

In addition to obtaining an evaluator's report that describes your child's talents, *parents* should keep their own *records and portfolio* of their child's work. Some gifted children are not happy in their school surroundings and will not work at their highest level. In this case, the parent must demonstrate the child's talents with actual samples of work completed at home or in a different school or class. Meet with your child's teacher to begin the conversation about your child's talents and educational needs. Smutny provides excellent strategies on effectively setting up and conducting these meetings.[11]

Characteristics of Effective Schools for Gifted Students

Here are a few things parents should look for while exploring their child's educational options. The schools that serve gifted students most effectively are likely to have some combination of the following characteristics in terms of policy, curriculum, and instruction:[12]

- clear policies about selection into gifted programs;
- curricula adapted to individual interests and abilities, including opportunities for students to direct their own learning;
- a strong base in knowledge of core subjects, as well as guided exposure to the arts;
- emphasis on thinking skills instead of "answers";
- adapting teaching strategies to the needs of the students;
- attention to individual students;
- appropriate, consistent feedback from the teacher;
- high value placed on learning and individual talents;
- balance of individual and group activities;
- encouragement of parent involvement by the teacher; and
- students and teachers who enjoy the teaching/learning relationship.

Parent-School Partnerships

Many people are involved in the educational well-being of the gifted child. Each has important information, skills, or both to bring to the arrangement. The key is coordination: Everyone involved is best served by access to information and resources from a wide variety of connected sources. Before we discuss the logistics of developing partnerships to serve gifted kids in school, I'll briefly describe the main partners involved in elementary education.

Who Are the Partners?

In an elementary school, the main partners are the parents or guardian, teacher, school psychologist/guidance counselor, gifted coordinator, other school personnel, principal, and the child. I will briefly describe the role of each below. Although parents may not need to establish formal relationships with everyone, it might be helpful to know who's involved. Priscilla L. Vail recommends that one person serve as the coordinator (or "overseer") of a child's plans to ensure consistency and a constant source of support for the child, particularly if that child has large differences in his or her abilities in different areas or school problems.[13]

Parents, as the first "teacher" of the child, bring specific information and expertise to this partnership. Parents are most familiar with their children's personal characteristics, particularly with regard to the development of specific interests that can be linked to special talents. In general, parents are accurate at identifying when a child is gifted, although not all parents know how or when to ask for special services or evaluation for their gifted child.[14] For example, my husband and I were quite familiar with our son's passion for creating original paper airplanes, testing them, and adjusting them to fly in different ways; this activity occupied a great deal of his time at home beginning before kindergarten. Not realizing its relevance to academic abilities, we did not tell his teachers about this skill. In retrospect, and with the input of subsequent teachers who encouraged this activity, we recognize that this early interest reflected advanced spatial skills and potential for high achievement.

Despite a parent's unique expertise and special interest in a child, he or she is effectively complemented by a partnership with the child's elementary school *teacher*. In fact, this partnership can be a particularly powerful alliance that serves as the cornerstone for other family-school relationships. A child's experience in school, particularly during the elementary years, is directly impacted by the teacher. Teachers know children in a classroom setting and often have a particular understanding of a child's talents and motivations. Teachers are experts in curriculum and instruction, which is necessary for developing an educational plan to serve a gifted child, although many teachers have not received systematic instruction or support for teaching methods that are especially beneficial for gifted students. Furthermore, teachers set and enforce standards for academic and social behavior and can help gifted students by expecting them to work hard instead of just attempting to meet the minimum requirements of a given task.

Parents can learn a great deal about their children from the teacher. My husband and I were surprised to hear from our son's second-grade teacher that he was "obviously gifted in math." Although I had spent years studying gifted children, I did not fully recognize the signs in my own son. Fortunately, his teacher knew him in an instructional setting and had the skills and experience to advise us and help create a productive learning environment for him.

School psychologists or guidance counselors provide information to both parents and teachers.[15] Psychologists and counselors are generally the school experts in testing students, as well as in the regulations regarding placement in specialized programs for gifted students. School psychologists and counselors often serve as the facilitators or liaisons between parents and other school officials and are frequently involved in proactively setting up family-school relationships to benefit individual children.[16] Sometimes, a psychologist can add the missing piece of information to understand the puzzle of a child. For example teachers sometimes misread gifted students' boredom from lack of challenge in class as attitude or attention difficulties.[17] An expert in child behavior, like a psychologist, may be able to shed some light on the child's difficulties in a way that can be remedied by collaboration.

Schools use a variety of terms to refer to the individual responsible for providing specialized educational services to gifted students at the district or school level. This person might be the "special education director" and might work with exceptional students of all types; he or she might be termed the "gifted coordinator," "enrichment specialist," or "gifted and talented specialist" in charge of the "Talented and Gifted" (TAG) students or the "Academically Gifted"(AG) students; or others. Some districts support a district-level coordinator who trains and supports teachers, as well as a school-based specialist who works with teachers or individual students in an individual school. The availability of such specialists is often reflective of the school or district's economic resources. A friend of mine serves as the sole resource for the gifted children of an entire K–12 school district; she spends a short time each week at each school trying to support gifted students' learning. Clearly, students' benefits are related to the accessibility and amount of appropriate services.

Other teachers and school personnel can be valuable partners in the education of a gifted child. A visual arts teacher may be critical in supporting the needs of an artistically gifted child; a fourth-grade teacher skilled in math may be helpful in guiding a mathematically gifted first-grader. Other school personnel, such as media specialists or language specialists, can also play a significant role in creating and supporting the best learning opportunities for gifted students. The coordination of different services can be complicated, but a student will be best served if he or she has access to many of the school's resources.

The *principal* is instrumental in interpreting policy and creating an effective instructional climate. As the school's instructional leader, the principal helps establish gifted education practices and supports the teachers in implementing them. Principals can also affect the coordination of services for gifted students. Because principals have a broader view of the school than most other school personnel and they can determine the allocation of resources, the principal can play an important role in a gifted child's educational opportunities.

In our discussion of a child's school experience, we must not neglect the role of *the child* in creating an optimal learning environment. We want our children to be challenged, but not overwhelmed; motivated, but not compulsive; happy with friends, but not distracted from schoolwork. These are difficult balances for our gifted children to reach. Children themselves can be great sources of information about their school experiences—they can articulate how much they like or don't like school or how successful they are. Unfortunately, it's up to us as parents and teachers to ask the questions that will give us the information we need. As a first-grader, my son brought home a note from the enrichment teacher letting us know that he had not turned in the note cards he had been assigned. We had our first serious discussion with our child about the responsibility of being in school and having the opportunity to do special projects. He seemed confused, but assured us that he did want to continue being part of that group. That night, I found his note cards, beautifully completed, in his backpack. No one had asked him if he'd actually done the cards. The teacher assumed he hadn't done them because he didn't bring them to the group. My husband and I assumed the teacher had asked. We apologized to our child and told him that it would have been appropriate for him to tell any of us that he'd simply forgotten to take them out of his backpack. He was, after all, only 7 years old. We did not ask the questions that would have told us the whole story. After only one incident, we were concerned about his level of responsibility!

Children should have some say in their educational programming, but parents must be cautious and reasonable when evaluating their children's requests and reactions to school. A colleague and I recently spoke with the mother of a gifted sixth-grader who had been bored in her small private school for the past few years. Although the school was sympathetic to the mother's requests, the instructional resources were not available in that school to meet the girl's needs. The mother was further frustrated by the fact that the neighborhood public school was widely known for its gifted programming; why could she not obtain what she needed at the costly private school? But, the parents continued to enroll their daughter in the private school because she did not want to have to make new friends. Although it is difficult to make choices for children that they may not immediately like, sometimes parents need to look past a child's initial discomfort to the larger issues. We suggested to this particular mother that a school with programs for gifted children and a variety of educational resources was likely to provide her daughter with intellectual, as well as social, peers to support her through middle school and high school, critical years for keeping gifted students engaged in learning. Of course our children's feelings are important; but, as the parents, we sometimes have to consider long-term outcomes within the bigger picture.

Some parents will find that getting to know their child's teacher through visiting the class is enough to assure themselves that their gifted child is doing good work at an appropriately challenging level. Other situations will require that parents enlist the help of some of the other partners described, like the principal or gifted coordinator. Everyone needs to be flexible for this to work.

Benefits of Family-School Partnerships

Although coordinating the partners can be difficult, everyone seems to benefit from family-school partnerships.[18] *Parents* learn to be more supportive of their child's school activities and classwork and gain from the teacher's perspective on the child's skills and behaviors. *Children* gain not only in terms of increased school learning, but also from experiencing school and home life as mutually beneficial; this "unified front" can be a powerful factor in a child's belief that school is worthy and important and can keep him or her engaged in learning. *Teachers* gain from these partnerships by learning to appreciate parents' skills and talents. *School psychologists* can benefit by having the opportunity to fulfill a role they believe is important: bringing parents and teachers together to serve individual children.

How Do Parents Do It?

How can parents begin to establish these partnerships? Here are some strategies parents and school personnel can use to work together effectively.[19]

- Parents must do their homework. Parents must be actively involved in learning about their children's educational opportunities. Be prepared to spend some time!
- Begin with the teacher. It's especially important that parents and teachers learn to appreciate each other's perspectives and skills, so parents should get to know the teacher. Spend time in school and in class. Parents can volunteer in class, provide enrichment support for students in the class, or otherwise support the teacher's work.
- Understand the school hierarchy. Parents should begin their conversations about a child's educational options with the teacher and work with him or her to make sure the child's needs are met. Sometimes, teachers can't do what parents want them to because they might have too many other students to attend to or they may not have the instructional resources or training to do what the parents are asking. In this case, the partnership should broaden to include others in the school. If the teacher is unwilling to pursue this kind of arrangement, parents must understand the hierarchy of the school to get the help they need. The gifted coordinator or the principal may be able to find the right person or people to serve the gifted student or may help the parent evaluate his or her requests.

Presentation is important! Parents should be well-informed and cooperative to set the best tone for ongoing relationships. When parents and school personnel are working together, keep these general principles in mind:

- *We're all doing the best we can.* These relationships should be based on the assumption that everyone is doing the best he or she can to serve these children. Everyone is busy and stretched to meet multiple demands, but we're all dedicated to the same effort.
- *Honor multiple perspectives.* Partnerships are strengthened by the varying perspectives of partners. Everyone won't always agree, but try to remember that the more ideas that are being shared, the greater the opportunity that the child will have a good experience.

- *Be aware of language issues.* Partnerships can be complicated by the use of jargon or highly technical language. Be sensitive to alternative viewpoints. Listen attentively and accurately.
- *Promote reciprocity.* Share information and the responsibility for meeting needs and solving problems. Work together in a way that values each member's contribution and expertise. Be mutually supportive of each other's goals. Be prepared to negotiate with reason and open-mindedness.
- *Responsibility is shared.* Since all the partners are dedicated to serving the educational needs of the gifted student, each member shares the responsibility of achieving these ends. These relationships should ease the frustration and isolation of working on difficult issues as individuals.
- *Focus on solutions.* If the group is working toward generating reasonable solutions, there's less likelihood that any one person will be blamed for any of the issues involved in the child's education. In a partnership, no one person is ever "at fault," anyway.

Specific Issues That Benefit From Partnership

Parents of gifted elementary children are faced with a variety of school-related challenges. Some of these are most effectively addressed within a partnership of family, teacher, and other school personnel.

How to Best Support the Gifted Child's Need for Challenging Material. A critical issue confronting nearly all parents and teachers of gifted children is the development of an appropriate educational plan. Since each partner has a unique perspective on the child's talents and well-being and each is invested in his or her future, the coordination of all members is most likely to develop an effective plan. Partnership is especially effective when the child's options will include a variety of teachers and other school personnel, such as a youngster who will be visiting a higher grade for reading or spending extra time in the art room on a supervised project.

When to Accelerate a Child. There are no hard and fast rules about when it's best to accelerate children through school or in a particular subject or how far to accelerate them.[20] This issue is best addressed through a series of conversations and work sessions involving all partners devoted to the child's education. The parent will have the greatest familiarity with the student's unhappiness in his or her current placement; the teacher will be most knowledgeable about teaching issues and curricular characteristics of the next grade(s); and the school psychologist will have an expert's view of how well suited the child is socially and emotionally for such a move. The successful implementation of this practice depends on effective coordination of everyone involved.

Choosing Supplementary Activities to Complement School Programs. Another educational topic that benefits from a supportive partnership is the quest to find appropriate activities and programs to supplement a gifted child's school experience. Weekend, summer, and other extracurricular school, community, or computer-based programs serve an important role in keeping bright children engaged in learning during off-times and are often associated with both personal growth and academic learning.[21] Applying for admission to some of these programs requires the collaborative efforts of the school counselor, teacher, and parent. See other chapters in this book for outside-of-school and supplemental activities for talented children in various domains.

Child's Social Issues With Peers. A parent-school partnership is especially helpful when a gifted child appears to be having trouble with peers. Gifted children sometimes have difficulties with other children their age, particularly if they feel different from them. A partnership can work like this: Parents report on how the child behaves and feels at home, teachers discuss how the child interacts with peers during school, and the counselor/psychologist discerns if these behaviors or emotions are appropriate. I remember well the evening my son, a first-grader at the time, told me tearfully at bedtime that he was the "loneliest boy in the world." I checked with his teacher and was reassured to hear that he spent his days happily surrounded by a variety of friends; in fact, I learned that his penchant for "hanging out" was occasionally interfering with his ability to complete his schoolwork, information that has helped me support his school learning at home. If I hadn't asked the teacher for her perspective, I would have had a very incomplete picture.

Underachievement. Even the brightest students do not always do as well in school as we expect them to. This is a complicated issue involving a complex pattern of individual, family, and school factors. Solving the problem of underachievement requires hard work over a long period of time from parents, teachers, and school psychologists. Everyone supporting the child must be prepared for frequent conversations to develop a strategy to keep the child on course and to check in on his or her progress. There are no easy "fixes" for a gifted child who is not doing well in school.[22]

Problems Will Happen

If these kinds of parent-school partnerships are so beneficial, why don't they happen all the time? The truth is, these relationships are not always easy to develop. Parents may have to get used to the idea of working together with teachers and psychologists as partners, especially if, during their own school years, they saw school personnel as the *only* experts in education. Similarly, parents who had negative experiences during their own school history may mistrust the school system in general or teachers and psychologists in particular. Parents may also be confused by the technical language or jargon used by teachers or school psychologists to discuss their child.[23]

Similarly, teachers are not always ready to accept parents as educational partners.[24] Teachers might feel that parents get in the way of the work they are trying to do in teaching the child. Effective partnerships are impacted by the willingness of parents, school officials, and even students to reflect on their attitudes and expectations about collaboration.[25]

Sometimes, despite everyone's best intentions, parents and school personnel disagree.[26] These conflicts can be extremely difficult for everyone to manage and can result in anger, frustration, and disappointment on the part of the parent or a school person. None of these issues is easy to resolve and all require the concerted effort of a number of individuals or groups. When these situations arise, all must remember the general principles described earlier while still holding fast to the overall goal of providing the best services to every child. The following are the "hot topics" about which parents and schools are most likely to disagree and general suggestions for parents faced with these issues.

Differing Views of a Child's Abilities. Parents and school personnel might disagree about a student's talents. This situation can result when a teacher or other school official does not recognize the characteristics of talent and the individual ways talent can be demonstrated in a child. This is particularly problematic for gifted students who underachieve in school. As we discussed earlier, it may be up to the parents to show the school evidence of their child's talents in the form of testing results or exceptional work. Parents of gifted children must keep careful records and a portfolio demonstrating their children's activities, interests, and quality of work.

Knowledge. Lack of knowledge or an imbalance of knowledge can lead to conflict between families and school officials. Parents tend to rely on school officials to be experts in rules and regulations regarding the education of their children; if these officials do not have the desired information or do not share that information appropriately and in a timely manner, parents may become frustrated and feel alienated from the school. Parents of gifted children must be prepared to solicit information about their individual children and about educating gifted children in general from a variety of sources. Parents must also be ready to share this information. In some schools or districts, the parents of gifted children serve as an important informational resource for teachers, administrators, and other parents. Parents can share articles, books, and even teaching assistance if they present the material and ideas to teachers in a cooperative way. As we mentioned earlier, everyone in the partnership benefits from the sharing of information and ideas.

Service Delivery. The availability and delivery of educational services such as pull-out programs or in-class enrichment can become a source of conflict if parents consider the available services inadequate. According to Paula Olszewski-Kubilius, many gifted programs are actually inadequate for the appropriate development of gifted students' development, such as those that are not considered essential and are in danger of losing funding, those that are inconsistent in terms of content or identification strategies, and those that are insubstantial with regard to curricular content.[27] These parents must be ready to work hard, beginning with the teacher, and follow the appropriate hierarchy if the child cannot be served adequately within that class. Parents may need to go to the principal or even the school district to find the right kind of educational match for their gifted children. This can be a long, painful process, and parents faced with this situation may want to garner support and information from other parents of gifted children.

Constraints. Conflicts between parents and schools can be caused or worsened by constraints in financial resources, time, personnel, and materials. This issue has come up for many parents of gifted students whose schools believe that talented students should be able to succeed in school with no special attention. However, even very bright students sometimes require motivational support to keep them engaged in school.

Conclusion

Everyone benefits from a collaborative partnership between family and elementary school personnel, but these partnerships are hard to achieve and maintain. However, since partnerships—particularly those between parents and teachers—are the best way to address several educational issues that are particularly pertinent to the parents of gifted children, parents and teachers should work together whenever possible to ensure that all students' needs are met.

Some parents have expanded their "partnerships" to include other parents and parent groups.[28] Serving gifted children is a complicated matter, and everyone involved should be ready to work with others to provide for our children successfully.

psychological
considerations
in raising
a healthy
gifted child

by

steven i. pfeiffer

This chapter departs from the majority of other chapters in this book and takes a different look at raising a gifted child. The other contributors provide specific advice and guidance on *how* to encourage the talent development process among elementary-age, gifted children. I will *not* provide specific advice to promote or further your son or daughter's talent in areas such as music, drama, language arts, math, or athletics. Rather, I will offer suggestions on what you can do to help prevent the development of psychological distress and problems to which gifted children are susceptible and promote their psychological health.

Should We Be Concerned
About the Mental Health of Gifted Children?

Many experts assume that gifted children enjoy relatively good social adjustment, vibrant mental health, and overall well-being. Our research at Duke University supports the view that intellectually gifted youth have better than average social adjustment.[1] However, few research studies have investigated the prevalence of psychological problems among gifted children with talents in areas other than the intellectual and academic. There are only a few case studies to help us understand the possible, unique vulnerabilities of children gifted in music, drama, the visual arts, academics, language arts, mathematics, and athletics.

The experience of professionals working with gifted children indicates that not all gifted children easily navigate the often challenging social and emotional waters of childhood and adolescence.[2] Quite a few children experience psychological problems as distressful as those experienced by their same-age nongifted peers.[3]

Many writers speculate that gifted children possess a unique set of behavioral characteristics that puts them at risk for psychological problems. For example, gifted children have been described—some might say stereotyped—as overly excitable, driven to perfection, nonconforming, and strong-willed.[4] If these behavioral characteristics are, in fact, more common among gifted children, then they very well could increase the gifted child's vulnerability to social and emotional difficulties.

We know that, in the U.S. today, the incidence of mental health problems is significant. Although growing up is never easy, today's children face new and more challenging pressures. Experts estimate that one in five students in school today have significant mental health problems such as depression, anxiety, low self-esteem, eating disorders, and social maladjustment.[5] We would be safe to assume that gifted children are not impervious to developing psychological problems. It also seems reasonable to conclude that what makes the gifted child special might paradoxically serve to increase their risk for social and emotional difficulties in some instances.

Promoting Healthy Psychological Development

Four principles serve as the foundation for discussion in this chapter. They are cornerstones supporting what I emphasize in terms of raising a psychologically healthy gifted child. I rely on these principles in my counseling and consulting practice and hope that you find them useful in working with your gifted child.

Before presenting the four principles, however, I should mention two important points. On the one hand, gifted children are different from children who are not gifted in many significant ways. As a result, gifted children, by the nature of their unique talents, experience the world differently.[6] I suspect that you have observed some of these differences with your own child.

For example, gifted children are oftentimes described as displaying a burning curiosity and seemingly unquenchable thirst for knowledge, keen observations skills, intense absorption in things that interest them, and tendency to get bored with schoolwork and tasks that are not challenging.[7]

On the other hand, gifted children share much in common with nongifted children. Parents should not forget that their gifted child has the same developmental, emotional, and social needs as other children who are not gifted, an important point that can be overlooked when raising a child who has special gifts.

I would like to introduce you to the four principles that are helpful in raising a young gifted child:

- Promote balance in your child's life.
- Normalize your child's experience.
- Set and enforce limits.
- Encourage social intelligence.

In discussing each principle, I include descriptions of one or more gifted children with whom I have worked. My goal is to illustrate by example the relevance of each principle to raising a psychologically healthy gifted child. The examples I have selected depict the kinds of psychological distress and problems most often reported among gifted children and youth.[8]

Promote Balance In Your Child's Life

Promoting balance in your child's life means that you need to protect your child (and yourself) from getting caught up in focusing on his or her special talent or talents to the neglect of other important developmental experiences. Parents of highly gifted children can be tempted to provide their child with *every* available opportunity and resource.[9] Nurturing your child's special gift is important—as we emphasize throughout this book. However, when the scales tip to place *excessive* emphasis—in terms of time, psychic energy, travel, rearranged schedules, and the like—on promoting the special talent, the gifted child can miss out on important socialization experiences, thus putting him or her at greater risk for developing psychological problems.

The following example illustrates the importance of promoting balance in your gifted child's life. I was counseling a preadolescent athlete who was ranked in the top 10 in the world in the 100-meter freestyle in his age group.

Raphael (the names of all the children in this chapter have been changed to protect their anonymity) was brought to see me by his parents, who were concerned that he had very few friends, acted in a depressed and socially withdrawn manner, and, although quite bright, was beginning to slip in his schoolwork. My work with Raphael and his family revealed that this 12-year old boy was suffering from spending excessive time training in the pool and weight room with other elite athletes. Few of the other swimmers were his age. Raphael had very little time or energy left for homework, relaxing, or socializing with school friends. He hesitantly acknowledged in one family session that he had been reluctant to confront his parents with his perceived dilemma because he felt that the family was making extraordinary sacrifices on his behalf—which they were! Raphael's story, fortunately enough, ended on a positive note. His family came to recognize in subsequent family counseling sessions that they needed to ease up on their son's rigorous training regime and encourage time for the unmet needs and social activities that were being given little attention. Raphael's parents showed great strength of character in acknowledging that they were overinvolved in their son's athletic life, in an almost self-absorbed attempt to experience the rewards of their son's athletic accolades and accomplishments.

Raphael decided to enroll in a Saturday art class that a classmate was attending—an activity he thought he would enjoy, but one in which he showed no extraordinary promise—and began attending a Wednesday evening church youth program. Raphael's competitive swimming continued, but was balanced with much-needed social and recreational activities and simple down time to relax and unwind.

This example illustrates that sometimes too much of a good thing in pursuit of developing your child's full potential—tutoring, lessons, practice, special classes, after-school programs, summer camps—can be detrimental to his or her overall psychological health. Raphael's case also illustrates the importance of providing your gifted child with enough time and opportunity to interact with same-age peers—not necessarily gifted children—in enjoyable, noncompetitive activities.

Normalize Your Child's Experience

Normalizing means providing your child with a range of social activities that are age and developmentally appropriate. This second principal is complicated by the fact that, for your gifted child, exposure to normalizing experiences includes experiences that are developmentally appropriate specific to his or her special talent and experiences that are age appropriate, but not necessarily specific to your child's talent.

Developmentally appropriate normalizing experiences provide your child with opportunities to interact with other equally gifted children who share similar interests. These type of normalizing experiences afford your child the opportunity to meet other gifted children and come to recognize—and even feel comfortable appreciating—that he or she is not alone because there are other children who share similar views, thoughts, and feelings.

Sara was 10 years old when I first met her, referred by her parents because she was feeling depressed, alone, and misunderstood by her peers. Sara was a bright child who was very dramatic, emotional, and expressive. Her teachers had long recognized her theatrical talent, and, since the first grade, she had enjoyed a reputation among the teachers as the school's most talented stage performer. However, her classmates were not enamored with Sara and viewed somewhat disparagingly her heightened emotional sensitivities and artistic talent. All too often, Sara was either teased or neglected by her peers. I encouraged Sara's parents to involve their daughter at a local repertory theater. Sara quickly fit in with the local actors and found a ready-made group of equally talented individuals who shared her passion for theater and performance. Although most of the performers were older then Sara, they quickly became an important normalizing group, reaffirming that Sara was neither alone nor weird in her passion for the arts. This experience, over time, ultimately helped Sara more effectively fit in with her same-age classmates.

Age-appropriate normative experiences, on the other hand, are activities that are distinct from the enriched, accelerated, or advanced type of experiences—such as Sara's theater involvement—that you provide in support of your child's special talent. Age-appropriate normalizing experiences are also important when raising a gifted child. Although providing these experiences makes good common sense as a parenting philosophy, it can become all too easy to stress your child's gifts and special needs since many schools provide so few resources for the gifted.[10] Many parents early in their gifted child's life recognize that they need to become their child's advocate if they hope to nurture their child's special talent. Like parents of other special needs students, such as the learning disabled and mentally and physically handicapped, sometimes families of the gifted unwittingly neglect to provide normalizing experiences for their exceptional child.[11]

Adam is an example of what can happen when parents neglect this principle. Adam's school referred this academically gifted fourth grader to my counseling practice because he was having difficulty getting along with his classmates. Adam's mother was on the computer science faculty of a nearby college and his father was a senior executive for a prestigious engineering consulting firm. Both parents were bright and well educated, and they placed a very high premium on their son's academic gifts.

During my first meeting with Adam, I was struck with how different he looked, dressed, and was treated by his well-intentioned parents. Adam's appearance was anything but typical for most fourth-grade boys in his neighborhood and school. Neither he nor his parents were interested in the fashions, music, or activities in which most other young boys were interested. Adam's 1950s-style eyeglasses and the legal briefcase he carried further accentuated the sense of a youngster who looked and acted like a little adult.

Adam's appearance and his parents' apparent insensitivity to youth culture were nonetheless minor issues relative to his unusual social and interpersonal style. Adam had been raised as if he was a very special young adult, rather than the 9-year-old gifted child that he was. Dinner discussions focused exclusively on conversations about politics, current events, the stock market, and other arcane or academic topics—conversations that one would expect to have at an evening faculty reception. Incredulously, this family never talked about Adam's social life, his (lack of) friends, peer relation problems, or child-related issues.

I quickly understood why this precocious child was having serious peer relation problems. Adam related to others—peers and adults alike—as if he were a caricature of a professor from an elite college: self-important, superior, and arrogant. Yet, when peers taunted and teased him, which happened often, given his insufferable attitude, he would fall apart emotionally and either cry or strike out physically. Unfortunately for Adam, neither his impulse control nor physical strength matched his intellectual prowess, and he was getting beaten up regularly.

My work with Adam and his parents focused on helping the family appreciate the value of providing Adam with age-appropriate normalizing experiences—activities that his classmates were involved in. This was no easy task, however. Adam's parents had to confront their own values and beliefs about raising a gifted child. Counseling challenged Adam's parents to ease up on their tendency to use every family interaction as an opportunity to further their son's intellectual development. In their mind, Adam was going to attend Princeton and their responsibility was to get him ready. David Elkind's book, *The Hurried Child: Growing Up Too Fast Too Soon*, does an excellent job of discussing the harm of "achievement overload" and pushing children to grow up too quickly.[12]

Adam's progress was slow, but positive. His peer relation problems subsided once his parents began treating him like a gifted, but otherwise normal, child who needed to learn how to interact and socialize in an age-appropriate, harmonious way with other children. Our work together included teaching Adam effective ways to deal with peer teasing, meanness, and bullying. We practiced simple anti-bullying techniques, such as staying calm and not reacting emotionally to name-calling, ignoring the teasing, and using simple, one-line comeback lines when all else fails (e.g. "Somebody already told me that" or "Thanks for telling me that, but I've heard it since preschool").

At the conclusion of my work with this family, Adam was participating in a swim program at the YMCA, was being invited by classmates to birthday parties, and was registered to attend a martial arts class. Most important, his newly learned social skills helped him avoid displaying the kind of intolerable behavior that previously caused his peer problems.

Set and Enforce Limits

Clearly stated limits, rules, and expectations for conduct help your child become a successful, worthwhile human being. Setting and enforcing age-appropriate limits provides the structure that allows children to learn how to get along with others, maintain friendships, deal with conflict, and recognize that they are part of the larger social world. All children need limits because limits are instrumental in teaching appropriate behavior and they communicate a sense of security and a message of parental love.

Some authorities in the gifted field[13] have suggested the idea that gifted children may need fewer constraints than others, although there is no evidence to support this position. As a parent, it is tempting to think that your gifted child has better judgment and is more socially mature then other children his or her age. This is not necessarily true, as the following three vignettes illustrate.

Debra was a 7-year old gifted child with extraordinary talents in academics and music. Her parents, school, and violin instructor considered her to be a child prodigy, yet she was disliked by her classmates and viewed by her parents as almost impossible to manage. Although her violin instructor excused her emotionally labile or variable temperament, overexcitability, and bossiness as characteristic of highly gifted children, her parents came to recognize that Debra lacked age-appropriate social skills such as sharing, taking turns, and being cooperative, courteous, and friendly. My work with Debra revealed that her parents had been unable to discipline their daughter effectively because they were intimidated by Debra's extraordinary gifts. They granted Debra almost total freedom without expecting appropriate or responsible behavior in return.

Shane was referred to my practice because of chronic power struggles at his school. An intellectually gifted and strong-willed 10-year old, Shane challenged authority and struggled for control with his teachers. Shane's parents were reluctant to set any limits on their son, concerned that they would curtail, in their words, "his creativity and individuality." Shane's parents employed a laissez-faire parenting style, believing that the unlimited freedom they allowed their child would serve him well in the long run, in spite of his present conduct problems. They perceived Shane as misunderstood by his teachers and the school principal.

I met 11-year-old Janelle when she was playing soccer for the highly competitive Olympic Development Program. A gifted female athlete and accomplished dancer, she had gained considerable attention the year before for her stellar performance on a boys' traveling soccer team. Janelle's parents were concerned because their daughter's perfectionism was causing her psychological problems. For the first time in her life, Janelle encountered competition that challenged her sense of being "the best." Janelle's intense frustration over no longer being number one created behavioral and emotional problems. She criticized and fought with other players on the team, argued with her coach, and developed migraines. Part of Janelle's dilemma was that her parents were reluctant to set appropriate limits for her conduct both on and off the field. Janelle's parents were immobilized around their daughter's declining status as a soccer star and implicitly sanctioned Janelle's acting out, believing that perhaps it was her teammates or coach who caused Janelle's fall from stardom.

Debra, Shane, and Janelle had three things in common. First, all three displayed problematic behaviors and lacked age-appropriate social skills important in problem solving and getting along with others. Second, all three had personality characteristics often described as being typical of the gifted: emotionally labile (highly emotionally variable), overexcitability, strong-willed, perfectionism, and fierce independence. Third, all three had parents who employed laissez-faire parenting styles and were reluctant to set reasonable limits, rules, or expectations.

Children often test limits. It is perfectly normal to expect your child to challenge the rules you set. Gifted children in particular are curious in wanting to understand your rationale for each rule, what you will do if they break a rule, and whether you will be consistent in enforcing a rule. Two suggestions that are helpful in enforcing rules are holding regular family meetings to discuss family rules and using constructive discipline when your child breaks a rule or misbehaves.[14]

Family meetings have been used in the mental health field for almost 50 years as a way for families to discuss problems, resolve conflicts, plan family events, and celebrate individual family member accomplishments. Family meetings should be democratic, participatory, enjoyable, and held regularly—once weekly works well. Agenda items can include both parent- and child-generated topics. For example, parent-generated agenda items might include establishing or revising family rules, expressing concern over rule breaking, and identifying recurring problems. Agenda items that gifted children frequently suggest at family meetings include dealing with jealousy of nongifted peers, unrealistic teacher expectations for perfect performance, sibling rivalry (particularly between gifted and nongifted siblings), coping with perfectionism and excessive competitiveness, and classroom boredom. During these meetings, your child will have the opportunity to learn effective communication skills, be exposed to different points of view, observe problem solving and consensus making in action, express strongly held feelings in the comfort of the family, and practice cooperation.

Constructive discipline is a second technique that supports limit setting. The first part of constructive discipline is using "I messages" rather than "you messages." When your child breaks a rule, communicate your disapproval starting your message with *I* instead of *you*. "I messages" sound less critical and focus on the misbehavior and not your child's self-worth. For example, a "you message" might be: "*You* are acting like a spoiled brat. Nobody will want to play with you if you keep acting like a baby." In contrast, an "I message" in the same instance might be: "*I* don't like to see you act immature like that. Other kids might think that you would be no fun to play with if they saw you act so childish."

The second part of constructive discipline is separating your child from his or her misbehavior. Effective discipline should teach your child how to correct misbehavior while respecting self-worth. Done properly, the corrective message tells your child what he or she did wrong and what alternative behavior you expect. For example, "*I* want to hear what is bothering you, but

I can't understand you when you yell and cry." A less effective communication, which does not separate the misbehavior from the child, sounds like this: "Stop screaming and crying. No other kids your age act like this."

Four resources that are helpful in learning more about setting limits and positive discipline are *Between Parent and Child*,[15] *Parents Do Make a Difference*,[16] *The Educated Child*,[17] and *Twenty First Century Discipline*.[18]

Encourage Social Intelligence

The fourth principle, encouraging social intelligence, ensures that your child develops the skills to be courteous, a good listener, likable, helpful, trustworthy, a team player, able to get along with others, and empathetic. These important social skills have been variously labeled as *emotional intelligence*,[19] *social competence, social maturity*,[20] and *interpersonal intelligence*.[21] I like to consider these skills part of *social intelligence*. Simply stated, helping your child to develop social intelligence will increase the likelihood that he or she will enjoy a rich, satisfying, and successful life.

The publication of Daniel Goleman's *Emotional Intelligence*[22] made popular the importance of being able to rein in emotional impulse, accurately read social cues and other people's feelings, delay need for immediate gratification, tolerate frustrating situations, and handle relationships smoothly. Employing a neuropsychological view of human intelligence, Goleman suggests,

> In a sense we have two brains, two minds—and two different kinds of intelligence: rational and emotional. How we do in life is determined by both . . . ordinarily the complementarity of limbic system and neocortex, amygdala and prefrontal lobes, means each is a full partner in mental life.[23]

Children with well-developed social intelligence are at ease with peers and adults, self-confident, and able to master stressful situations. They are able to present themselves as friendly and appealing, almost as if they have taken a Dale Carnegie course in "How to Make Friends and Influence People."[24] It is important to remember that children's social intelligence may not be as advanced as their intellectual development or special talent. In fact, it would be surprising if their emotional maturity were as highly developed.

Sarah was an intellectually gifted 7-year old who was quickly gaining a bad reputation in her private school as a troubled child. I was invited by her parents to observe Sarah in her school, where I found that Sarah's problems represented underdeveloped social intelligence. Specifically, Sarah did not share with others or respect other children's property, was reluctant to wait her turn, was uncooperative in group activities, and demonstrated little respect for teacher authority.

Rather than viewing Sarah as a troubled child with deep-seated emotional problems, her parents and I embarked upon a course of treatment that focused on teaching Sarah important social skills. Over eight family counseling sessions, we focused on identifying friendship-making problems and how to correct them, taught social etiquette and good sportsmanship, and provided Sarah with an extensive vocabulary of emotional words to help her better identify feelings in others. Sarah's parents used literature as a means of building social skills. They asked Sarah to describe which characters in books she would want to have as a best friend and why. Sarah's parents used television as another means to help build her social intelligence. After watching popular TV programs together, Sarah was asked to identify good and bad social behavior among the various characters.

Children don't come into the world knowing these important skills. Even gifted children need to learn from their parents about virtuous habits, good manners, and social skills. This is the all-important process of character development. The ingredients for teaching social intelligence are:

- Set a good example. There is nothing more influential than teaching by quiet example.
- Make standards clear and expectations high, but not unreasonable. Gifted children, like all children, enjoy living up to their parents' expectations.
- Talk about right and wrong. Discuss the way the world works and the way people ought to live and treat one another. Don't preach, but rather hold Socratic dialogues with your gifted child. This type of conversation works especially well at family meetings.
- Avoid rescuing your child. Although it is tempting to want to solve your child's problems, it robs your child of the opportunity to develop problem-solving skills, confidence, and self-sufficiency.
- Look for warning signs. If your child displays any of the following behaviors, then you need to give greater attention to his or her social intelligence: doesn't have a friend, acts like a poor loser, lacks confidence, plays too aggressively, is easily upset or quickly becomes

angry, acts bossy, doesn't share or respect others' property, is uncooperative and doesn't do well in group situations, doesn't respect
authority, rarely compromises, shows little empathy for others' feelings, acts discourteously, and doesn't enjoy socializing with peers. If
you think your child is displaying one or more of the above warning signs to a degree that is excessive, unreasonable, or adversely
impacting upon his or her academic, social, or family life, I recommend that you consider seeking professional help. One organization
you can contact is the National Register for Health Service
Providers in Psychology. The National Register lists licensed psychologists nationwide and their areas of specialization. A second
resource to contact to help identify a referral is the school psychologist in your child's school. He or she may know a psychologist or
child psychiatrist in your community who specializes in working
with gifted children.

Four resources that are helpful in learning more about strengthening
your child's social intelligence are *How to Raise a Child With a High EQ
(Emotional Quotient)*,[25] *More than Manners! Raising Today's Kids to Have Kind
Manners and Good Hearts*,[26] *Stress-Proofing Your Child*,[27] and *Teach Your
Child Decision Making*.[28]

Conclusion

One parent with whom I had the pleasure of working said that raising
her gifted child was like competing in an Iron Man triathlon. Although
financially well off and highly educated, she was apprehensive about whether
she was doing enough for her daughter, Celeste, much less preparing her for
a secure and happy future. Caught up in a weekly schedule of shuttling
Celeste to a local community college, violin and piano lessons, a church
youth group, and SAT prep course, this parent began to wonder if, in some
way, she was robbing her daughter of the joys of childhood. At the time that
I saw Celeste, she was an anxious, unenthusiastic, and stressed-out 12-year
old who was preoccupied with getting into Dartmouth, where her dad was
an alumnus.

Celeste was missing out on important normalizing childhood experiences simply because of well-intentioned parents who wanted to ensure that

she had every opportunity to develop to her full potential. Celeste is an example of when too much of a good thing can become bad for a child, particularly in terms of their psychological health.

In this chapter I have emphasized the importance of not neglecting the psychological health of your gifted child. Although most gifted children enjoy better-than-average social adjustment, some gifted children do experience distressful psychological problems. As a parent, you have the responsibility and opportunity to help your gifted child learn to navigate the often challenging social and emotional waters of childhood and adolescence.

The four principles I have discussed can help you raise a more resilient and better-adjusted child. I encourage you to promote balance in your child's life, normalize your child's experience, set limits and rules for appropriate behavior, and teach social skills, virtuous habits, and good manners. Make family time a priority and don't overload your child's schedule to the point where achievement becomes the only important thing in his or her life.

Raising a gifted or talented child is no easy job. Enjoy parenthood and the joys and wonder of raising such a special child. Give your child the right kind of guidance and wisdom about life. You play a key role in teaching your children about themselves and the world around them.

end notes

chapter 1

1. Benjamin S. Bloom, *Stability and Change in Human Characteristics* (London: Wiley, 1964).
2. Ann M. Clarke and A. D. B. Clarke, *Early Experience: Myth and Evidence* (New York: Free Press 1976).
3. Linda S. Gottfredson, "Editorial: Mainstream Science on Intelligence. An Editorial with 52 Signatories, History and Bibliography," *Intelligence 24*, no. 1 (1997): 13–24.
4. Ibid., 14.
5. Joseph S. Renzulli, "Three Ring Conception of Giftedness," in *Conceptions of Giftedness*, ed. R. J. Sternberg and J. E. Davidson (New York: Cambridge University Press, 1990), 53–92.
6. Howard Gardner, *Frames of Mind: The Theory of Multiple Intelligences* (New York: BasicBooks, 1983)
7. Ellen Winner, *Gifted Children: Myths and Realities* (New York: BasicBooks, 1996).
8. Jane Piirto, *Understanding Those Who Create* (Dayton: Ohio Psychology Press, 1992).
9. Ellen Winner and Gail Martino, "Giftedness in the Visual Arts and Music," in *International Handbook of Research and Development of Giftedness and Talent*, ed. K. A. Heller, F. J. Mönks, and A. H. Passow (New York: Pergamon Press, 1993), 253–282.
10. Ibid.
11. Nancy E. Jackson and E. J. Klein, "Gifted Performance in Young Children," in *Handbook of Gifted Education*, 2nd ed., ed. N. Colangelo and G. A. Davis (Boston: Allyn and Bacon, 1997), 460–474.
12. Martha J. Morelock and David Henry Feldman, "Prodigies and Savants: What They Have to Tell Us About Giftedness and Human Cognition," *International Handbook of Research and Development of Giftedness and Talent*, ed. K. H. Heller, F. J. Mönks, and A. H. Passow (New York: Pergamon, 1993), 171. See also David Henry Feldman, *Nature's Gambit. Child Prodigies and the Development of Human Potential* (New York: BasicBooks, 1986).
13. François Gagné, "From Giftedness to Talent: A Developmental Model and Its Impact on the Language of the Field," *Roeper Review 18*, no. 2 (1995): 103–111.
14. Benjamin Bloom, *Developing Talent in Young People* (New York: Ballantine, 1985).
15. Mihalyi Csikszentmihalyi and O. Beattie, "Life Themes: A Theoretical and Empirical Exploration of Their Origins and Effects," *Journal of Humanistic Psychology 19*, no. 1 (1979): 45–63.

16. Mihalyi Csikszentmihalyi, *Flow: The Psychology of Optimal Experience* (New York: Harper and Row, 1990).

17. Rena F. Subotnik and Paula Olszewski-Kubilius, "Restructuring Special Programs to Reflect the Distinctions Between Children's and Adult's Experiences with Giftedness," *Peabody Journal of Education 72*, no. 3–4 (1997): 101–116.

18. Paula Olszewski, Marilyn J. Kulieke, and Thomas Buescher, "The Influence of the Family Environment on the Development of Talent: A Literature Review," *Journal for the Education of the Gifted 11*, no. 1 (1987): 6–28.

19. R. Ochse, *Before the Gates of Excellence: The Determinants of Creative Genius* (Cambridge, England: Cambridge University Press, 1983); Paula Olszewski-Kubilius, "The Transition From Childhood Giftedness to Adult Creative Productiveness: Psychological Characteristics and Social Supports," *Roeper Review 23*, no. 2 (2000): 65–71.

20. Dean Keith Simonton, "The Child Parents the Adult: On Getting Genius From Giftedness," in *Talent Development: Proceedings From the 1991 Henry B. And Jocelyn Wallace National Research Symposium on Talent Development*, ed. N. Colangelo, S. G. Assouline, and D. L. Ambroson (New York: Trillium, 1992), 278–297; Ochse, *Before the Gates of Excellence.*

21. Milhalyi Csikszentmihalyi, Kevin Rathunde, and Samuel Whalen, *Talented Teenagers: The Roots of Success and Failure* (Cambridge, England: Cambridge University Press, 1993).

22. William A. Therival, "Why Mozart and Not Salieri," *Creativity Research Journal 12*, no. 1 (1996): 67–76.

23. Paula Olszewski-Kubilius, *The Transition From Childhood Giftedness to Adult Creative Productiveness: Psychological Characteristics and Social Supports.*

24. Rena Subotnik and Paula Olszewski-Kubilius, "Restructuring Special Programs to Reflect the Distinctions Between Children's and Adult's Experiences with Giftedness."

chapter 2

1. American Association for the Advancement of Science, *Benchmarks for Science Literacy* (New York: Oxford University Press, 1993); National Research Council, *National Science Education Standards* (Washington, D.C.: National Academy Press, 1995).

2. Paul Brandwein, *Science Talent in the Young Expressed Within Ecologies of Achievement* (Storrs, Conn.: National Research Center on the Gifted and Talented, 1995).

3. G. Toppo, "Test: Few Students Know Science," *Washington Post*, 21 November 2001.

4. American Association for the Advancement of Science, "Heavy Books Light on Learning," http://www.project2061.org/newsinfo/research/textbook/article/heavy2.htm.

5. Paul Brandwein, "Science Talent: In an Ecology of Achievement," in *Gifted Young in Science: Potential Through Performance,* ed. P. Brandwein and A. H. Passow (Washington, D.C.: National Science Teachers Association, 1988), 73–103.

6. Susan Johnsen and Anne Corn, *Screening Assessment for Gifted Elementary and Middle School Students*, 2nd ed. (Austin, Tex.: PRO-ED, 2001)

7. J. A. Ross and F. J. Maynes, "Development of a Test of Experimental Problem-Solving Skills," *Journal of Research in Science Teaching 20*, no. 1 (1983): 63–75.

8. Cheryll M. Adams and Carolyn M. Callahan, "The Reliability and Validity of a Performance Task for Evaluating Science Process Skills," *Gifted Child Quarterly 39*, no. 1 (1995): 14–21.

9. B. Cross, "A Passion With Reason: The Human Side of Process," *Science and Children 27*, no 4 (1990): 16–21.

10. R. Pollack, "Science as a Creative Process," *Liberal Education 74*, no. 2 (1988): 15.

11. Paul Brandwein, "Science Talent: In an Ecology of Achievement," in *Gifted Young in Science: Potential Through Performance,* ed. P. Brandwein and A. H. Passow (Washington, D.C.: National Science Teachers Association, 1988), 73–103.

12. D. W. MacKinnon, "Childhood Variables and Adult Personality in Two Professional Samples: Architects and Research Scientists," in *Creativity at Home and in School,* ed. F. E. Williams (St. Paul, Minn.: Macalester College, 1968), 123–147; R. G. Mansfield, *The Psychology of Creativity and Discovery: Scientists and Their Work* (Chicago: Nelson Hall, 1981); Ann Roe, *The Making of a Scientist* (New York: Dodd, Mead, 1952); E. G. Ypma, "Prediction of the Industrial Creativity of Research Scientists From Biographical Information" (Ph.D. diss., Purdue University 1968).

13. B. Ghiselin, *The Creative Process* (New York: Mentor, 1901).

14. Robert S. Root-Bernstein, *Discovering: Inventing and Solving Problems at the Frontiers of Scientific Research* (Cambridge, Mass.: Harvard University Press, 1989).

15. Mansfield, *The Psychology of Creativity and Discovery: Scientists and Their Work.*

16. Root-Bernstein, *Discovering: Inventing and Solving Problems at the Frontiers of Scientific Research.*

17. Dana Johnson, Linda Boyce, and Joyce VanTassel-Baska, "Science Curriculum Review: Evaluating Materials for High-Ability Learners," *Gifted Child Quarterly 39*, no. 1 (1995): 36–44; Joyce VanTassel-Baska, "Developing Science Curriculum for High Ability Learners, K–8" (paper presented at the annual meeting of the Northern Virginia Council for the Gifted and Talented, Woodbridge, Va., November 1992).

18. B. Wellman, "Making Science More Science-Like," in *Developing Minds: A Resource Book for Teaching Thinking,* ed. A. Costa (Alexandria, Va.: ASCD, 1991), 159–163.

19. D. Freedman, "Science Education: How Curriculum and Instruction Are Evolving," *Curriculum Update* (Fall 1998): 1.

20. For an extended discussion of gifted girls in science, see Cheryll M. Adams, "Gifted Girls and Science: Revisiting the Issues," *Journal of Secondary Gifted Education 7*, no. 4 (1996): 447–457.

21. If you would like information on gender equity, you may wish to send for a catalog from WEEA Equity Resource Center, Education Development Center, Inc., 55 Chapel St. D–12000, Newton, Mass. 02458-1060.

chapter 3

1. Office of Educational Research and Improvement, U.S. Department of Education, *National Excellence: A Case for Developing America's Talent* (Washington, D.C.: U.S. Government Printing Office, 1993), 1.

2. Michael C. Thompson, *Classics in the Classroom* (Unionville, N.Y.: Royal Fireworks Press, 1990).

3. Joyce VanTassel-Baska, *Excellence in Educating Gifted and Talented Learners* (Denver: Love, 1998), 451.

4. Michael C. Thompson, "Mentors on Paper: How Classics Develop Verbal Ability," in *Developing Verbal Talent*, ed. J. VanTassel-Baska, D. T. Johnson, and L. N. Boyce (Boston: Allyn and Bacon, 1996), 63.

5. Michael C. Thompson, *Classic Words,* computer software (Unionville, N.Y.: Royal Fireworks Press, 2001).

6. James G. Gallagher, *Teaching the Gifted Child,* 2nd ed. (Boston: Allyn and Bacon, 1975), 198.

7. Michael C. Thompson, *The Word Within the Word,* rev. ed. (Unionville, N.Y.: Royal Fireworks Press, 2000).

8. Thompson, *Classic Words.*

9. Gallagher, *Teaching the Gifted Child,* 181.

10. Michael C. Thompson and Myriam Borges Thompson, "Reflections on Foreign Language Study for Highly Able Learners," in *Developing Verbal Talent,* ed. J. VanTassel-Baska, D. T. Johnson, L. N. Boyce (Boston: Allyn and Bacon, 1996), 149–179.

11. Barbara Clark, *Growing Up Gifted,* 3rd ed. (Columbus: Merrill, 1988), 337.

12. VanTassel-Baska, *Excellence in Educating Gifted and Talented Learners,* 450.

13. Clark, *Growing Up Gifted,* 337.

14. Ibid, 337.

15. Joan Franklin Smutny, "Parenting Young Gifted Children: How to Discover and Develop Their Talents at Home," *Parenting for High Potential,* http://www.nagc.org/Publications/Parenting/Smutney.htm.

16. Ken W. McCluskey, "The Importance of Being Early: A Case for Preschool Enrichment," press release for the March 2000 issue of *Parenting for High Potential,* http://www.nagc.org/Publications/Parenting/early.htm.

17. Ibid.

18. VanTassel-Baska, *Excellence in Educating Gifted and Talented Learners,* 340.

19. Robert J. Kirschenbaum, "Interview with Dr. A. Harry Passow," *Gifted Child Quarterly 42,* no. 4 (1998): 198.

20. VanTassel-Baska, *Excellence in Educating Gifted and Talented Learners,* 450.

21. Ibid.

22. Ibid.

23. Paula Olszewski-Kubilius, "Interview with Joyce VanTassel-Baska," *Journal of Secondary Gifted Education 12,* no. 2 (2001): 57–61, 60.

24. J. A. Kulik and C. C. Kulik, "Meta-analytic Findings on Grouping Programs," *Gifted Child Quarterly 36,* no. 2 (1992): 73–77.

25. VanTassel-Baska, *Excellence in Educating Gifted and Talented Learners,* 357.

26. Jeanette Plauché Parker, *Instructional Strategies for Teaching the Gifted* (Boston: Allyn and Bacon, 1975), 191.

chapter 4

1. Stanislas Dehaene, *The Number Sense: How the Mind Creates Mathematics* (New York: Oxford University Press, 1997).

2. Brian Butterworth, *What Counts: How Every Brain is Hardwired for Math* (New York: The Free Press, 1999).

3. National Council of Teachers of Mathematics (NCTM), *An Agenda for Action: Recommendations for School Mathematics of the 1980s* (Reston, Va.: National Council of Teachers of Mathematics, 1980), 18.

4. Linda Sheffield, Jennie Bennett, Manuel Berriozábal, Margaret DeArmond, and Richard Wertheimer, "Report of the Task Force on the Mathematically Promising,"*NCTM News Bulletin 32* (December 1995): 3–6.

5. Linda Jensen Sheffield, "Characteristics of Mathematically Promising Student," *KAGE Update: The Newsletter of the Kentucky Association for Gifted Education* (Fall 2000): 7–8.

6. Dehaene, *The Number Sense: How the Mind Creates Mathematics*; Butterworth, *What Counts: How Every Brain is Hardwired for Math*.

7. Glenn and Janet Doman, *How to How to Teach Your Baby Math: More Gentle Revolution* (New York: Putnam, 1993).

8. Linda Jensen, "A Heuristic for Creative Mathematical Problem Solving" (paper presented at the International Congress on Mathematical Education, Berkeley, Calif., 1980)

9. Linda Jensen Sheffield, ed., *Developing Mathematically Promising Students* (Reston, Va.: National Council of Teachers of Mathematics, 1999), 45.

10. Sheffield, Bennett, Berriozábal, DeArmond, and Wertheimer, "Report of the Task Force on the Mathematically Promising."

chapter 5

1. Irene Deliège and John Sloboda, *Musical Beginnings: Origins and Development of Musical Competence* (Oxford: Oxford University Press, 1996).

2. D. N. Stern, *The Interpersonal World of the Infant* (New York: BasicBooks, 1985); Mechthild Papousek, "Intuitive Parenting: A Hidden Source of Musical Stimulation in Infancy," in *Musical Beginnings: Origins and Development of Musical Competence*, ed. Irene Deliège and John Sloboda, 88–112.

3. H. Moog, *The Musical Experience of the Pre-school Child*, trans. C. Clarke (London: Schott, 1976); Lyle Davidson and Larry Scripp, "Conditions of Giftedness: Musical Development in the Preschool and Early Elementary Years," in *Beyond Terman: Contemporary Longitudinal Studies of Giftedness and Talent*, ed. Rena F. Subotnik and Karen D. Arnold (Norwood, N.J.: Ablex, 1994), 155–85; P. E. McKernon, "The Development of First Songs in Young Children," *New Directions in Child Development* 3 (1979): 43–58.

4. Arnold Bentley, *Musical Ability in Children and Its Measurement* (New York: October House, 1966); Rosamunde Shuter-Dyson and Clive Gabriel, *Psychology of Musical Ability* (London, Methuen, 1968); Davidson and Scripp, "Conditions of Giftedness: Musical Development in the Preschool and Early Elementary Years."

5. Michael Howe and John Sloboda, "Young Musicians' Accounts of Significant Influences in their Early Lives: 1. The Family and the Musical Background," *British Journal of Music Education* 8 (1991): 39–52.

6. John Sloboda and Michael Howe, "Biographical Precursors of Musical Excellence: An

Interview Study," *Psychology of Music 19* (1991): 3–21; Lauren A. Sosniak, "Learning to Be a Concert Pianist," in *Developing Talent in Young People*, ed. Benjamin Bloom (New York: Ballantine Books, 1985), 19–67.

7. Joanne Haroutounian, *Kindling the Spark: Recognizing and Developing Musical Talent* (New York: Oxford University Press, 2001); Joanne Haroutounian, "Nurturing Musical Potential—One Step At A Time," *Parenting for High Potential* (September 2001): 6–7, 26–27.

8. Joanne Haroutounian, "Talent Identification and Development in the Arts: An Artistic/Educational Dialogue," *Roeper Review 18*, no. 2 (1995): 112–117; Joanne Haroutounian, "The Academics of Artistic Thinking," *Think: The Magazine on Critical and Creative Thinking 5*, no. 2 (1994): 17–20.

9. K. A. Ericsson, R. T. Krampe, and C. Tesch-Romer, "The Role of Deliberate Practice in the Acquisition of Expert Performance," *Psychological Review 100* (1993): 363–406.

10. Edwin Gordon, *The Nature, Description, Measurement, and Evaluation of Music Aptitudes* (Chicago: G.I.A. Publications, 1986), 7–8.

11. Ibid.

12. Joanne Haroutounian, "Perspectives of Musical Talent: A Study of Identification Criteria and Procedures," *High Ability Studies 11*, no. 2 (2000): 137–160.

13. Liona Bresler, "Music in a Double-Bind: Instruction by Non-Specialists in Elementary Schools," *Bulletin of the Council for Research in Music Education 115* (1993): 1–13.

14. Benjamin Bloom, ed., *Developing Talent in Young People* (New York: Ballantine Books, 1985).

15. Haroutounian, *Kindling the Spark*; Haroutounian, "Nurturing Musical Potential—One Step at a Time."

16. Lauren Sosniak, "Phases of Learning," in *Developing Talent in Young People*, ed. Benjamin Bloom (New York: Ballantine Books, 1985), 409–38.

17. Mihalyi Csikszentmihalyi, Kevin Rathude, and Samuel Whalen, *Talented Teenagers: The Roots of Success and Failure* (Cambridge, N.Y.: Cambridge University Press, 1993).

18. Sosniak, "Learning to Be a Concert Pianist"; Haroutounian, *Kindling the Spark*; John Sloboda and Michael Howe, "Young Musician's Accounts of Significant Influences in the Early Lives: 2. Teachers, Practicing, and Performing," *British Journal of Music Education 7* (1991): 53–63

19. Joanne Haroutounian, "MTNA Winners After a Decade: Portraits of Commitment and Excellence," *The American Music Teacher 47*, no. 2 (1997): 20–25, 66.

20. Joanne Haroutounian, "Delights and Dilemmas of the Musically Talented Teenager," *Journal of Secondary Gifted Education 12*, no. 2 (2000): 3–16.

chapter 6

1. Madeleine L'Engle, *Walking On Water* (Wheaton, Ill.: Shaw, 1972), 72.

2. Dorothy Heathcote, *Collected Writings on Education and Drama* (London: Hutchinson & Co., 1984), 44.

3. Michael Grinder, *Righting the Educational Conveyor Belt* (Portland: Metamorphous Press, 1989), 6.

4. Nellie McCaslin, *Children and Drama* (New York: Longman, 1981), 386.

5. Viola Spolin, *Theatre Games for the Classroom* (Evanston, Ill.: Northwestern University Press, 1986), 3.

6. Adam Blatner, *The Art of Play: Helping Adults Regain Their Imagination* (New York: Human Science Press, 1980).
7. Nellie McCaslin, *Children and Drama*, 50.
8. Ibid., 50.
9. Dorothy Thames Schwartz and Dorothy Aldrich, *Give Them Roots and Wings: A Guide to Drama in Elementary Education* (Washington, D.C. : American Theatre Association, 1972), 60.
10. Ibid., 60.
11. Nellie McCaslin, *Children and Drama*, 30.
12. Constantin Stanislavski, *An Actor Prepares* (New York: Routledge/Theatre Arts Books, 1936), 54.
13. Heidi Priesnitz, "Asking Questions: The Key to Leaning," *Natural Life Magazine 40*, http://www.life.ca/nl/40/keytolearning.html.
14. Barry Oreck, Susan Baum, and Heather McCartney, *Artistic Talent Development for Urban Youth: The Promise and the Challenge* (Storrs: The National Research Center on the Gifted and Talented, University of Connecticut, 2000), 43.
15. Ibid., xi.
16. The President's Committee on the Arts and the Humanities and the Arts Education Partnership, "The Study's Findings," *Gaining the Arts Advantage: Lessons from School Districts That Value Arts Education* (1999), http://www.pcah.gov/gaa/study_findings.html.
17. George W. Noblit, et al., "Moving Towards Comprehensive School Reform: A+ After Year 3 Executive Summary," *The A+ School Program* (March 1999), http://www.aplus-schools. org/research.htm.
18. James Delisle, "Successful Parent-Teacher Conferences," *Gifted Children: Identification, Encouragement, and Development* (May 2002), http://www.gifted-children.com.
19. Nellie McCaslin, *Creative Drama in the Classroom and Beyond* (New York: Longman, 1981), 361.
20. Ibid., 373.
21. Ibid.
22. Robert Cohen, *Acting Professionally: Raw Facts About Careers in Acting* (Calif.: Mayfield, 1990), 8.
23. Lesley Hendy and Lucy Toon, *Supporting Drama and Imaginative Play in the Early Years* (Buckingham/Philadelphia: Open University Press, 2001), 28.
24. Ibid., 132.
25. Richard Courtney, *Dictionary of Developmental Drama* (Springfield, Ill.: Charles C. Thomas, 1987), 39.

chapter 7

1. Salvatore Dali, *Diary of a Genius* (New York: Prentice Hall, 1965); V. Frisch and J. T. Shipley, *Auguste Rodin* (New York: Frederick A. Stokes, 1939); W. Rubin, ed., *Pablo Picasso: A Retrospective* (New York: Museum of Modern Art, 1980); G. Scrivani, ed., *The Collected Writings of Willem de Kooning* (New York: Hanuman, 1988).
2. Karen L. Carroll, *Towards a Fuller Conception of Giftedness: Art in Gifted Education and the Gifted in Art Education* (Ed.D. diss., Teachers College, Columbia University, 1987);

Abraham J. Tannenbaum, *Gifted Children* (New York: MacMillan, 1983).

3. Karen L. Carroll, *Towards a Fuller Conception of Giftedness: Art in Gifted Education and the Gifted in Art Education*, 451.

4. Ibid., 37.

5. Victor Lowenfeld and W. L. Brittain, *Creative and Mental Growth*, 8th ed. (New York: MacMillan, 1987).

6. Al Hurwitz and Michael Day, *Children and Their Art*, 5th ed. (San Diego: Harcourt Brace Jovanovich, 1991).

7. Sandra I. Kay, "Developing Talent and Talent Developed: Assessing Qualities of Artistic Talent," in *Talent Development III: Proceedings from the 1995 Henry B. and Jocelyn Wallace National Research Symposium on Talent Development*, ed. N. Colangelo and S. G. Assouline (Scottsdale, Ariz.: Gifted Psychology Press, 1999), 379–382.

8. N. C. Meier, "Factors in Artistic Aptitude: Final Summary of a Ten Year Study of a Special Ability," *Psychological Monographs 51*, no. 5 (1939): 140–158.

9. Michael Piechowski and K. Cunningham, "Patterns of Overexcitability in a Group of Artists," *The Journal of Creative Behavior 19*, no. 3 (1985): 153–174.

10. Sandra I. Kay, "Spatial Ability in Female Artists' Performance," in *Remarkable Women*, ed. K. Arnold, K. D. Noble, and R. F. Subotnik (Cresskill, N.J.: Hampton Press, 1996): 317–334.

11. Sandra I. Kay, "Developing Talent and Talent Developed: Assessing Qualities of Artistic Talent."

12. Sandra I. Kay, *Differences in Figural Problem Solving and Problem Finding Behavior Among Professional, Semi-Professional, and Non-Artists* (Ann Arbor, Mich.: University Microfilms International, 1989).

13. Ibid.

14. Sandra I. Kay, "On the Nature of Expertise in Visual Art," in *Talents Unfolding*, ed. R. C. Friedman and B. M. Shore (Washington, D.C.: American Psychological Association, 2000), 217–232.

15. Al Hurwitz and Michael Day, *Children and Their Art*.

16. Ibid.

17. Ellen Winner, *Gifted Children* (New York: BasicBooks, 1996).

18. Stephanie Z. Dudek and R. Cote, "Problem Finding Revisited," in *Problem Finding, Problem Solving, and Creativity*, ed. Mark A. Runco (Norwood, N.J.: Ablex, 1994), 130–187; J. W. Getzels and M. Csikzentmihalyi, *The Creative Vision: A Longitudinal Study of Problem Finding in Art* (New York: John Wiley, 1976); Sandra I. Kay, *Differences in Figural Problem Solving and Problem Finding Behavior Among Professional, Semi-Professional, and Non-Artists*.

19. Vimla L. Patel and Marco F. Ramon, "Cognitive Models of Directional Inference in Expert Medical Reasoning," in *Experise in Context: Human & Machine*, ed. Paul F. Feltovich, Kenneth M. Ford, and Robert R. Hoffman (Menlo Park, Calif.: AAAI/MIT Press, 1997), 67–99.

20. Sandra I. Kay and Rena F. Subotnik, "Talent Beyond Words: Unveiling Spatial, Expressive, Kinesthetic, and Musical Talent in Young Children," *Gifted Child Quarterly 38*, no. 2 (1994): 70–74.

21. Karen L. Carroll, "Artistic Beginnings: The Work of Edvard Munch," *Studies in Art*

Education 36, no. 1 (1994): 7–17; David Pariser, "The Juvenile Drawings of Klee, Toulouse-Lautrec, and Picasso," *Visual Arts Research 13* (1987): 53–67.

22. Sandra I. Kay, "Shaping Elegant Problems for Visual Thinking," in *Creating Meaning Through Art: Teacher as Choice Maker,* ed. J. W. Simpson, J. M. Delaney, K. L. Carroll, C. M. Hamilton, S. I. Kay, M. S. Kerlavage, and J. L. Olson (Upper Saddle River, N.J.: Prentice Hall, 1998), 260–288.

23. Benjamin Bloom, *Developing Talent in Young People* (New York: Ballantine Books, 1985).

24. Christine Davis, ed., "NAEA Policy on Contests and Competitions," *Advisory NAEA,* (Summer 2001).

25. Ibid.

26. Sandra I. Kay, "A Method for Investigating the Creative Thought Process," in *Problem Finding, Problem Solving, and Creativity,* ed. Mark A. Runco (Norwood, N.J.: Ablex, 1994), 130–187.

chapter 8

1. J. Nicholls, *The Competitive Ethos and Democratic Education* (Cambridge, Mass.: Harvard University Press, 1989).

2. M. D. Walling, J. L. Duda, and L. Chi, "The Perceived Motivational Climate in Sport Questionnaire: Construct and Predictive Validity," *Journal of Sport and Exercise Psychology 15,* no. 2 (1993): 172–182.

3. D. Treasure and G. Roberts, "Relationship Between Female Adolescents' Achievement Goal Orientation, Perceptions of the Motivational Climate, Belief About Success, and Sources of Satisfaction in Basketball," *International Journal of Sport Psychology 30,* no. 3 (1998): 63–82.

4. S. Harter, "Effective Motivation Reconsidered," *Human Development 21* (1978): 34–64.

5. K. A. Klint and M. R. Weiss, "Perceived Competence and Motive for Participating in Youth Sports: A Test of Harter's Competitive Motivation Theory," *Journal of Sport Psychology 9,* no. 2 (1987): 55–65.

6. E. T. Braathen and S. Sveback, "Motivational Differences Among Talented Teenage Athletes: The Significance of Gender, Type of Sport, and Level of Excellence," *Scandinavian Journal of Medicine and Science in Sports 2,* no. 3 (1992): 153–159.

7. D. L. Gill, J. R. Gross, and S. Haddelston, "Participation and Motivation in Youth Sports," *International Journal of Sports Psychology 30,* no. 1 (1983): 41–62.

8. E. T. Braathen and S. Sveback, "EMG Response Patterns and Motivational Styles as Predictors of Performance and Discontinuation in Explosive and Endurance Sports Among Talented Teenage Athletes," *Personality and Individual Differences 17,* no. 4 (1994): 545–556.

9. A. Moran, *Psychology of Concentration in Sport Performance* (East Sussex, England: Psychology Press, 1996); D. S. Kirschenbaum and R. M. Bale, "Cognitive-Behavioral Skills in Gold," in *Psychology of Sports: Methods and Application,* ed. R. M. Suinn (Minneapolis: Burgess), 334–343.

10. G. Winter and C. Martin, *Sport "Psych" for Tennis* (Adelaide: South Australia Sport Institute, 1991).

11. R. H. Cox, *Sport Psychology: Concepts and Applications* (Madison, Wis.: Brown and Benchmark, 1994).

12. Schmid and Pepper, "Training Strategies for Concentration," in *Applied Sport*

Psychology: Personal Growth to Peak Performance, 2nd ed., ed. J. M. Williams (Mountain View, Calif.: Mayfield, 1994), 262–273.

13. T. Orlick, *In Pursuit of Excellence* (Champaign, Ill.: Leisure Press, 1990).

14. A. Moran, *Psychology of Concentration in Sport Performance* (East Sussex, England: Psychology Press, 1996).

15. G. A. Klein, "Using Knowledge Engineering to Preserve Corporate Memory," in *The Psychology of Expertise: Cognitive Research and Empirical AI,* ed. R.R. Hoffman (New York: Springer-Verlag, 1992), 170–190.

16. D. J. Garland and J. R. Barry, "Cognitive Advantage in Sport: The Nature of Perceptual Structures," *American Journal of Psychology 104,* no. 2 (1991): 211–228.

17. Abernathy, "Visual Search Strategies and Decision-Making in Sport," *International Journal of Sport Psychology 22,* no. 3/4 (1991): 189–210.

18. A. Moran, *Psychology of Concentration in Sport Performance.*

19. Ibid.

20. J. Munzert and D. Hackfort, "Individual Preconditions for Mental Training," *International Journal of Sport Psychology 30,* no. 1 (1999): 41–62.

21. I. Schwartzwold, "Self-Concept of Middle School Students: Its Meaning for Religion Education," *Megamot 4,* no. 1 (1979): 580–587.

22. Y. Parat, D. Lufti, and G. Tenebaum, "Psychological Components Contribute to Select Young Female Gymnasts," *International Journal of Sport Psychologists 20,* no. 4 (1989): 279–286.

23. G. Privette and C. Bundrick, "Psychological Process of Peak, Average, and Failing Performance in Sport," *International Journal of Sport Psychology 28,* no. 4 (1997): 323–334.

24. Ibid.

25. T. O. Bompa, *Theory and Methodology of Training: The Key to Athletic Performance* (Dubuque, Iowa: Kendall/Hunt, 1983).

26. J. S. Raglin and G. S. Wilson, "Overtraining in Athletes," in *Emotions in Sport,* ed. Y. L. Hanon (Champaign, Ill.: Human Kinetics, 2000), 191–207.

27. J. Lewko II and M. E. Ewing, "Sex Differences and Parental Influences in Sport Involvement of Children," *Journal of Sport Psychology 2,* no. 1 (1980): 62–68.

28. Ibid.

29. Ibid.

30. G. M. Hill, "Youth Sport Participation of Professional Baseball Players," *Sociology of Sport Journal 10,* no. 1 (1993): 107–114.

31. D. P. Valentiner, C. J. Holohan, and R. H. Moos, "Social Support, Appraisals of Event Controllability, and Coping: An Integrative Model," *Journal of Personality and Social Psychology 66,* no. 6 (1994): 1094–1102.

32. S. C. Greendorfer, "Shaping the Female Athlete: The Impact of the Family," in *The Sporting Woman,* ed. M.A. Boutilier and L. San Giovanni (Champaign, Ill.: Human Kinetics, 1983), 135–155.

33. M. A. Messner, *Power of Play: Sports and the Problem of Masculinity* (Boston: Beacon Press, 1992).

34. G. H. Sage, *Power and Ideology in American Sport* (Champaign, Ill.: Human Kinetics, 1990).

35. K. R. Baily, *The Girls Are the Ones With the Pointy Nails: An Exploration of Children's Conception of Gender* (London: Althouse Press, 1993).
36. G. G. Solomon and R. J. Bredemeier, "Children's Moral Conception of Gender Stratification in Sport," *International Journal of Sport Psychology 30*, no. 3 (1999): 350–68.
37. S. Birrell, "Discourse on the Gender/Sport Relationship: From Women and Sport to Gender Relations," *Exercise and Sport Science Review 16*, no. 4 (1988) 459–502.

chapter 9

1. Harleen S. Vickers and Kathleen M. Minke, "Family Systems and the Family-School Connection," in *Children's Needs II: Development, Problems, and Alternatives*, ed. G. G. Bear, K. M. Minke, and A. Thomas (Bethesda, Md.: National Association of School Psychologists, 1997), 547–558.
2. Ibid.
3. Kristen R. Stephens and Frances A. Karnes, "State Definitions for the Gifted and Talented Revisited," *Exceptional Children 66*, no. 2 (2000): 219–238.
4. Paula Olszewski-Kubilius, "Talent Search," *Journal of Secondary Gifted Education 9,* no. 1 (1998): 96–113.
5. Joyce VanTassel-Baska, "Theory and Research on Curriculum Development for the Gifted," in *International Handbook of Giftedness and Talent*, ed. K. A. Heller, F. J. Mönks, R. J. Sternberg, and R. F. Subotnik (New York: Elsevier, 2001), 345–366.
6. Shirley W. Schiever and C. June Maker, "Enrichment and Acceleration: An Overview and New Directions," in *Handbook of Gifted Education*, ed. N. Colangelo and G. A. Davis (Boston: Allyn and Bacon, 1997), 113–125.
7. Joan Franklin Smutny, *Stand Up for Your Gifted Child* (Minneapolis: Free Spirit, 2001).
8. Sandra Page, "When Changes for the Gifted Spur Differentiation for All," *Educational Leadership 58*, no. 1 (2000): 62–65.
9. Rebecca Belcher and F. Fletcher-Carter, "Growing Gifted Students in the Desert: Using Alternative, Community-Based Assessment and an Enriched Curriculum," *Teaching Exceptional Children 32*, no. 1(September/October 1999): 17–11.
10. Jonathan A. Plucker and Jay McIntire, "Academic Survivability in High-Potential, Middle School Students," *Gifted Child Quarterly 40* (1996): 7–14.
11. Smutny, *Stand Up for Your Gifted Child.*
12. Olszewski-Kubilius, "Talent Search"; Page, "When Changes for the Gifted Spur Differentiation for All"; Smutny, *Stand Up for Your Gifted Child*; Priscilla L. Vail, *Smart Kids With School Problems: Things to Know and Ways to Help* (New York: Plume Books, 1987); Joyce VanTassel-Baska, "Appropriate Curriculum for the Talented Learner," in *Excellence in Educating Gifted and Talented Learners*, ed. J. VanTassel-Baska (Denver: Love, 1998), 339–361.
13. Vail, *Smart Kids With School Problems: Things to Know and Ways to Help.*
14. Belcher and Fletcher-Carter, "Growing Gifted Students in the Desert: Using Alternative, Community-Based Assessment and an Enriched Curriculum"; Olszewski-Kubilius, "Talent Search."
15. Marcia S. Scott, Ruth Perou, Richard Urbano, Anne Hogan, and Susan Gold, "The

Identification of Giftedness: A Comparison of White, Hispanic, and Black Families," *Gifted Child Quarterly 36,* no. 3 (1992): 131–139; Reva C. Friedman (Jenkins) and Thomas J. Gallagher, "The Family With a Gifted Child," in *Collaboration With Parents of Exceptional Children,* ed. M. J. Fine (Brandon, Vt.: Clinical Psychology Publishing, 1991), 257–276; Vail, *Smart Kids With School Problems: Things to Know and Ways to Help.*

16. Vickers and Minke, "Family Systems and the Family-School Connection."

17. Lynn E. Pelco, Roger R. Ries, Lisa Jacobson, and Susan Melka, "Perspectives and Practices in Family-School Partnerships: A National Survey of School Psychologists," *School Psychology Review 29,* no. 2 (2000): 235–251.

18. Marilyn S. Ford, Robin Follmer, and Kathleen K. Litz, "School-Family Partnerships: Parents, Children, and Teachers Benefit!" *Teaching Children Mathematics 4,* no. 6 (1998): 310–313; Kim R. Galant, Carol M. Trivette, and Carl J. Dunst, "The Meaning and Implications of Empowerment," in *Children's Needs II: Development, Problems, and Alternatives,* ed. G. G. Bear, K. M. Minke, and A. Thomas (Bethesda, Md.: National Association of School Psychologists, 1997), 681–688; Dorothy Knopper, *Parent Education: Parents as Partners* (Boulder, Colo.: Open Space Communications, 1994); Althier Lazar and Frances Slostad, "How To Overcome Obstacles to Parent-Teacher Partnerships," *Clearing House 72,* no. 4 (1999): 206–211; Elizabeth A. Meckstroth, "Guiding the Parents of Gifted Children: The Role of Counselors and Teachers," in *Counseling Gifted and Talented Children: A Guide for Teachers, Counselors, and Parents,* ed. R. M. Milgram (Norwood, N.J.: Ablex, 1991), 95–120; Carol Strip and Gretchen Hirsch, "Trust and Teamwork: The Parent-Teacher Partnership For Helping the Gifted Child," *Gifted Child Today 24,* no. 2 (2001): 26–30, 64.

19. Vail, *Smart Kids With School Problems: Things to Know and Ways to Help*; Sandra L. Christenson, "Best Practices in Supporting Home-School Collaboration," in *Best Practices in School Psychology—III,* ed. A. Thomas and J. Grimes (Washington, D.C.: National Association of School Psychologists, 1995), 253–267; Friedman (Jenkins) and Gallagher, "The Family With a Gifted Child"; Knopper, *Parent Education: Parents as Partner;* Sylvia T. Rimm, "Parenting the Gifted Child: Special Problems, Special Joys," in *Understanding the Gifted Adolescent: Educational, Developmental, and Multicultural Issues,* ed. M. Bireley and J. Genshaft (New York: Teachers College Press, 1991), 18–32; Smutny, *Stand Up for Your Gifted Child*; Strip and Hirsch, "Trust and Teamwork: The Parent-Teacher Partnership For Helping the Gifted Child."

20. Susan Winebrenner, *Teaching Gifted Kids in the Regular Classroom* (Minneapolis: Free Spirit, 2001).

21. Vail, *Smart Kids With School Problems: Things to Know and Ways to Help*; Cheryll A. Adams and Tracy L. Cross, "Distance Learning Opportunities for Academically Gifted Adolescents," *Journal of Secondary Gifted Education 11,* no. 2 (1999): 88–96; Tracy L. Riley and Frances A. Karnes, "Forming Partnerships with Communities Via Competitions," *Journal of Secondary Gifted Education 10,* no. 3 (1999): 129–133; Vicki B. Stocking, "'What I Did This Summer': Summer Options for Gifted Students," *National Association for Secondary Schools Principals Bulletin 82,* no. 595 (1998): 93–99; Alice W. Terry, "An Early Glimpse: Service Learning From an Adolescent Perspective," *Journal of Secondary Gifted Education 11,* no. 3 (2000): 115–135.

22. Hilary Lee-Corbin and Pam Denicolo, "Portraits of the Able Child: Highlights of Case Study Research," *High Ability Studies 9*, no. 2 (1998): 207–219; Meckstroth, "Guiding the Parents of Gifted Children: The Role of Counselors and Teachers"; Sally M. Reis and D. Betsy McCoach, "The Underachievement of Gifted Students: What Do We Know and Where Do We Go?" *Gifted Child Quarterly 44*, no. 3 (2000): 152–170; Vail, *Smart Kids With School Problems: Things to Know and Ways to Help*; Rimm, "Parenting the Gifted Child: Special Problems, Special Joys."

23. Marilyn Sapon-Shevin, "Explaining Giftedness to Parents: Why It Matters What Professionals Say," *Roeper Review 9* (1987): 180–183.

24. Lazar and Slostad, "How to Overcome Obstacles to Parent-Teacher Partnerships."

25. Friedman (Jenkins) and Gallagher, "The Family With a Gifted Child"; Vickers and Minke, "Family Systems and the Family-School Connection."

26. Friedman (Jenkins) and Gallagher, "The Family With a Gifted Child"; Jeannie F. Lake, "An Analysis of Factors That Contribute to Parent-School Conflict in Special Education," *Remedial and Special Education 21*, no. 4 (2000): 240–252; Lazar and Slostad, "How to Overcome Obstacles to Parent-Teacher Partnerships"; Olszewski-Kubilius, "Talent Search."

27. Olszewski-Kubilius, "Talent Search."

28. Knopper, *Parent Education: Parents as Partners.*

chapter 10

1. Sidney M. Moon, Kevin R. Kelly, and John F. Feldhusen, "Specialized Counseling Services for Gifted Youth and Their Families: A Needs Assessment," *Gifted Child Quarterly 41*, no. 1 (1997): 16–25.

2. James T. Webb, Elizabeth A. Meckstroth, and Stephanie S. Tolan, *Guiding the Gifted Child* (Scottsdale, Ariz.: Gifted Psychology Press, 1994).

3. Steven I. Pfeiffer and Vicki Stocking, "Vulnerabilities of Academically Gifted Students," *Special Services in the Schools 16*, no. 20 (2000): 83–93.

4. Linda K. Silverman, "The Moral Sensitivity of Gifted Children and the Evolution of Society," *Roeper Review 17*, no. 2 (1994): 110–115.

5. Steven I. Pfeiffer and Linda A. Reddy, "School-Based Mental Health Programs in the United States: Present Status and a Blueprint for the Future," *School Psychology Review 27*, no. 1 (1998): 84–96.

6. Tracy L. Cross, *On the Social and Emotional Lives of Gifted Children* (Waco, Tex.: Prufrock Press, 2001).

7. William J. Bennett, Chester E. Finn, Jr., and John T. E. Cribb, Jr., *The Educated Child: A Parent's Guide* (New York: Touchstone, 2000).

8. LeoNora M. Cohen and Erica Frydenberg, *Coping for Capable Kids* (Waco, Tex.: Prufrock Press, 1996).

9. Steven I. Pfeiffer, "The Editor's View," *Duke Gifted Letter 2*, no. 2 (2002): 3.

10. John Feldhusen, "Programs for the Gifted Few or Talent Development for the Many," *Phi Delta Kappan 79*, no. 10 (1998): 735–738.

11. Steven I. Pfeiffer and Linda A. Reddy, *Inclusion Practices With Special Needs Students: Theory, Research, and Application* (Binghamton, N.Y.: Haworth Press, 1999).

12. David Elkind, *The Hurried Child: Growing Up Too Fast Too Soon*, 3rd ed. (Cambridge, Mass.: Perseus Publishing, 2001).
13. Webb, Meckstroth, and Tolan, *Guiding the Gifted Child*
14. Michele Borba, *Parents Do Make a Difference* (San Francisco: Jossey-Bass, 1999).
15. Haim Ginott, *Between Parent and Child* (New York: Avon, 1972).
16. Borba, *Parents Do Make a Difference*.
17. Bennett, Finn, and Cribb, *The Educated Child: A Parent's Guide*.
18. Jane Bluestein, *Twenty-First Century Discipline* (Albuquerque, N.M.: Instructional Support Services, 1998).
19. Daniel Goleman, *Emotional Intelligence* (New York: Bantam Books, 1995).
20. Steven I. Pfeiffer, "Emotional Intelligence: Popular But Elusive Construct," *Roeper Review 23*, no. 3 (2001): 138–142.
21. Howard Gardner, *Frames of Mind: The Theory of Multiple Intelligences* (New York: BasicBooks, 1983).
22. Goleman, *Emotional Intelligence*.
23. Ibid., 28.
24. Elkind, *The Hurried Child: Growing Up Too Fast Too Soon,* 28.
25. Lawrence E. Shapiro, *How to Raise a Child With a High EQ (Emotional Quotient)* (New York: HarperCollins, 1997).
26. Letitia Baldrige, *More Than Manners! Raising Today's Kids to Have Kind Manners and Good Hearts* (New York: Rawson Associates, 1997).
27. Sheldon Lewis and Sheila Kay Lewis, *Stress-Proofing Your Child* (New York: Bantam, 1996).
28. John F. Clabby and Maurice J. Elias, *Teach Your Child Decision-Making* (New York: Doubleday, 1987).

about
the authors

editors

Paula Olszewski-Kubilius is the director of the Center for Talent Development at Northwestern University and an associate professor in the School of Education and Social Policy. She has worked at the Center for 20 years, during which time she has conducted research and published widely on issues of talent development, particularly the effects of accelerated educational programs and the needs of special populations of gifted children. She was the recipient of the Early Scholar Award of the National Association of Gifted Children. She has designed and conducted educational programs for learners of all ages, as well as workshops for parents and teachers. She is active in national and state-level advocacy organizations for gifted children. She currently serves as editor of *Gifted Child Quarterly* and previously edited the *Journal of Secondary Gifted Education*. She has served on the editorial advisory boards of the *Journal for the Education of the Gifted, Gifted Child International*, and *Roeper Review*.

Lisa Limburg-Weber is an assistant director at Northwestern University's Center for Talent Development. She has served as an administrator with the Center's gifted programs since 1992. She has developed educational programs for gifted students at all levels of schooling. She recently coauthored a publication for parents, *Designs for Excellence*, which describes educational program options for gifted secondary students. She holds a Ph.D. from Northwestern University.

Steven I. Pfeiffer is executive director of Duke University's Talent Identification Program (TIP). At Duke, he holds faculty appointments in psychology, education, and child and family policy. Dr. Pfeiffer received his Ph.D. from the University of North Carolina and served as a clinical psychologist in the U.S. Navy Medical Service Corps. He is a Fellow of the

American Psychological Association, a Diplomate of the American Board of Professional Psychology, and is listed in the National Register of Health Service Providers in Psychology. He has published more than 100 articles and book chapters and coauthored the Pfeiffer-Jarosewich Gifted Rating Scales and the Devereux Behavior Rating Scales. His present interests include counseling high-risk gifted youth, parent and family therapy, and working with young elite athletes.

contributors

Cheryll M. Adams is the director of the Center for Gifted Studies and Talent Development at Ball State University. She received her doctorate from the University of Virginia and was a research assistant at the National Research Center on the Gifted and Talented. She served two years as the Director of Academic Life for the Indiana Academy for Science, Mathematics, and Humanities at Ball State and has a 15-year background in teaching science and math in both public and private schools. She teaches courses on gifted education and has presented widely at local, state, and national conferences, particularly on differentiating instruction in mathematics and science and gifted females. She has served on the board of directors of the National Association for Gifted Children and serves on the executive board of the Indiana Association for the Gifted.

Maria Chrysanthou is a graduate of the University of North Carolina at Chapel Hill with a degree in performance studies. During her time as a student, she toured with the Tar Heel Tale Tellers, a company that performed contemporary children's literature in schools and bookstores in North Carolina. Upon graduating, she traveled to Montevideo, Uruguay, where she taught drama to teenagers and adults. When she returned to Chapel Hill, she became a member of StreetSigns Center for Literature and Performance, appearing in the educational productions *Reading On Your Feet* and *Look At Me! The Big Adventures of Little People*. Over the past 2 years, she has taught drama to children at the ArtsCenter in Carrboro and Chapel Hill-Carrboro City Schools. She recently interned at the Science Museum of Minnesota, where she performed and helped develop educational theatre presentations. She currently lives in Los Angeles, where she continues to work in the theatre and film industry.

Karen L. Drill, a former Regional All-America softball pitcher for Princeton University, received her master's degree from Northwestern University in counseling psychology. She has coached softball at the middle and high school levels, as well as provided private pitching lessons for clients of all ages. As an advocate for gifted education, Karen has worked for Northwestern University's Center for Talent Development summer program for many years and continues to develop holistic approaches to the social and emotional elements of giftedness.

Julie K. Fishell is a member of the faculty of the Department of Dramatic Art at the University of North Carolina at Chapel Hill, where she teaches and directs. Her professional theatre experience spans over 20 years and includes training and performing with The Juilliard Drama Division, the Moscow Art Theatre School, The Acting Company, Hartford Stage Company, Theatre for a New Audience, and PlayMakers Repertory Company. Professor Fishell is the recipient of the Michel and Suria St. Denis Theatre Award from The Juilliard School. Her community collaborations include teaching, directing, and consulting with churches, public schools, continuing education foundations and professional companies. She has received numerous educational grants for work with drama students and has served on the curriculum review board for the North Carolina Public Schools Arts Education Standard Course of Study. She currently serves on the board of Inspiration Theatre, a nonprofit touring company bringing theatre to hospitals and care facilities and is designing curricula for PlayMakers Repertory Company's DRAMAQUEST and THEATREQUEST summer drama camps.

Joanne Haroutounian serves on the piano faculty of George Mason University, consults nationally in the fields of music and gifted/arts education, and has edited and written numerous music teaching publications. Dr. Haroutounian is the founder, president, and executive director of the MusicLink Foundation, which provides long-term private music instruction to promising students in financial need and promotes independent study credit for musically talented teenagers. Dr. Haroutounian's articles on musical talent development have appeared in *Roeper Review*, *Arts Education Policy Review*, *High Ability Studies*, and *American Music Teacher*. She was guest editor of the *Journal of Secondary Gifted Education*'s fall 2000 special issue on musical talent development. Her book, *Kindling the Spark: Recognizing and Developing Musical Talent*, is a valuable resource for parents.

Lynn Johnson is an actress and director who is committed to community cultural development and has been teaching students of all ages for over a decade. After receiving her theater degree from Northwestern University, she founded TurnStyle Teen Theatre, an ensemble of teenagers who work together over the course of a school year to create an original, movement-based production to present to a variety of audiences throughout their community. While in Chicago, she was a member of Child's Play Touring Theatre, which travels all over the United States performing stories and poems written by kids. Lynn relocated to Chapel Hill, North Carolina, in 1999 as a member of the StreetSigns Center for Literature and Performance. There, she designed and directed a number of educational programs, including *Reading On Your Feet*, a high-energy touring show and workshop aimed at encouraging elementary school students to become passionate readers, and *Wave When You Pass*, an intergenerational production exploring notions of home and identity and featuring residents of Chatham County, North Carolina. Through her work with StreetSigns, she was able to found and direct the Village Whippersnapper Ensemble, a group of homeschooled children ages 4–12 who, along with their mothers, perform original plays as a service to their community. Lynn has also taught for Burning Coal Theatre Company of Raleigh, the Durham Arts Council, the ArtsCenter, Chapel Hill-Carrboro City Schools, Raleigh Little Theatre, the Opera Company of North Carolina, and the Raleigh School of Ballet.

Sandra I. Kay is the district coordinator of gifted programs at Monroe-Woodbury Central School District. She holds an Ed.D. and M.A. in special education from Teachers College, Columbia University. Her publications include journal articles in *School Arts, The Journal of Aesthetic Education, Design for Arts Education, Roeper Review, Creativity Research Journal, Gifted Child Quarterly*, and *Teaching Exceptional Children*. She has also written numerous book chapters and is the co-author of an art education textbook. In addition, Sandy has been the chair of the Research and Evaluation Division of the National Association for Gifted Children and vice president of the NYS AGATE Association. Her research interests focus on developing talent/expertise and on the problem-finding aspects of creative thought, visual thinking, and other habits of mind that engage the imagination and promote self-directed inquiry in children and adults.

Linda Sheffield is a Regents Professor of Mathematics Education at Northern Kentucky University. She received her M.Ed. and Ph.D. in mathematics education from the University of Texas at Austin. She has written numerous books and articles for both teachers and students and has conducted seminars for teachers around the world. Her books include PreK–2 NCTM Navigations series, a series of math problem-solving books for children in third through eighth grade, and a math methods book for elementary and middle school teachers. She is past-president of the School Science and Mathematics Association (SSMA) and was chair of the Task Force on Promising Students for the National Council of Teachers of Mathematics (NCTM). She was also editor of the NCTM book *Developing Mathematically Promising Students* and the SSMA special journal issue on gifted and talented mathematics and science students.

Vicki Stocking received her Ph.D. in educational psychology from Stanford University in 1990. She worked for many years with the Research Division of the Duke University Talent Identification Program (TIP), first as a postdoctoral fellow and then as the director of that division. She recently joined Duke's Program in Education, where she teaches courses in education and psychology and directs Duke's Secondary Teacher Preparation Program for undergraduates. She is part of the service learning faculty and works to integrate service into undergraduate instruction. Her research interests include self-concept, academic talent, adolescent development, and contextual effects on achievement, and she supports student community-based research projects that illuminate contexts appropriate for optimal development. She is married and has two elementary-aged children.

Michael Clay Thompson is the editor of *Our Gifted Children* magazine and the author of numerous books concerning language arts for gifted children, including *The Word Within the Word* and *The Magic Lens*. He has served as president of the Indiana Association for the Gifted and as a member of the board of directors for the National Association for Gifted Children.